Public Record Office Handbook No. 27

A GUIDE TO CHANCERY EQUITY RECORDS AND PROCEEDINGS 1600-1800

Henry Horwitz
Professor of History
University of Iowa

PRO Publications
Public Record Office
Ruskin Avenue
Kew
Surrey
TW9 4DU

© Crown copyright 1998

First published by HMSO in 1995

ISBN 1 873 162 63 4

A catalogue card for this book is available from the British Library

CONTENTS

Note on Form	v
Glossary	vi
List of Tables	ix
List of Illustrations	x
Preface	xi
Preface to Second Edition	xiii

Introduction — 1

    A: The Court of Chancery — 1
    B: The Handbook — 6

1 How the Court of Chancery Conducted its Business — 8

    A: Introduction — 8
    B: The Procedure of the Court: the Manuals of Practice — 12
    C: Observations upon Procedure in Practice — 24

2 The Jurisdiction of the Court of Chancery Between the Early Seventeenth and the Early Nineteenth Centuries — 30

    A: Introduction — 30
    B: The Broader Context — 31
    C: The Volume of Chancery Business — 32
    D: The Subject Matter of Chancery Suits — 35
    E: The Identity of the Litigants — 41
    F: Conclusions — 48

3	**The Records and the Finding Aids**	**51**
	A: Introduction: the Survival of the Records	51
	B: The Organization of the Records	56
4	**Searching the Chancery Equity Records**	**90**
	A: Some Successful Searches	90
	B: Specimen Searches	92
	C: Conclusion	104

Appendixes

	I: Memorandum on the Filing of the Pleadings	105
	II: The Samples	109

Bibliography   **111**

Index   **120**

NOTE ON FORM

All dates in the text and of documents are new style, with the year beginning on 1 January.

In Public Record Office (PRO) terminology, documents are organized into classes, classes into boxes (or bundles or volumes); boxes, in turn, may be subdivided into individual pieces (which may themselves contain one or several linked documents). Throughout, the terms 'box' and 'boxes' have been used, even if the documents are bundled or comprise a single volume. A reference in the form of C 6/285/24 indicates the class C 6, box 285, piece 24; a reference in the form of C 33/1098 indicates class C 33, box 1098 (here, a volume). Any further reference will be to a folio or page number.

As explained in the discussion of finding aids in Chapter Three, a 'listing' refers to a list of a class (usually box by box, sometimes by piece), an 'index' denotes a modern fully-alphabetized listing of the contents of all or part of a class, and an 'alphabet' is a listing (usually made by the officers of the Court) by the suit title - ie, by the first letter of the surname of the first plaintiff and giving the surname of the first defendant (eg, Smith v Jones, and very occasionally *John* Smith v *Ralph* Jones).

Throughout, the decree and order books (C 33) of the Court of Chancery have been referred to as the 'book(s) of orders' both for the sake of brevity and to emphasize that the volumes contain much of significance in addition to the decrees.

Document citation: all documents, unless otherwise noted, are from the PRO. Only documents from other repositories are cited with the name of the repository.

GLOSSARY

Administrator: court-appointed representative of one who died without making a will (*see also* Executor).

Affidavit: a voluntary written statement made under oath.

Amended Bill: *see* Bill (of complaint).

Answer: the first pleading by the defendant (*see also* Demurrer, Disclaimer, Plea; also Cross Bill).

Attachment: initial process of contempt, normally to enforce the taking of securities for appearance in court; attachment with proclamations issued if the initial process fails. *See also* Sequestration.

Bill (of complaint): the initial statement of the plaintiff's case. The plaintiff, in light of the contents of the defendant's answer, might amend the original bill or might, depending on the stage the suit had reached, be required instead to file a supplemental bill if he wished to make changes (*see also* Cross Bill).

Bill (of review): petition, normally alleging an error in law, to reopen a case after a decree had been enrolled.

Bill (of revivor): petition to revive a suit which had abated because of the death of a party or other contingency such as the marriage of a female plaintiff.

Commission of Rebellion: process of contempt if attachment with proclamations failed; usually empowered sheriff to arrest the person in contempt (*see also* Sequestration).

Commissioners of the Great Seal: individuals (usually three) named by the King to act collectively in lieu of appointing either a Lord Chancellor or a Lord Keeper.

Cross Bill: bill which a defendant was allowed to exhibit for the same cause against the original plaintiff, and thereby seek discovery from the plaintiff.

de bene esse: evidence, usually in the form of depositions, allowed provisionally but which could subsequently be ruled inadmissible.

Decree: judgment.

dedimus potestatem: commission authorizing persons to perform official acts outside of London and its immediate environs such as the taking of a defendant's answer or the conducting examinations of witnesses.

Demurrer: a pleading by defendant seeking discharge on grounds of lack of jurisdiction by the court or of technical insufficiency in the plaintiff's bill of complaint.

Depositions: witness's statements on oath, taken down in secrecy before an Examiner or commissioners under *dedimus potestatem*, in reply to written interrogatories prepared by the parties; depositions were supposed to be kept sealed until order for publication (*see below*). (Depositions might also be taken in Masters' proceedings upon a reference.)

Disclaimer: express denial by a defendant that the matter in the plaintiff's bill concerned him in any way.

Dismission: order, with the force of a decree, whereby a bill of complaint was dismissed. Dismission might be for failure to proceed or because the Court adjudged the bill without merit.

Docquet: generally, an abstract of some official action; specifically, the text of a decree prepared for enrolment.

Examination: the formal interrogation of witnesses (or parties) either prior to the hearing (the principal form of evidence in Chancery cases) or to elucidate matters of fact upon a reference to a Master. Normally, examination was by interrogatories and the testimony taken by writing, but *viva voce* examination was possible at the hearing of a case under special circumstances (eg, the authentication of documents).

Exception: formal allegation by a party that a prior pleading or a Master's report was insufficient or in error, specifying the grounds for the exception.

Executor: person(s) named by a testator to execute the provisions of his/her will.

Exemplification: certified and official copy of a document.

in forma pauperis: an arrangement whereby poor suitors were assigned legal representatives free of charge and allowed to proceed with their suits without the payment of official fees.

Injunction: an order of Chancery enjoining something upon a party; the common injunction was to require the party to halt litigation in another court; the special injunction secured possession of property or restrained potentially irremediably damaging acts such as breach of copyright or waste.

in perpetuam rei memoriam: depositions taken and kept out of the normal course as a means of preserving testimony from aged or sick persons or those leaving the realm.

Interrogatories: written questions formulated by the parties to put to witnesses to elicit their testimonies by deposition.

Interlocutory: matters arising in the course of a suit, notably proceedings on injunctions (*see also* Motion, Petition).

Lord Keeper: the equivalent in function of a Lord Chancellor but an appointment carrying less prestige.

Motion: an oral application by a party's legal representative to the bench.

Ne exeat regnum: a writ forbidding a person to leave the country.

Petition: a written application by a party's legal representative to the bench. In addition to petitions on procedural questions during the course of a suit ('ordinary' petitions), proceedings for a rehearing of an enrolled decree were initiated by a petition for review.

Plea: a response to a bill of complaint raising a point of law which, if upheld, would free the defendant from answering the bill.

Pleadings: formal preliminary statements by parties in suits including the bill of complaint and the various responses possible by a defendant (*see also* Rejoinder, Replication, Surrejoinder and Surrebutter).

Probate: certificate of the church court having jurisdiction over a deceased person's testament that it had been proved and might be executed.

Publication: when both sides in a suit had completed the examination of their witnesses, the Court would order the hitherto-sealed depositions to be opened for perusal and for the making of copies.

Quer[ent]: complainant (plaintiff) in Chancery suit.

Rejoinder: second pleading of a defendant's case, and made in response to the plaintiff's replication.

Replication: second pleading of a plaintiff's case, and made in response to the defendant's answer.

Sequestration: taking custody of property into the hands of the Court, either temporarily or for disposition.

subpoena: initial process of Chancery requiring that the defendant appear under penalty. Other versions of the writ could be used to enforce the attendance of a witness (*subpoena ad testificandum*) or to produce material evidences (*subpoena duces tecum*).

Supplemental Bill: *see* Bill (of complaint).

Surrejoinder and Surrebutter: third pleadings, respectively, of the plaintiff's and defendant's cases.

Terms: the legal year was divided into four terms: Michaelmas (roughly mid-October to late November); Hilary (mid-January to early February); Easter (early April to early May); Trinity (early June to early July). The long vacation ran from the end of Trinity term to the beginning of Michaelmas term.

LIST OF TABLES

One:	Duration of Suits in Chancery	28
Two:	Bills of Complaint Exhibited in Chancery	32
Three:	'Active' Cases in Chancery	33
Four:	New versus Ongoing Business in Chancery	33
Five:	Subject Matter of Chancery Sample Suits	36
Six:	Estimates of Types of Active Cases	37
Seven:	Status/Occupation of All-Named Plaintiffs	42
Eight:	Status/Occupation of First-Named Male Plaintiffs	43
Nine:	Status/Occupation of First-Named Male Defendants	44
Ten:	Status/Occupation of First-Named Male Parties	45
Eleven:	Place of Residence of all First-Named Plaintiffs	45
Twelve:	Place of Residence of all First-Named Defendants	46
Thirteen:	Place of Residence of all First-Named Parties	46

LIST OF ILLUSTRATIONS

Diagram: Chancery Equity Process and Associated Records.	13
Bill (only) of complaint (undated, but addressed to Francis Bacon as Lord Verulam, Lord Chancellor: hence between 7/1618 and 1/1621) of Alice ap William widow against Thomas ap William Lloyd. (C 2/Chas 1/W102/23)	63
Answer (with bill) sworn 5 May 1615 of Mathew Bacon gent to the bill of Sir Thomas Bendysh bart et al. (C 2/James 1/B11/9/2)	64
A portion of the accounts submitted with the answer sworn 12 Sept 1787 of James Hayling to the bill of William Taylor esq 'proprietor of the King's Theatre or Opera House in the Haymarket'. (C 12/2147/14)	65
Deposition of James Collee of the Middle Temple, gent, aged 40 years or thereabouts, sworn 15 April 1736, in the suit of Ketelbey v Ketelbey. (C 22/951/13)	66
A single sheet of the 'B' order book for 1619. (C 33/138)	67

The cover illustration is entitled *The First Day of Term*, 1730 (from an engraving by C Modley, after a drawing by Gravelot).

PREFACE

This handbook aims to facilitate and hence to promote research in the records of Chancery equity proceedings. Of course, as anyone who has explored them has quickly realized, what would most encourage their use - what would most stimulate the exploitation of the riches they hold for economic, social, local and cultural history - would be to index the records comprehensively by name, subject and place. But since Chancery handled approximately 750,000 suits between 1600 and 1800, the effort required for such a project would be massive, and is unlikely to be forthcoming in the foreseeable future. Hence, this handbook is an attempt to make these materials more accessible than they have been in order to ease the aversion syndrome that seems to afflict so many enquirers contemplating searching in Chancery equity records.

This limited and exploratory scheme could not have been contemplated without the support of generous and far-seeing institutions. The Leverhulme Trust of the United Kingdom made available to the Institute of Historical Research of the University of London the funds with which to employ for two full years Dr Charles Moreton as the invaluable research assistant in the gathering of the samples of pleadings and of the tracing of sample suits which forms the backbone of this enterprise. The National Endowment for the Humanities of the United States under grant no RC21981-81 provided the funds to enable the author to spend one academic semester and two summers working at the PRO. And the author's own institution, the University of Iowa, provided the support for an additional academic semester in Chancery Lane, as well as extended leave of absence to work in London between 1991 and 1994.

The author is also indebted to many individuals for advice and assistance. From the outset, this project received the backing of successive heads of the one-time department of Early Modern Records in the PRO - Jane Cox and Dr John Post. Dr Alice Prochaska, then Secretary of the Institute of Historical Research, took the initiative in deciding to take the project under the Institute's wing, thereby facilitating the task of securing funding. Subsequently, the author has had all the help he has sought from members of the PRO staff, and especially from Dr Trevor Chalmers who has been indispensable in overcoming the difficulties of programming and making operational a data base for the samples drawn from the records.

Fellow scholars have also been of enormous help. Without the encouragement of Juliet Gardiner and of Professors Robert Hume and Judith Milhous, I doubt that I would have persisted in the inevitable resubmissions of grant proposals, while Professor Henry Snyder gave me the benefit of his long experience in preparing such documents. In the actual research that has gone into the handbook, no one has been more important than Dr Patrick Polden, and here I want gratefully to acknowledge - as I do also at the relevant points in the text - that the nineteenth-century data drawn on in Chapter Two and elsewhere are the product of his research, research which has enabled me to put in much clearer perspective my own results for the preceding two centuries.

In addition, I have learned much from two other authors of recent guides to the Chancery records - guides particularly designed for the family and local historians who collectively probably constitute the largest number of searchers. Mr Dorian Gerhold has generously shared the fruits of his experience, not least earlier versions of his *Courts of Equity A Guide to Chancery and other Legal Records*.[1] At a later stage, I also benefited from the exchange of information with Mr Guy Lawton, the author of a very helpful series of articles on using the Bernau Index and the Bernau Notebooks; I have also, with his permission, drawn on his draft 'Chancery Court Proceedings for the Family Historian'.[2]

Many others have offered suggestions, information, and comments on earlier drafts of this work. In particular, I am grateful to Dr Christopher Brooks, Mr D E C Yale, Professor Louis Knafla, Professor Henry Roseveare, Professor James Oldham, Professor John Baker, and Mr Duncan Harrington. I hope they, and those who have occasion to use the handbook, will feel that the effort has been worth it.

---

[1] Published by Pinhorns in 1994 as 'Pinhorn Handbooks: Ten'.
[2] The articles appear in *Family Tree Magazine* (for specifics, see the Bibliography); the draft guide was prepared for the Public Record Office.

PREFACE TO SECOND EDITION

This edition has been prepared to make the handbook more accessible to users and to take account of the reorganization of finding aids in the wake of the PRO's consolidation at Kew. Several additions and revisions have been made, chief of them the incorporation of several new listings of certain Chancery equity materials and more detailed explanations of how to use the Bernau index for locating documents. Bibliography and notes have also been updated.

Since the completion of the first edition, the PRO has also launched an 'Equity Pleadings Database' by which existing and new listings can be entered and searched; as this database is gradually enlarged it should prove a very valuable tool for locating Chancery equity records, as well as those of other English equity courts. The first fruits of this endeavour will be the inputting of the present C 5 - C 10 finding aids, thereby allowing these six classes to be searched simultaneously.

I am grateful to Dr Amanda Bevan and Mr Aidan Lawes, both of the PRO, for their assistance and support in the preparation of this edition. I should also like to thank Dr Richard Hoyle for the suggestion that the List and Index Society print the sample data, thereby making it easily accessible to other researchers.

INTRODUCTION

A. The Court of Chancery

No reader of *Bleak House* is likely to forget its scathing portrayal of the deficiencies of the early nineteenth-century Court of Chancery, and page after page of the *Parliamentary Papers* of that era document Dickens' 'bill of complaint' on such scores as delay and expense, procedural technicalities and inconclusiveness of outcome.[1] Yet, half a millennium earlier in the reign of Edward III when the Lord Chancellor (the principal minister of the Crown and then normally a cleric) began to serve frequently as an ad hoc hearer of civil disputes among subjects, he was responding to petitioners complaining of an inability to secure justice through the conventional legal channels.[2] The problems that such petitioners had encountered in existing jurisdictions varied considerably, but a common thread in their stories was that the standard procedures and practices of existing courts, especially the common law courts, left them unjustly at risk or unable to secure what was rightfully due them.

Two hundred and fifty years later, by the death of Elizabeth I in 1603, Chancery had developed into one of the leading royal central courts for the resolution of a wide range of disputes between subjects - a coequal, and sometimes more, with the common law courts of King's Bench and Common Pleas, but with its own distinctive procedures and remedies.[3] Over these centuries, what had begun as an ad hoc channel for the sorting-out of civil disputes in an 'equitable' fashion - unconstrained by the rules and norms of common law practice - had evolved into an institution with a complex body of rules, an elaborate array of records, a substantial cadre of officials, and a mushrooming caseload.

Some key developments had come in Henry VIII's reign. On the one hand, some common lawyers in the 1520s appear to have been fearful that Lord Chancellor (and Cardinal) Thomas Wolsey meant to encroach upon the established boundaries of common law jurisdiction. But Wolsey's fall was followed by a succession of common lawyers as heads of the Chancery,

---

1   Sir William Holdsworth, *Charles Dickens as a Legal Historian* (1928); cf D Hamer, 'Dickens: The old Court of Chancery', *Notes and Queries*, new series 17 (1970), 347. The principal parliamentary inquiries of the first half of the nineteenth century about the operation of Chancery since the mid-eighteenth century are *Parliamentary Papers* 1810-11 (244) iii; 1826 (143) xvi; 1836 (370) xliii.
2   J H Baker, *An Introduction to English Legal History* (3rd edn, 1990), 116 ff [hereafter, Baker, *Introduction*]; cf Robert C Palmer, *English Law in the Age of the Black Death 1348-1381* (1993), 107ff. As Baker explains, well before the equity or 'English' side of the Chancery evolved, there was a common law or 'Latin' side (the Petty Bag) handling personal actions involving the Chancery staff and the Petty Bag jurisdiction persisted throughout the early modern era.
3   For an in-depth treatment, see William J Jones, *The Elizabethan Court of Chancery* (1967) [hereafter, Jones, *Chancery*].

beginning with the ill-fated Sir Thomas More.[4] To be sure, in 1603 a substantial majority of the Chancellor's principal subordinates, the Master of the Rolls and the eleven Masters in Ordinary, were still Doctors of Civil Law, trained mainly at Oxford and Cambridge.[5] Nonetheless, by the end of the sixteenth century what surviving potential there was for conflict between Chancery and the common law courts was being eroded by the increasingly prominent role of common lawyers in Chancery. Civil lawyers were a declining minority among the Masters by the second half of the seventeenth century, while it had always been barristers who argued suitors' cases before the Lord Chancellor and the Master of the Rolls.

Hence, when the famous feud erupted between Sir Edward Coke and Lord Chancellor Ellesmere (both common lawyers) in the middle years of James I's reign, what was at issue was not the substance of the relevant law (that is, 'equity' as practiced in Chancery versus actions in the common law) but rather the scope of Chancery's authority vis-à-vis the Courts of King's Bench and Common Pleas - in particular, whether Chancery on grounds of equity could reopen decided cases at common law. Moreover, once the sound and fury of that controversy had been stilled by Coke's dismissal and Ellesmere's death, there was no repetition of such contretemps, though in the critiques of Chancery's operation voiced by MPs in early Stuart parliaments some echoes of the challenge to the Court's jurisdiction can be heard.[6] Rather, the dominant note, as earlier, was co-operation between the Court of Chancery and the common law courts, with the judges often sitting in Chancery outside the law terms in order to assist in processing its voluminous caseload and with the Chancellor showing greater restraint in using the power of injunction to suspend proceedings at common law.[7]

As the first half of the sixteenth century saw the last of the great clerical Lord Chancellors, so in the years immediately after Wolsey's fall three of what became the Court's principal series of records, in addition to the pleadings themselves (bill and answers, now PRO classes C 1 and following), began to be kept by its officers. First to appear were the decree rolls in 1534-1535 (C 78 and C 79). Second, and surviving as a continuous series down into the

---

[4] John A Guy, *The Public Career of Sir Thomas More* (1980). There was a reversion to clerical Chancellors under Queen Mary, while Sir Christopher Hatton was probably never called to the bar. For lists of Chancellors (and Lord Keepers and Commissioners of the Great Seal) along with lists of Masters of the Rolls, the ordinary Masters, the Six Clerks, and other principal officers of the Court, see Thomas D Hardy, *A Catalogue of the Lord Chancellors...and Principal Officers of the High Court of Chancery* (1843). Hardy's lists have been amended, with respect to holders of the Great Seal, by *Handbook of British Chronology* (Royal Historical Society, 3rd edn, 1986); with respect to Masters of the Rolls by Sir John Sainty, *The Judges of England 1272-1990* (Selden Society supp ser 10, 1993); and, with respect to the ordinary Masters by Edmund Heward, *Masters in Ordinary* (1990).

[5] A significant number of Masters in Chancery also served as Masters in Request and as judges in the Court of Admiralty.

[6] For these criticisms, many of which anticipate the fiercer attacks of the 1640s and 1650s, see *Commons Debates 1621* (7 vols, 1935), ed Wallace Notestein, II, 264-266, and VII, 568 ff. See also D X Powell, 'Why was Sir Francis Bacon Impeached? The Common Lawyers and Chancery Revisited: 1621', *History* 81 (1996), 522-526. As late as the turn of the century, there is evidence in some legal circles of opposition to the scope of Chancery's jurisdiction: see British Library, Stowe Ms 303 ff, 232 ff, 239 ff, 250 ff, (various proposals for the reform of Chancery and for restriction of its jurisdiction with respect to money bonds, parol trusts, and certain claims for legacies); also Sir Richard Atkyns, *Inquiry into the jurisdiction of the Chancery in causes of Equity* (1695).

[7] D E C Yale, *Lord Nottingham's 'Manual of Chancery Practice' and 'Prolegomena of Chancery and Equity'* (1965) [hereafter Yale, *Manual*], introduction, pp 7-16, 69-73; Baker, *Introduction*, pp 124-126.

nineteenth century, were the books of orders and decrees (hereafter referred to as the books of orders) which began in 1544-1545 (C 33). And third, surviving in significant numbers from the late sixteenth century onwards, were the reports of the Masters in Ordinary on questions referred to them by the Court (C 38 and C 39).[8] Thus, during the course of the sixteenth century Chancery became a tribunal in which the main stages in a suit (pleadings, proofs, references, and decrees and orders) were recorded in writing - ample testimony to the Court's commitment to investigate thoroughly each complaint brought before it.

The shape of the Court's evolving structure of records reflected the distinctive character of its process and procedure - including those features which attracted litigants who, for one reason or another, felt that the chances of gaining their aims were better in 'equity' than in actions at common law. By the early seventeenth century, the contrast between common law and Chancery process (and hence, in no small part, the differences between the extant records of the respective law courts) can be summed up as follows. First, whereas a civil suit at common law was usually begun with the purchase of a specific writ *in Latin* allowing the litigant to initiate a particular type of action (eg, an action in debt on contract), a case in Chancery was begun with the submission by the suitor of a bill of complaint *in English* detailing in non-technical language his situation and asking for appropriate relief.[9] More or less simultaneously, the complainant in Chancery would secure the issuance of a subpoena ordering the defendant(s) to appear and to answer under oath the bill of complaint. The bill and the defendant's answer, along with any further statements of their cases by the parties, are known collectively as 'the pleadings', and the employment of the vernacular in this and subsequent stages of the suit led contemporaries to employ the phrase 'English bill procedure' to characterize not only Chancery process but also that of analogous jurisdictions. In other words, English bill procedure meant that the complainant in Chancery was not bound to choose one specific form of action (each with its own rules about pleading) from among a range of hundreds of possibilities in the registers of common law writs. Second, one form of intermediate, or 'interlocutory', relief that the Court of Chancery could provide, and that was not available at common law, was the injunction. The injunction was an order of the Court barring the defendant either from continuing an ongoing action in another court over the matter raised by the complainant in Chancery (the so-called 'common injunction') or, alternatively, from engaging in any other action that might be irremediably damaging to the complainant (the 'special injunction' - eg, to bar the committing of waste on a tenement in which the plaintiff claimed an interest). The interlocutory injunction would remain in force until the defendant had appeared and answered or, in some circumstances, *until* the controversy was heard in Chancery.[10] Third, whereas the proofs in an early modern civil suit at common law that went to trial consisted of the testimony (and cross-examination) of each side's witnesses before a jury (and for the most part not recorded in writing), the proofs in a Chancery case by 1603 generally consisted of the testimony of witnesses whose depositions were taken out of court by either officials or commissioned agents of Chancery

---

8   C 38/1 starts with a single report misdated as of 1544 but in fact 1594; the remainder in this volume are from Elizabeth's reign with the earliest of 1562.
9   Note, however, that during the later fifteenth and the sixteenth centuries, the court of King's Bench 'developed its own bill system', partly in competition with Chancery; Baker, *Introduction*, pp 48, 49.
10 Requests for injunctions were commonly made in the bill of complaint; injunctions were allowed as a matter of course, until the defendant answered, if the defendant was answering by commission in the country.

and recorded in writing for subsequent use.[11] Consequently, the evidence involved in a Chancery suit is rather more likely to survive than the 'evidence' in a common law suit.[12] Witnesses in and around London were deposed by the Examiners; those in the country by specially-commissioned persons (often local officials in the early seventeenth century; more commonly solicitors a century later) named for the purpose. Thus, it was possible to interrogate witnesses from anywhere in England without requiring them to travel long distances. Moreover, where common law would not, save under special circumstances, allow sworn testimony from a party on grounds of the person's interest in the dispute, no such formal constraint operated in Chancery. Indeed, since a defendant's answer was submitted under oath (unless the plaintiff agreed to dispense with this requirement, as in a consent suit), it was possible, though uncommon, in Chancery to proceed to a hearing - if the parties so chose - simply on the allegations of the complainant and the answer of the defendant.

Fourth, it was possible for the Court to refer matters of fact (including the scrutiny of lengthy documents, such as business accounts) to a Master (usually one of the eleven, later ten, Masters in Ordinary but also, if the inquiry was to take place outside London, to a Master Extraordinary), thereby allowing an examination in depth of matters that might well have been too complex to be assimilated by a jury at common law.[13] Masters' reports of their findings in such references survive in considerable numbers for the seventeenth and eighteenth centuries, often providing further insight into the background and nature of the dispute.

Finally, the Lord Chancellor or the Master of the Rolls (who could only hear causes when the Chancellor was not sitting), upon assessment of the evidence submitted by the parties and reviewed in Masters' reports (if any), and after hearing the arguments of their counsel, would render a decision, recorded verbatim in the book of orders. And this decision, preceded by summaries of the contents of bills of complaint and answers thereto, depositions of witnesses, and Masters' reports, might then (upon payment of the requisite fees) be formally written out on parchment and enrolled, giving the 'decretal order' a greater measure of finality. Instead of simply seeking a rehearing, the losing party - to contest an enrolled decree - had to initiate a more formal reconsideration by way of a bill of review.

Chancery's civil jurisdiction was broad, but by no means all-encompassing.[14] Nor is it easy to define, save to say that the Court exercised jurisdiction over issues with which the common law courts had not been prepared to deal as Chancery evolved. This can be illustrated with respect to disputes over land. In principle, Chancery could not decide *legal* title in land (ie, title in fee simple or fee tail); by definition, *legal* title had been and remained the province of the common law courts. Yet Chancery might well consider disputes centring on land, if a trust or mortgage were involved or if what was at issue was possession or use rights. Hence,

---

11 Pre-trial depositions, to be sure, were often taken in criminal cases at common law. Again, it should be noted that up to the early seventeenth century, the common action of debt on contract was normally decided by wager at law, rather than by testimony before a jury; Baker, *Introduction*, pp 87-88.
12 Thus, a litigant at common law might initiate a Chancery suit for the purpose of discovery and deposition - in particular, to depose a witness who, by reason of age or expected departure from the realm, might not be present when the litigant's common law case came before a jury at trial.
13 Conversely, certain disputed issues of fact - in particular, those involving title to freehold and tithe claims - would normally be sent by Chancery for trial by jury as 'feigned issues' of law, with the Court retaining jurisdiction on the 'equity reserved'.
14 See Chapter Two for a quantitative analysis of the subject matter of disputes coming before Chancery.

what came to be known as *equitable* title, rights to land enforced in Chancery, also took shape.[15] Moreover, to enforce its decisions, Chancery could make permanent an injunction against waste or to quiet possession; it could also decree 'specific performance' (ie, order a party to perform a given act such as to convey title to a piece of land the party had originally contracted to sell). Insofar, then, as the Court could and did direct the behaviour of the parties with respect to the controversy, it was in a position to compel conduct that, at least for the duration of the parties' interests in the property in question, came close to resolving a range of land disputes.[16] And to enforce its decisions, it could punish the recalcitrant party by contempt process (imprisonment till he conformed) or even sequestration of that party's property until compliance.[17]

Here, it should be observed that the Court of Chancery was only the most important of a number of courts employing variants of English bill procedure in the early seventeenth century. A host of such jurisdictions existed in the provinces, including the 'equity side' of the Councils of the North and of Wales and also more geographically-circumscribed jurisdictions such as the Chancery Court of Dover. While Chancery's position in relation to these jurisdictions was one of 'dominance' as a central court of equity vis-à-vis provincial ones, their business in the early 1600s was extensive.[18] At the same time, other central courts using English bill procedure included the Court of Star Chamber and the Court of Requests. Thus, at Westminster, too, litigants seeking equitable remedies had a number of choices, though in Star Chamber 'the criminal aspect was more to the fore ... by Stuart times', while Chancery appears to have valued Requests principally as an 'alternative channel for smaller and trivial litigation' which did not meet its own jurisdictional thresholds (ten pounds in value or six acres in extent or a tenement yielding at least forty shillings yearly).[19]

As the Councils of the North and of Wales fell victim to attack by the Long Parliament and the Court of Requests perished of attrition under the conditions of civil war, Chancery itself was perhaps the most prominent target of the legal reformers once the first Civil War ended in 1646. Attacked for its linkage with the royal prerogative (the Chancellor, after all, was the crown's principal minister for matters of law) and, even more vociferously, for many

---

15 Hence, the equity of redemption - the right of a borrower upon mortgage to redeem the property despite an earlier failure to satisfy the terms of the mortgage. See Baker, *Introduction*, pp 356-357.
16 Edith G Henderson, 'Legal Rights to Land in the Early Chancery', *American Journal of Legal History* 26 (1982), 97-122, points out that many early Chancery decrees concerned land, with the complainant often alleging that he was in pursuit of the deeds of title. By the Restoration, the Court had made it a rule that a plaintiff suing for deeds must put in an affidavit swearing he was not in fact in possession of them.
17 Similarly, it is often said that Chancery could not order damages - that its particular remedy for a breach of a contract or the like was specific performance. But on occasion, it did impose monetary damages. One instance is the case of Eyre v Wortley (1627-1633; decree at C 78/458/5) in which the judgment against the defendant included a form of damages - ie, compensation for his delay of seven years in paying over the legacies which the Court found the Eyres to be entitled to; such damages were to be computed by a Master. See also Peter McDermott, 'Jurisdiction of the Court of Chancery to Award Damages', *Law Quarterly Review* 108 (1992), 652-673.
18 W J Jones, 'Palatine performance in the seventeenth century', in *The English Commonwealth 1547-1640* (1979), ed Peter Clark *et al*, 189-204.
19 Baker, *Introduction*, p 137; Jones, *Chancery*, p 382. Requests, to be sure, was not simply a poor man's Court by the early 1600s, and in any case Chancery did admit an occasional litigant *in forma pauperis* - that is, providing legal assistance and waiving fees.

of the deficiencies that Dickens and other nineteenth-century reformers would decry, the Court was made the target of a resolution calling for its abolition passed by the Nominated Parliament in 1653. But in fact, Chancery was less tainted by politics than Star Chamber and also too useful to be abolished, at least if a total revamping of the judicial system was not to be undertaken. Rather, in the hope of reducing costs and delays, Oliver Cromwell - acting upon the advice of moderate reformers - instituted a series of changes by executive decree in 1654. However, the so-called 'Ordinance of 1654' expired in 1658, so that even before the restoration of the monarchy two years later the Court's officials had revived its traditional procedures - procedures that would for the most part remain in use until the judicial reforms of the mid-nineteenth century.

Perhaps, then, the major consequences for Chancery of the storm over law reform of the mid-seventeenth century were twofold. First, after 1660 provincial jurisdictions in equity counted for less than they had before 1640. Second, what competition Chancery now had to face at Westminster came not from Star Chamber or Requests but from the 'equity side' of the Court of Exchequer. Already before 1640, the Exchequer's jurisdiction in equity had attracted a growing volume of business. Yet access to the Exchequer still seems to have been limited by its enforcement of the requirement that the complainant be entitled to invoke its jurisdiction by reason of a debt owing to the Crown. But from the late 1640s onwards, the Court of Exchequer ceased to look behind allegations by suitors that their complaint somehow involved a debt owing to the Crown.[20] If only, then, by reason of external shifts in terms of parallel and competing jurisdictions, Chancery emerged from the Civil War decades in a somewhat different position. On the one hand, the competition of the provincial courts of equity was diminished. But on the other, litigants now had the choice, in many matters, of pursuing their claims either in Chancery or in Exchequer.

It is, then, the unreformed Court of Chancery as the premier, but by no means the only equity court of the land in early modern England that is the focus of this handbook, and the surviving records of its proceedings during the seventeenth and eighteenth centuries that figure as its principal subject.

B. The Handbook

Although the searcher exploring the records of the Chancery's proceedings in equity in the seventeenth and eighteenth centuries does not, for the most part, have to struggle with formulaic Latin, there remain formidable hurdles to identifying and locating materials either in a given suit or in a category of suits. These may be briefly summarized. First, there is the enormous volume of paper and parchment that the Court's caseload and increasingly drawn-out process generated. Second, there is the fact that the materials for any suit are not grouped together; instead, the 'classes' in which the records of the Court's proceedings in equity are at present organized are largely based on the type of document involved (and/or by the office of the

---

20 Jones, *Chancery*, pp 342-344; W H Bryson, *The Equity Side of the Exchequer* (1975), p 24 and App 1. See also R M Ball, 'Tobias Eden, Change and Conflict in the Exchequer Office, 1672-1698', *Journal of Legal History* 11 (1990), 70-89.

Court charged with its making or receipt). Thus, pleadings are to be found in a series of pleading classes (depending on their date and in part also with which of the Six Clerks they were originally filed), depositions in another series (depending on date and whether taken in the metropolis or the provinces), Masters' reports and other Masters' documents in a variety of other classes (reflecting in part the various divisions of the Masterships), and so on. Third, there is the absence of any comprehensive index, by name or by place or by subject, to these suits. For the most part, there are merely lists and/or indexes to individual classes, and these - with but few exceptions - suffer from a variety of limitations. Relatively few are topographical, even fewer are by subject, and the nominal indexes to individual classes - many of them contemporaneous with the documents themselves - all too often list only the last name of one plaintiff and one defendant in 'alphabets' compiled term by term.

It is these very difficulties in utilizing the extremely rich Chancery records that have occasioned the production of this handbook. At the outset, a choice had to be made between a scheme to deal with all Chancery equity materials from the later fourteenth century at least up to the mid-nineteenth century reforms of the central courts, or a handbook covering a more limited time span. The decision to opt for the latter was based on a series of overlapping considerations, not least constraints of time and money, but above all the desire to carry out in-depth sampling of the records for the period to be studied. The starting and ending dates are arbitrary, but made sense partly in terms of the extensive work already done on the Elizabethan Chancery by Professor W J Jones and partly because it has been possible to carry the analysis of substantive issues up to 1820, thanks to the good fortune in discovering before work got underway the ongoing researches of Dr Patrick Polden on Chancery in the early 1800s.

In turn, no little of the value of this work rests on the four samples taken at four different points over the two centuries under scrutiny - altogether 969 sets of pleadings drawn from the years 1627, 1685, 1735 and 1785. The results of these researches, taken in conjunction with Dr Polden's 1818-1819 sample of 149 suits, will be considered in the chapters that follow in connection with a variety of questions.

The handbook itself is organized in four chapters. The first discusses how the Court did its business, and describes the work of the various officials and offices of the Court. The second examines the range and scope of Chancery's jurisdiction and analyses the character of the litigants who came before the Court. The third provides an annotated listing of the relevant Chancery classes and of the existing finding aids to those classes. The final chapter consists mainly of a series of 'specimen' searches, intended to illustrate in step-by-step fashion how searchers may be able to locate specific information or types of documents within the records of Chancery equity proceedings.

The text is supplemented by a glossary, a bibliography of printed and manuscript materials, and two appendixes: (1) an eighteenth-century account of the procedures of the Six Clerks for handling the pleadings records, and (2) a description of how the four samples were designed and compiled. The samples themselves have been published separately in *Samples of Chancery Pleadings and suits: 1627, 1685, 1735, and 1785* (List and Index Society, vol 257, 1995), compiled by Henry Horwitz and Charles Moreton.

CHAPTER ONE:
How the Court of Chancery Conducted its Business

A. Introduction

The conduct of Chancery business can be viewed from two different, if overlapping perspectives. The first is that of the litigant - especially the complainant who initiated the suit. Basically, the complainant was seeking some form of assistance from the Court. Ostensibly, and often in fact, that was the remedying of a wrong done to him or the warding off of an injustice. However, the litigant might have other aims in view as well, as an opponent of Sir Nicholas Barbon, the notorious London speculative builder of the later seventeenth century, indicated when he alleged that Barbon had threatened 'to keep the said [Edward] Proby in suit in Chancery about two years, and in that time will make out and convert all the brick-earth' on the premises in dispute.[1]

Among the more common objectives of complainants in Chancery, in addition to the righting of a wrong or preventing an injustice, were:

(1) securing the Court's formal sanction for a course of action upon which the parties were already agreed (ie, a collusive proceeding, most often encountered in the administration of a trust or estate);[2]
(2) putting pressure upon an opponent to compromise or to settle a dispute by the threat of expense and delay involved in judicial proceedings;
(3) blocking - at least for a time - adverse action in another court;
(4) using Chancery process as a means of making his opponent disclose his own position or situation by putting him under a compulsion to file an answer under oath; and /or
(5) securing discovery via the taking of depositions that might be used in cases in other courts.

From a somewhat different perspective, it could be said that a complainant was seeking either (a) some kind of formal action from the Court (whether a binding judgment or an interlocutory remedy (the injunction) or (b) some kind of leverage against an opponent which did not require any definitive decision from the Court. And here it should be noted that the worst that could happen to a complainant was to have his bill formally dismissed (a dismission); Chancery would not actually issue a decree against him on the sole basis of his original suit.[3]

As complainants came into Chancery with diverse aims, so the Court and its officials also had a variety of concerns. For one thing, the various officers had their own material

---

1 C 8/260/63, quoted by Elizabeth McKellar, 'Architectural Practice for Speculative Building in Late Seventeenth Century London', Royal College of Arts PhD, 1992, p 218.
2 An indicator of a collusive proceeding is that the complainant (and hence the Court) allows the defendant to answer without being under oath. Such collusive proceedings appear to become rather more common in the eighteenth century.
3 However, see the discussion below at p 15 of cross bills.

interests to serve; most of the subordinate officials of Chancery, as those of other courts, depended on the fee income derived from the performance of their functions (a common feature of governmental administration of the era). New offices had been created in Chancery as its business expanded and as its recordkeeping apparatus was elaborated over the course of the sixteenth and early seventeenth centuries, and there were recurrent boundary disputes among them which could sometimes affect how the complainants and their representatives were compelled to proceed. Of these internecine conflicts, the longest-running was between the Six Clerks and their one-time under-clerks, subsequently known as the Sworn Clerks and the Waiting Clerks.[4] Nor was the Lord Chancellor himself immune from such considerations. He had a substantial annual stipend from the Crown, but also he could and did profit from the sale of offices of the Court in his gift.[5]

Beyond the pursuit of and occasional conflict over such material interests, the Court as an institution was greatly affected by two concerns which pulled it in different directions. One was the commitment in principle of the Lord Chancellor to get to the bottom of the individual complaints brought before the Court in order to render appropriate relief, and especially in cases where fraud might have been committed. As one student of Chancery has observed: 'the first object of inquiry in Equity is the defendant's conscience, rather than the plaintiff's right', by contrast to the common law.[6] The other was the pressure to deal with the rising tide of cases that washed over Chancery (to be discussed in Chapter Two) along with the other central courts, in the later sixteenth century and for much of the seventeenth century. This surge of business (and a subsequent revival in the early nineteenth century) tended, not surprisingly, to prolong suits, especially since the Court was short of judges. Besides the Chancellor, only the Master of the Rolls could decide causes, and he could sit to do so only when the Chancellor was not himself sitting in Court. To be sure, that left the Master of the Rolls considerable opportunity, for given his many other official responsibilities the Chancellor could not be a full-time judge. Nonetheless, the Master of the Rolls' judgments were subject to rehearing by the Chancellor. Moreover, the Master of the Rolls' authority, even after a clarifying act of parliament of 1730 (3 George II, c 30), was limited in other respects, too: in part, by the requirement that he act in conjunction with at least two either of the Masters in Ordinary or of the common law judges (out of term), in part by the rule that enrolment of all decrees required the signature of the Chancellor.

All in all, then, the way in which the Court and its officials handled the cases that came before them was a mixture of genuine idealism and bureaucratic self-interest, compounded by

---

4   Together, the two are sometimes styled 'the Clerks in Court' in the eighteenth century. The 'Waiting Clerks', as their name suggests, were men qualified by an apprenticeship to become Sworn Clerks and serving in a subordinate position waiting for a Sworn Clerkship to become vacant.
5   Charges of judicial corruption (admittedly driven by political aims) brought down Sir Francis Bacon in 1621; what toppled Lord Chancellor Macclesfield little more than a century later, amidst a larger scandal focussing on defalcations by several of the Masters with respect to litigants' funds in their safekeeping, was the sale of the Masterships and other offices in his disposal. The financial scandal led to the creation of a new post, the Accountant-General (who became one of the eleven Masters in ordinary), to safeguard the mounting volume of funds in court. The records of the Accountant General survive from the time of the post's creation in the mid-1720s; they were never deposited in the PRO and are presently in the keeping of the Court Funds Office.
6   Yale, *Manual*, p 23.

overwork and complicated by the manoeuvres of the opposing parties for whom delay and obfuscation might well be advantageous.

These intersecting concerns and perspectives can, in turn, be discerned both in the formal orders of the Court and in the ways litigants behaved and the channels through which their suits progressed. The earliest recorded order of Chancery regulating the conduct of proceedings in equity dates from the mid-sixteenth century, and thereafter they multiplied, not least when reforming Chancellors of the later sixteenth and early seventeenth centuries - Sir Nicholas Bacon, Lord Ellesmere, and Sir Francis Bacon - delineated their concerns in revised and amplified sets of orders.[7] But however meticulously Chancellors spelled out the standards and rules of the Court, enforcement of these orders was by no means assured. Indeed, by the eighteenth century, it appears that some rules were more honoured in the breach than in the observance, reflecting the informal supersession in current practice of older standards. Yet, newer ways were rarely embodied in orders of court, thus further complicating the solicitor's task in managing suits. As Lord Chancellor Eldon remarked in an 1813 case: 'Much of the modern practice will, I fear, be found inconsistent with subsisting orders, without any contradiction of them by subsequent orders; and, upon principle, repeated decisions, forming a series of practice, as it must be, against an order, may with safety be taken to amount to a reversal of that order.'[8]

As the Court's concerns and conduct were articulated in its orders and then modified over time by shifting patterns of observance, so complainants' diverse aims and objectives were mirrored in the conduct of their suits. It is, indeed, noteworthy that many complainants did not pursue their suits very far. For over one-quarter of the suits in the period, there survive only the bills of complaint, and in most of these instances there is no evidence that an answer was ever made.[9] So we must presume that for a sizeable minority of complainants, filing of the bill (or even the securing of a subpoena ordering their opponents to answer an as-yet unfiled bill) sufficed to promote an informal settlement *or* otherwise exhausted their commitment to action in Chancery.[10] For the majority of suitors who did pursue their cases further, there were significant costs. Not only did they have to pay fees to Court officials for the performance of their functions, but there were also the expenses incurred in employing their own legal representatives. Whereas in the early days of Chancery the Six Clerks had acted for individual

---

7   The orders, taken from C 33 and a number of ancillary sources, are printed in George W Sanders, *The Orders of the High Court of Chancery* (1845) [hereafter Sanders, *Orders*].
8   In the case of *Boehm v De Tastet* (1813) quoted in Joseph Parkes, *A History of the Court of Chancery* (1828), p 451.
9   See Chapter Three for a discussion of the issue of wastage and loss of Chancery equity records. The Six Clerks frequently filed such 'single bills' separately, a practice illustrated by the old alphabet to C 6.
10 It was possible for a potential complainant in Chancery to secure the issuance of a subpoena to a potential defendant before the complainant filed his bill; a penalty would attach, however, if he failed to file by the time the defendant appeared. While there was frequent criticism of this aspect of Chancery process as allowing the unscrupulous to harass their enemies, one Interregnum defender of the Court - noting that 'in this last year' some 9,000 subpoenas to answer had been issued but only 6,000 bills of complaint exhibited - read this as evidence that the issuance of a subpoena often sufficed to promote out-of-court settlements: *A View of the Regulation of the Chancery* (1654), p 2. See below pp 15-16.

suitors (a role already being assumed by their under-clerks in the later sixteenth century), during the seventeenth and eighteenth centuries most suitors also employed their own solicitors to look after the management of their suits and feed counsel to advise on strategy and to argue their positions when formal hearings were held.[11]

In dissecting the course of a suit in Chancery, two other general features need to be kept in mind. In the first place, as it was the complainant who took the initiative at the outset, so thereafter it was the respective parties who largely determined the pace at which the suit proceeded. The Court had rules and deadlines, but it was up to the parties or their representatives to see to their observance - for example, it was up to the defendant to move for the dismissal of a suit if a plaintiff had failed to respond with a replication to the defendant's answer within the requisite time and it was also up to the defendant to make counter-arguments if under such circumstances a plaintiff came into Court, sought to excuse his previous failure to act, and asked for an extension.

In the second place, in pursuing their courses of action, the parties had to manoeuvre within the framework of the Court's bureaucratic structure and the requirements of the various offices and officers involved in the course of a suit. While the principal offices of the Court were sited on or close by Chancery Lane (The Rolls Chapel, The Masters' Offices ['the Public Office'], the Six Clerks' Office, the Subpoena Office, the Examiners' Office, the Affidavit Office, and the Register's Report Office), the Lord Chancellor - who also presided over the House of Lords when parliament sat - was mainly based at Westminster. The parties, or their representatives, had also to bear in mind the Court's calendar. Thus, during term (according to the published schedules of the eighteenth century) the Lord Chancellor heard causes only on Mondays, Tuesdays, and Fridays at Westminster, with rehearings on Saturdays; the Master of the Rolls heard causes, rehearings, 'further directions' (in cases in which the Court retained a continuing jurisdiction), and a variety of other matters on Monday, Tuesday, and Thursday evenings at the Rolls Chapel.[12] And besides such complications, suitors had also to be mindful of other matters of timing, not least the hours of attendance and the means of appointment for carrying on references before a Master.

Like the common law courts, Chancery observed four terms - Michaelmas, Hilary, Easter, and Trinity - and entries in the books of orders, compiled by the deputy registers and their clerks, were grouped by term.[13] But while the common law judges went on assizes through the kingdom twice yearly, the Lord Chancellor and his judicial staff remained in London, and so it was possible to transact many kinds of business out of term - in particular, the Master of Rolls would continue to hear causes during the intervals between terms, though with a break during the long summer vacation.

What, then, were the stages of a Chancery suit from the filing of a bill of complaint to the formal hearing of the cause? The account that follows is based on two principal sources:

---

11 For a detailed and term by term breakdown of the Court and legal costs that various types of suits might entail by the later 1700s, see [Samuel Turner], *Costs in the Court of Chancery* (2nd edn, 1795). The Clerks in Court took on a double role in some instances - acting as solicitors (or London agents for country solicitors) as well as officers of the Court.
12 In addition, the Lord Chancellor heard exceptions, pleas and demurrers on Wednesday and Friday afternoons in term at Lincoln's Inn Hall, a venue first resorted to in the early eighteenth century.
13 The Register was a sinecurist.

first, the practice manuals (listed in the Bibliography) published in increasing number from the late sixteenth century onwards for the use of would-be practitioners in Chancery (and the other central courts); second, the evidence accumulated in tracing samples of Chancery suits. On the one hand, the practice manuals are informative about the technical requirements parties had to satisfy, though Mr Jackson (a Clerk in Court), making a submission to a parliamentary inquiry on Chancery in the mid-1820s, suggested that 'although correct in many points ... yet in others [the practice manuals] most grievously mislead the practitioner' - a problem he attributed to the complexity of the Court's (unpublished) rules of practice.[14] On the other hand, the samples indicate, in a way that goes beyond the technical descriptions of the manuals, how parties to those particular suits actually proceeded.

B. The Procedure of the Court: the Manuals of Practice

The first published manual exclusively devoted to practice in the Court of Chancery, *The Practice of the High Court of Chancery Unfolded*, appeared in late 1651, well after Chancery's emergence as the fourth of the great central courts of the realm. However, *The Practice* appears to reflect the workings of the Court in the early seventeenth century, and it had precursors in older works which often combined reports of cases and information about practice in a variety of courts.[15]

The Practice proved useful enough to reprint in 1672, but it was eventually overtaken by larger-scale offerings such as William Brown's *Praxis Almae Curia Cancellariae* (published first in two volumes in 1694) and William Bohun's *Cursus Cancellaria* (1715). Nor did these works sate the market. The middle decades of the eighteenth century saw the publication of a number of purportedly comprehensive manuals (including those by Richard Boote, Jeffrey Gilbert, and Joseph Harrison), with their authors often proclaiming their expertise - if not always providing their names - by styling themselves 'a Gentleman of Lincoln Inn', 'a solicitor of the Court', and the like. The later 1700s were distinguished by the appearance of even more specialized publications - notably John Mitford's treatise on pleading in Chancery, Samuel Turner's works on costs in Chancery, and the anonymous *Collection of Interrogatories for the Examination of Witnesses in Courts of Equity, as Settled by the most eminent Counsel*, penned 'by an old solicitor' and published first in 1775.

There is, then, ample evidence from the early seventeenth century onwards for the outlines and, increasingly, the nuances of Chancery practice, and the following account is a distillation from these sources.

I The First Stage: Pleadings and the Six Clerks

The initial stage of a Chancery suit was the filing of a written bill of complaint. In principle, bills were supposed to follow a standard tripartite format, with the complainant (giving his

---

14 *Parliamentary Papers* 1826 (143) xvi, app B(24) 552.
15 Perhaps the most important of these were William West's *Three Treatises, of the second part of Symbolograephia ... whereto is annexed another Treatise of Equitie* (1594) and Thomas Powell's *The Attourneys Academy* (1623). The Bibliography lists the most important practice manuals, and many secondary ones, of the seventeenth, eighteenth and early nineteenth centuries.

How the Court of Chancery Conducted its Business

Diagram: Chancery Equity Process and Associated Records

1 **Pleadings** ---→ 2 **Proofs** ---→ 3 **Hearings & Decrees (and related masters' papers and proceedings)** ---→ 4 **Enforcement & Rehearings**

Pleadings:
- Bills of Complaint
- Response(s)
- C 2 - C 12
- Subpoenas C 33

Proofs:
- Interrogatories and Depositions
- C 21 - C 22
- C 24 - C 25
- (and C 11 - C 12)

Hearings & Decrees:
- C 33
- C 78 - C 79
- C 38 - C 40
- C 101 - C 129

Enforcement & Rehearings:
- C 33
- C 36

INTERLOCUTORY (may be submitted at any stage)

INJUNCTIONS — C 38 - C 40
MOTIONS — C 33
PETITIONS — C 28

13

name, status and/or occupation, and place of residence) stating on parchment the relevant facts of his complaint, going on to allege that it was impossible to secure a remedy without the Court's action, and praying relief - relief which normally include a request for a subpoena and often a request for an injunction. By the later eighteenth century, this relatively simple format had been elaborated, but the crux of the matter remained the statement of the facts of the complaint. Of the nine parts distinguished by practice manuals of later date, perhaps the only one worthy of additional remark was the standard allegation of confederacy between the named defendant(s) and other unnamed parties. If this formula had any specific function, it was to allow for the subsequent inclusion of additional defendants to the case.[16] The bill was to be signed by the complainant's counsel; his signature attested to his belief that the complainant was not acting frivolously or without cause.

The bill was to be filed in one of the Six Clerks' offices and dated as of the day of filing. In origin, the Six Clerks were the attorneys of Chancery with a monopoly of acting for complainants in the Court. By the 1620s, having just rebuilt their offices in Chancery Lane after a fire destroyed their previous quarters, the Six Clerks were well on their way to becoming sinecurists, with much of their original work being done by those whom they styled their 'under-clerks', some seventy-two in number by Charles I's reign (reflecting the rapid expansion of the Court's business) and who usually secured their places by purchase from the respective Six Clerk in whose division they acted.[17] But if the 'under-clerks', eventually transmuted into the 'Sworn Clerks' by Lord Keeper Bridgeman's order of 1668, took over in the seventeenth century much of the representative function once exercised by the Six Clerks, the Six Clerks remained in control of recording and keeping of the 'pleadings'. Meanwhile, the work of the Sworn Clerks and the Clerks in Waiting as 'attorneys' to the litigant was increasingly supplemented by the parties' employment of their own 'solicitors' to look after their cases in Chancery in conjunction with one or another of these Clerks in Court.

Once a bill of complaint was filed, the next issue was getting the defendant to appear (ie, to acknowledge the Court's jurisdiction) and to make a response, again in writing. Several different kinds of responses might be offered, in addition or in alternative to the usual - the sworn answer.[18] One, the disclaimer, took the defendant wholly out of the suit by disavowing any interest in the matter in dispute and ceding any claim that he might be thought to have in the matter to the complainant. A second, the demurrer, sought to evade the force of the complaint by admitting the truth of the complainant's factual allegations but then going on to argue that

---

16 John Wyatt, *The Practical Register in Chancery* (1800), p 63 [hereafter cited as Wyatt, *Register* (1800)]. Wyatt's is a composite work reprinting a manual of 1714, with substantial additions of his own, the former printed in brackets. See also C Churches, '"Equity against a purchaser shall not be:" a seventeenth-century case study in landholding and indebtedness', *Parergon* new series 11 no 2 (Dec 1993), p 78 (speaking of the allegation of confederacy in a bill of 1674 exhibited by Sir John Lowther: 'Lowther very well knew there was no such confederacy'; his purpose was to secure 'from the other parties their assurance that their claims [against the principal defendant] had been met in full or else of what remained outstanding, the whole to be put on record in the court.')

17 E 215/498 and 501 (documents submitted to the Commissions on Fees of Charles I's reign, the former dated 26 Nov 1629).

18 Sir William Holdsworth, *A History of English Law* IX (1926), has a full and informative discussion of pleading at pp 376-408, including examples of bills and an answer.

these charges did not present any cause to which the defendant might reasonably be expected to answer. A third, the plea, amounted to the raising of a ground in law, frequently jurisdictional in nature, to forestall the complainant - eg, that the matter in question was not one of equity and hence not to be heard in Chancery but in some other court, usually either a court of common law or an ecclesiastical court. Defendants' demurrers were normally referred to a Master for a recommendation as to acceptance or rejection; however, the Court itself would usually refer pleas involving a clear-cut point of law to the common law judges.[19] Should a demurrer or a plea be rejected, the defendant would have to submit an answer. Defendants might choose at the outset to respond in the alternative submitting simultaneously, for instance, both a demurrer and an answer; if the former was rejected, the suit would then go forward on the basis of the answer. However, for a defendant less interested in expedition (and perhaps with a bigger purse than his opponent), the opportunity for delay inherent in first offering a plea or demurrer (or even an insufficient answer) was substantial. Although, in principle, an overruled plea or demurrer (or an answer found insufficient) was to be followed within eight days by the submission of a further answer without need for enforcement by a new subpoena, this rule, made an order of court by Lord Keeper Bridgeman, was not enforced, 'and by this means it has happened a Plaintiff has been two or three years getting a sufficient answer.'[20]

Basically, a sufficient answer involved a denial (unless the suit was a collusive one), to be attested under oath by the party, of all or some of the relevant or material factual allegations of the complainant; the denial would commonly go hand in hand with the defendant's own version of the controversy or disputed transaction. Besides disclaimer, plea, demurrer, or answer, one other option was open to some defendants. That was to file a cross bill - to make the complainant the defendant in a second but inter-linked suit. This was a course the defendant could pursue if he thought the original bill itself (inadvertently) opened the door for a claim by him against the complainant. A cross bill might be filed at any time during the pleadings stage, and thereafter proceedings on the two bills would usually move forward together. Under such circumstances, it was possible for a complainant to have his original bill dismissed and judgment found against him on the defendant's cross bill.

Although defendants had a variety of options by way of response to the bill of complaint, it was not always easy to get a named defendant to appear and respond. Hence, the complainant's invocation of the Court's power to subpoena (an order to appear and answer, subject to penalty for failure) - a power which the complainant might seek to utilize even before filing his bill of complaint or might request as part of the relief prayed for in the bill itself. Paradoxically, since the filing of pleadings was the province of the Six Clerks while the issuance of a subpoena was not, often the first notice in the Court's books of orders (kept by the deputy registers and their clerks) of a suit concerns the issuance of a subpoena or other process to enforce the defendant's appearance. Subpoenas had since 1575 been the work of the newly-established Subpoena Office, with quarters in the southeast corner of the Rolls Yard, adjacent to the Rolls Chapel in Chancery Lane where the Master of the Rolls presided. From the viewpoint of the individual summoned, the subpoena's principal disadvantage was that it did not specify the nature of the

---

19 Jones, *Chancery*, p 208; Yale, *Manual*, pp 100-101.
20 *Observations on the Dilatory and Expensive Proceedings in the Court of Chancery* (1701), pp 2-3.

complaint to which he was to respond. This difficulty was compounded by the fact that subpoenas were frequently (though not always) issued before the actual filing of the bill for the 'ease', according to Thomas Powell, of suitors.[21] Though the parliamentary act of 1706 for amending the law (which included several provisions relating to the conduct of Chancery business) specified that bills be exhibited before subpoenas issued, the requirement of the act seems, by the testimony of the eighteenth-century practice manuals, to have been more honoured in the breach than in the observance, thus perpetuating a long-standing grievance.[22] Costs, however, would be assessed by the Court if the plaintiff failed to file his bill by the time the subpoena was returnable.

This is not to say that a subpoena alone would bring every defendant to appear, and the Court had more drastic powers of compulsion at its disposal, including the power of attachment (imprisonment until compliance) and even the power to sequester a defendant's property. But it was not until 1732 that parliament legislated to provide for the problem of the failure of the defendant to appear at all; under that legislation, after public advertisement in *The London Gazette*, Chancery might proceed *ex parte* and, if need be, render judgment by default.[23] Yet, no small part of the cause of delay in the initial stage of a suit even after 1732 was the Court's reluctance to proceed to judgment without the appearance of and answer by the defendant. Under most circumstances, a defendant need not appear in person; an appearance by his legal representative would suffice. Nor need he journey to London to file an answer (or other response); the Court would allow parties resident outside London to give in their answers to a commission named for that purpose. For this purpose, the commissions were accompanied by a copy of the complainant's bill until the requirement for the making of such copies, a charge to the defendant, was, after recurrent complaints of the unnecessary cost, abolished by the act of 1706 (with the Sworn Clerks compensated for the loss of the fees involved at the expense of the Six Clerks).[24]

But whether the written answer was submitted in town or to commissioners in the country, it was - unlike the plaintiff's bill - to be made under oath (save in special circumstances), and the defendant was bound by whatever admissions he made therein that were germane to the suit.[25] Answers, in turn, might be backed up by documentation intended to support the defendant's position, and such material - often in the form of schedules of account - would be attached to and filed with the answer itself.[26]

With the defendant appearing and answering, the stage was set for further exchanges between the parties. On the one hand, the complainant might offer exceptions to the answer

---

21 *The Attourneys Academy* (1623), p 1.
22 4/5 Anne, c 3; Wyatt, *Register* (1800), pp 44-45.
23 5 George II, c 25. On Chancery's inclusion within the ambit of a statute first passed with respect to the courts of common law, see Stephen C Yeazell, 'Default and Modern Process', *Legal History in the Making* (1991), ed W M Gordon & T D Fergus, esp pp 129-132.
24 For contemporary pamphlet material on the various episodes of the quarrels between the Six Clerks and the Sworn Clerks, see the Bibliography.
25 As sworn documents, answers from earlier suits might be introduced in evidence in subsequent ones if the party making the answer were no longer alive (just as depositions from witnesses no longer alive or out of the realm might similarly be used). The usual reason for the Court to waive the requirement that the answer be sworn was that the suit was collusive and the plaintiff had petitioned for such a waiver.
26 Occasionally, a plaintiff might also submit detailed accounts or the like.

itself, on the grounds that it contained impertinent or scandalous matter or, more commonly, that it was insufficient - that it did not either deny or admit the material allegations of the complaint. If the defendant failed in due time to put in a 'further answer' satisfying such exceptions, the original answer and the exceptions would be referred to the consideration of one of the Masters. And if the Master's report to the Court pronounced the answer insufficient, 'scandalous', or otherwise defective, and if the Court accepted this report, the defendant would be bound to submit a revised answer (the 'further answer') that met these objections.[27] Normally, only this subsequent, satisfactory answer, if submitted, would be preserved among the Court's records.

Once an acceptable answer had been submitted, the complainant was required within three terms to respond with his replication. Failure to meet this deadline entitled the defendant to move to dismiss the bill of complaint. A replication might be *pro forma*, a brief paragraph or two in formulaic terms intended to close out the pleadings (by eschewing any new facts or arguments that the defendant would need to controvert), or the plaintiff might introduce new factual allegations, supportive of, yet not deviating in essentials from the statements he had already made in his complaint. To this, the defendant might enter a rejoinder - a reiteration of the principal assertions of his answer, with any possible elaborations he thought useful, especially in the light of his opponent's replication. Indeed, even further exchanges beyond the replication and rejoinder were allowed under the Court's rules, but these possibilities were rarely exploited. As one practice manual observed in 1800: 'According to the present course of the Court, rejoinders, surrejoinders, rebutters, and surrebutters are disused.'[28] By then, the replication was almost always *pro forma* and used to close the pleadings stage so as to advance to those of the proofs and the hearing. Thus, by the eighteenth century, and to a fair measure even earlier, bill, answer, and replication constituted the normal pleadings, followed by the issuance by the plaintiff to the defendant of a subpoena to rejoin - a step which would be followed by the beginning of the process of taking depositions unless both parties agreed to proceed directly to a hearing.

Not surprisingly, occasions arose when the rules governing the content of replications were felt to be unduly constraining. Hence, the Court would allow the submission of an 'amended' bill (the original bill with alterations made to it, with the date of such alterations) - an increasingly common phenomenon in the eighteenth century. The amendment sought usually involved a change in the identity of the parties on the opposing side - the addition of a new defendant as a 'necessary party' (ie, someone whose interests would be directly affected by a judgment for the plaintiff) or, on occasion, the omission of an individual named in the original bill. Such amendments might also be prompted by material in a defendant's answer. Hence, upon payment of the stipulated fees, an amended bill could also be filed after the defendant's answer. (Indeed, it was possible even after a rule for publication had passed - that is, after witnesses' depositions had been taken - to add new parties if at this stage it became apparent that not all the proper parties were included.) Naturally, such amendment would prolong the

---

27 '[A]nything ... alledged in a ... pleading, in such language as is unbecoming the Court to hear, or as is contrary to all good manners' or 'which chargeth some person with a crime not necessary to be shewn in the cause ... is accounted scandal': Wyatt, *Register* (1800), p 383.
28 Wyatt, *Register* (1800), p 372.

pleadings since the defendant, if he had already answered, would have to be allowed time to alter his answer (under these circumstances, he would also be allowed costs); as a consequence, the date by which the complainant had to file his replication would have to be extended.

However, if the plaintiff had already submitted his replication, new substantive matter coming to his attention could only be incorporated in his case by way of a 'supplemental' bill. Such a supplemental bill could be filed as a matter 'of course' - that is, without the prior permission of the Court.

In turn, all the pleadings - complainant's bill(s), defendant's response(s), and complainant's replication - were supposed to end up on file (usually held together by string or drawing pins) in the office of the particular Six Clerk with whom the original bill had been entered.[29] The Six Clerks kept track, at least from the early seventeenth century onwards, of the bills and other pleadings filed in their respective offices by entering their titles (ie, the names of the first plaintiff and of the first defendant) in books of record, respectively the bill book which covered all the bills exhibited in that legal year in all the Six Clerks' offices, and the cause books of each of the Six Clerks (which tracked the various stages of the pleadings). Files of pleadings were held in the respective Six Clerks' offices for a limited period (standardized as six terms in the eighteenth century). They were then transferred to the Six Clerks' record repository. Finally, at irregular intervals, the Six Clerks would transfer the overflow of records from their record room to the Court's long-term repository, first the Rolls Chapel, and later the Tower of London.

Not everything, of course, went so smoothly, and there were indeed many opportunities for slippage. In the first place, the division of responsibility among the Six Clerks, with opposing parties having different Six Clerks, made for complications. In the second place, since the real work as attorneys in the Court was being conducted by the Sworn Clerks, not the Six Clerks, it was often either the Sworn Clerk for the plaintiff or his counterpart for the defendant who had possession of the originals as the suit proceeded. (Possession of the originals was needed for various purposes, but above all for the making of copies, from which both the Sworn Clerks and the Six Clerks derived a significant proportion of their income.) And in the third place, even if all the documents ended up back in the appropriate Six Clerk's office, there was no guarantee that he (or his deputy) would maintain the necessary listings and do the requisite work of filing and safekeeping.

The related problems of misplacement and loss of Chancery pleadings and other documents will be discussed in detail in Chapter Three. For the moment, this account of the pleadings stage may be concluded with the observation that as it was the Six Clerks' responsibility to list and to safeguard the original pleadings, so should there be any dispute in the course of the suit as to whether a particular pleading had been filed or the date of its filing, it was the Six Clerks' duty to certify the state of the matter to the Court on the basis of the original documents presumed to be in their custody.

---

29 A complainant was free to choose any one of the Six Clerks to file his bill. In practice, by the later 1600s the choice was which of the Sworn Clerks or Waiting Clerks he (or his solicitor) would choose as 'attorney', since that Sworn Clerk was committed to filing bills he accepted in the particular Six Clerk's division of which he was a member. During Charles I's reign and again during Charles II's reign, there were experiments in allocating plaintiffs (by the first letters of their surnames) to one or another of the six divisions but these experiments foundered on the opposition of the Sworn Clerks.

II Interlocutory relief and interlocutory process

If a complainant sought an injunction, whether to restrain his opponent from pursuing proceedings in another court (the 'common injunction') or from carrying out some potentially irremediable act before his present suit in Chancery could be adjudicated (the 'special injunction' - eg, to halt the sale of a book to which the plaintiff held copyright), he might do so in his bill of complaint or, after filing his bill, by motion to the Court. If the defendant sought permission to answer in the country or failed to appear and answer promptly, the Court authorized the issuance of the writ of injunction (under the signature of the Chancellor or Master of the Rolls) as a matter of course. But once a defendant had answered, the burden would be on the complainant to show cause for any continuation of the injunction, with such questions sometimes being referred to a Master for investigation of the relevant circumstances. Should a defendant wish for any reason to seek an injunction (a rather uncommon occurrence), he could do after filing his answer.

In the early seventeenth century, a goodly proportion of plaintiffs did seek injunctions (indeed, for some it was their principal aim); by the eighteenth century, and reflecting Chancery's somewhat narrowed scope of business, such requests for injunction became less frequent.[30] But whatever the frequency of such requests, it was understood that the party who obtained an injunction must prosecute his case in Chancery without delay or risk a prompt challenge from his opponent for termination of the injunction. By and large, then, the records with respect to proceedings on the issuance of an injunction consist of formal entries in the Court's books of orders. However, the texts of the Masters' reports on injunctions (and on pleadings) are preserved in the volumes of Masters' reports which were filed in the Report Office maintained by the deputy registers.

As the books of orders note motions for the grant and dissolution of injunctions, so they record a range of other interlocutory matters, some made as motions in Court, others submitted in writing as petitions. Such requests ranged in significance from matters of course to matters of consequence, and might be made at virtually any stage of a suit. If substantive, such requests would require formal consideration by the Court, with the representatives of the opposing parties being heard, and might eventuate in the issuance of a formal order by the Chancellor or the Master of the Rolls. Their frequency is suggested by the lament of one mid-seventeenth century account of Chancery practice: 'Motions more then needful, and not tending to the end of the Cause, are many times the cause of long and tedious suits'.[31] And their elaboration is suggested by the detailed accounts of types of motions in later practice manuals. Thus, Maddock, writing in the early 1800s, listed no less than eleven different motions that might be made by the plaintiff after filing his bill and before answer was made, fifteen different motions that the defendant might make during the same stage, eighteen that might be made between filing of an answer and hearing of the cause, and thirteen more after a decree had been pronounced.[32]

---

30 By contrast, the frequency of injunctions was increasing in the Court of Exchequer's equity business.
31 *The Practice of the High Court of Chancery Unfolded* (1651), p 30.
32 Henry Maddock, *A Treatise on the Principles and Practice of the High Court of Chancery* (1820), II, 216-505.

III Proofs: Interrogatories, Depositions, and Exhibits

The next stage of a Chancery case, the presentation of proofs, began after the exchange of pleadings had ended, unless both parties were prepared to go to a hearing simply on the strength of the cases they had made out in the pleadings (including the attachments, usually accounts, submitted by some parties). The principal, though not the invariable, mode of proof was the taking of testimony from the witnesses designated by the opposing sides. Normally, testimony was taken out of Court (though it was possible with special permission to examine witnesses *viva voce* at the hearing of the cause for a limited number of purposes, as, for example, to authenticate a document). And while the parties themselves were rarely summoned as witnesses (though occasionally some defendants in the case were transmuted into witnesses, by consent), it should be borne in mind that the defendant's answer was on oath and he was bound by whatever he had therein admitted. The taking of testimony was the responsibility of the Office of Examiners (also situated in Chancery Lane in Symonds' Inn, just north of the Rolls Chapel) with respect to witnesses normally residing in or near London. The interrogation of witnesses residing in the provinces, long a matter of dispute between the Examiners and Six Clerks, was from Charles I's reign regularly delegated to specially-named commissioners from the localities concerned (to be chosen by both parties) with witnesses' depositions to be returned, along with the interrogatories, to the Six Clerk for the plaintiff in the suit.[33]

Whoever was charged with the taking of testimony, their responsibility was strictly confined to that task. The witnesses were simply asked to answer under oath to lists of written questions (interrogatories) drawn up by the respective parties. While each side might supply interrogatories for some or all of the witnesses of the opposing side, they could not cross-examine them in the conventional sense. Rather, the questioner simply put the interrogatories to the witnesses, memorialized in writing the answers of the witnesses (the depositions), and then read back their statements to the deponents. If deposition was by commission in the country, the interrogatories and depositions were supposed to be filed with the pleadings; the Examiners' Office kept custody of all those taken in London.[34]

Once both sides in a suit had all their witnesses deposed, the Court, at the motion of one of the parties (usually the plaintiff), issued a rule for 'publication' - that is, set a day when the depositions in the case were 'published' in open court. It was only at this stage that the two sides were permitted access to the statements of each other's witnesses - though allegations of pre-publication disclosures were occasionally made. At this juncture, either party was free to file exceptions in the Examiners' Office against the credit of the other side's witnesses (provided that the objecting party had not, in effect, 'established' a particular witness by including him or her among its own list of witnesses).

By this stage, too, the parties would have been obliged to bring in any documentary evidence they wished to offer themselves or had sought, usually by motion, from the opposing side. Such materials would be received by the Usher of the Court, as one of his multifarious

---

33 An account of this dispute is given by Lord Chancellor Nottingham; Yale, *Manual*, pp 153-154. See also Jones, *Chancery*, pp 137-142. It would appear that while it was common for Justices of the Peace and other local notables to serve as commissioners in the early 1600s, by the later 1700s it was more common for lesser local men, notably solicitors, to act.

34 In fact, country depositions are filed separately from the pleadings until the eighteenth century.

ministerial tasks. Documentary evidence submitted as exhibits varied in substance depending on the nature of the dispute; it might include title and other property documents, account books, or any other materials deemed useful by either side. It might be submitted voluntarily, as, for instance, via an attachment to a party's bill or answer, but it might also be produced under Court order upon the motion or petition of one side or the other.

The efficacy of the Chancery's procedures for examining witnesses was frequently criticized in the later seventeenth and eighteenth centuries on a variety of grounds, chiefly the lack of flexibility and also the lack of opportunity to test the witnesses' veracity before the Court. And indeed, the Court, after reviewing the depositions and any other proofs at a hearing of the cause, might, if in doubt, refer a question of fact to trial at common law on a 'feigned issue', before proceeding to come to a decision informed by a jury's verdict.[35] Just how common this practice was is not easy to determine. Various contemporaries, including a House of Commons committee of 1705-1706 and some of the witnesses before the parliamentary inquiry on Chancery in the mid-1820s, stated that such directions were frequently issued by Chancery.[36] And certainly, this procedure was understood by the Court to be required if the relevant factual question was a rectorial right to tithes or a matter of right in an heir at law. However, the assertion that such 'feigned issues' were frequent in the later 1600s and the 1700s cannot stand unqualified. In the first place, informed opinion was by no means at one on the point; others of the witnesses before the parliamentary committee of inquiry of the mid-1820s flatly contradicted their fellows. Thus, John Bell KC, answering the question as 'to the number of issues directed in proportion to the causes', replied: 'they are very few in number'.[37] In the second place, the detailed examination of cases does not support the assertion: of the 246 suits traced from the 1685 and 1785 samples, only five saw this course adopted.[38] On the whole, then, it would appear that even in the eighteenth century, the usual mode of proof in a Chancery suit was by deposition, with recourse to common law juries an occasional expedient, and one resorted to only after depositions had been taken and a hearing held.

IV Hearing, Master's Report, and Decree

In principle, the stage was now set for the fixing of a date for the hearing before the presiding judge - the Lord Chancellor or the Master of the Rolls. But in practice, the road was not so

---

35 Wyatt, *Register* (1800), p 263 [the following quotation comes from the early eighteenth-century portion of the text]: 'If upon hearing, the proofs and facts are so doubtful, that the Court cannot well tell which way to determine the matter, especially where the question is touching a title of inheritance or freehold; the Court commonly orders and directs an issue at law to be tried by the jury, for the better informing and guiding the conscience of the Court.' By contrast, when such a problem arose on the equity side of Exchequer, it was simply referred to the common law side; Henry Maddock, *A Treatise on the Principles and Practice of the High Court of Chancery* (1820), II, 474.
36 These are the sources relied upon by Sir William Holdsworth, *A History of English Law* IX (1926), 357 and note 3. See also Yale, *Manual*, p 220.
37 *Parliamentary Papers* 1826 (143), xvi, app A(1), p 8. Bell excepted tithe cases from his general response, but in any case tithe cases were chiefly the province of the equity side of Exchequer and only a very limited number were litigated in Chancery. See also ibid, A(27), p 341, testimony of George Boone Roupell.
38 Again, of 268 decrees issued by Chancery in 1785, at most four seem to have involved directed issues at common law.

smooth. For one thing, if any party had died in the months (and years) of the intervening stages of the case, the suit would have 'abated' and would have to be restarted by way of filing a bill of revivor to reinstate the litigation in the posture it had stood at the time of the death. The same requirement applied if a plaintiff who was a single woman married, for in that case her husband (under the common law doctrine of *coverture*) became a necessary party. Conversely, a married woman who was widowed in the course of litigation had the option of putting in a new bill or answer. Often, a bill of revivor would be accompanied by a supplemental bill to enable the plaintiff to add to or to enlarge his pleadings.

As death or, in the case of a woman, marriage (or remarriage) not infrequently interrupted Chancery suits, so progress to the hearing of a cause was often slowed by the Court's burden of business. The Court could only hear so many causes in a day (a dozen appears to have been the norm in the eighteenth century), and even with a day fixed on the Court's lists there might be further delays when parties (or sometimes their counsel) failed to attend.

Beyond the problems of scheduling the hearing and securing the requisite attendance, it was not uncommon for hearings to end without a definitive resolution, at least in detail. Frequently, after reviewing the pleadings, the depositions, and any other evidence submitted, the presiding judge would pronounce on the general issue and then make a 'reference': that is, refer the cause to one of the Masters in Ordinary with instruction to review some or all of the facts of the matter in the light of the judgment on the general issue and then to report back to the Court on how the judgment should be implemented - eg, how a disputed estate should be handled in terms of ascertaining of debts, marshalling of assets, reconciling conflicting claims among the beneficiaries, and providing for the guardianship and upbringing of minor beneficiaries.

It was, then, the responsibility of the parties to attend the Master so named. In principle, the Master's task was to inquire into disputed or simply relevant factual questions, not to get involved with the rights and wrongs of the matter, but this was not always a line easy to draw or to observe. And since the fees of the Master's clerks were dependent in large part upon the length of the Master's written reports, there was a constant temptation to extend the scope of the reference and to become involved in the general issue.[39] In any case, it was open to Masters not only to review the proofs in detail but also, if they saw fit, to question on oath, either via written interrogatories or *viva voce*, any of the witnesses or parties. Drafts of the report, when prepared, were then to be submitted for comments to each side.

As the opposing parties might try to influence the Master's view of the matter by their own or their legal representatives' presentations, so it was open to them, if they objected to the substance of the report after it was made, to lay exceptions (confined to submissions previously made to the Master) before the Court and have them argued there. The Court, then, might confirm the report or send it back to the Master to reconsider in light of some or all of the objections.

Thus, for those causes - a substantial minority - which involved review of a complex pattern of facts or necessitated detailed plans of implementation, the Master's proceedings could be as important in practice as the Court's decisions were in principle. Once the Master's

---

39 The Masters themselves had originally derived the bulk of their income from fees for non-equity business. Under the act of 5/6 George III, c 28, their annual salary of one hundred pounds was trebled.

report was approved by the Court, a supplementary decretal order incorporating its results would usually be entered.

Once the Court had made up its mind, it was open to either party to have the decree enrolled on parchment. In the later sixteenth and the seventeenth century, many - though by no means all - decrees were enrolled, usually at the initiative of the winning party. In form, an enrolled decree incorporated a summary of the pleadings and of the proofs along with the formal text of the decretal order as it had been taken down by a deputy register in Court and subsequently entered verbatim in the book of orders. Enrolments were the province of the Six Clerks and subsequently of the Sworn Clerks, and the practice of including an extensive summary of the cause, beginning with the bill of complaint, was a source of added income for them and their copyists.

Perhaps more important, the enrolled decree in some measure reinforced the Court's decision. Before a decree was enrolled, it technically had the force only of an interlocutory order; it could be altered upon a rehearing or sometimes even on motion. Rehearings, indeed, appear to have become increasingly frequent, and there were repeated complaints during the eighteenth century of the delays they caused. But once a decree was enrolled, it gained a greater degree of finality. Challenges to it in Chancery could ordinarily only be made by way of a bill of review. Those seeking reconsideration via a bill of review were limited to evidence before the Court at the time of the original decree (unless they could show cause why any new evidence could not have been available to them on the earlier occasion) and also had to show that they had conformed to the terms of the original decree.[40] In these ways, enrolment could create a substantial barrier to any attempt by the losing side to reopen the cause and so might be worth the additional costs and efforts to the winning party. Why enrolment should have become much less common over the course of the eighteenth century is not altogether clear. Certainly, from the 1620s onwards, parties had another alternative to a bill of review - appeal to the House of Lords.[41] And however expensive an appeal to the Lords would be, since the cause would be reviewed by all the peers and since the common law judges might exert a considerable influence, counsel might judge it preferable to a bill of review.[42] On this logic, winning parties might have been dissuaded from undertaking the costs and troubles of enrolment, at least in part, by reason of this new route of appeal for their opponents. But this is speculative.[43] What we do know is that the Court itself was discouraging enrolment. The practice manuals of the later eighteenth and early nineteenth century suggest that the reason

---

40 The Court was prepared to make limited exceptions to these requirements when what was sought was an alteration of the enrolled decree in order to correct mistakes of copying and computation; [Richard Boote], *The Solicitor's Practice in the High Court of Chancery Epitomized* (5th edn, 1782), p 19.
41 The invention of the appeal to the Lords is described by James S Hart, *Justice upon Petition The House of Lords and the Reformation of Justice 1621-1675* (1991).
42 The requirement for an appeal to the Lords was the same as for the proceeding by bill of review - that is, the challenging party had to show that the decree itself contained disabling error. So, the appellant was limited to the terms of the original case and was not allowed to allege any new matter (save under exceptional circumstances), and he must also have shown his good faith by conforming to the terms of the decree against which he was now appealing.
43 In this regard, it is also relevant that the House, by a standing order of 1725, would not accept an appeal from Chancery if enrolment had occurred more than five years previously.

for the Court's attitude was the expense to the parties of altering enrolled decrees in matters of account; 'it ties up their hands from relieving, if there should have been any defect in the directions [the detailed provisions] of the decree'.[44]

Whatever the explanation, the facts are clear: first, that the practice of enrolment fell off sharply in the eighteenth century (for details, see below, section C); second, that the Court itself encouraged this development despite a loss of fees to some of its officers. Indeed, we find at least as early as the 1690s that Masters, in taxing costs, would on occasion make provision (by consent) that if the losing party paid the assessed costs promptly, the winning party would forego enrolment, with the result that the losing party might reduce its obligation by the amount that an enrolment would otherwise have cost. Thus, for instance, Master Meredith, in the case of Shaw v Clarke (1696), stipulated: 'in case the said plaintiff shall pay the said costs to the said defendant upon the service of a subpoena for that purpose, without putting the said defendant to the charge of signing and enrolling the dismission then the said plaintiff is at liberty to deduct five pounds' (from a total of nearly thirty-one pounds) assessed as costs.[45]

V Post-decree proceedings

Post-decree proceedings, apart from rehearings and bills of review (and appeals to the House of Lords), mainly involved the taxation of costs to the losing side by the Master (if requested), processes of enforcement against a recalcitrant loser, and/or requests for adjustments to the terms of decrees necessitated usually by changes of circumstance or by omissions or mistakes in the decree itself. Parties were most likely to come back to Court for 'further directions' on a decree in situations where the decree itself called for continuing action over months and years - most notably, in cases involving the administration of estates.

C. Observations upon Procedure in Practice

While descriptions of practice in Chancery, as found in manuals for practitioners and other contemporary works, provide considerable insight into process and the kind of documents that a suit might generate, a survey of the course of suits - based on samples drawn from the records - serves both to amplify and to qualify these general accounts. The 1627 sample comprises 285 bills (that is, approximately one in twenty out of an estimated total of 6000 bills filed for the year); the 1785 sample comprises 140 suits (approximately one in ten out of a total of approximately 1500 bills for the year). Both sets of suits have been traced from the filing of the bill to their outcomes. Two other samples of bills were taken: one from 1685 consisting of 250 bills (a one-in-twenty sample of the bills exhibited in that year) and one from 1735 consisting of 294 bills (a one-in-ten sample for that year). In addition, 146 of the 250 sample bills of 1685 were traced through the record in comparable fashion to the work of tracing completed for the 1627 and 1785 samples, so that of the total of 969 sample suits 571

---

44 Wyatt, *Register* (1800), p 156.
45 C 38/253, Master Meredith, 29 Feb 1695[-6]. For other instances, C 38/253, Pace v Fletcher, Master Holford 10 Feb 1695[-6]; C 38/250, Ward v Bowater, Master Holford, 8 Dec 1694.

have been fully traced.[46] The following discussion, then, relies primarily on these 571 traced suits, with the other 398 sets of pleadings drawn upon where relevant.

Two broad points stand out. First, many suits never went beyond the bill of complaint, and many more never went beyond the pleadings. And second, procedure and process changed in some important ways over these two centuries, with consequent changes in documentation.

I *The course of suits*

The sample sizes reflect sharp fluctuations in the volume of the Court's business over the seventeenth and eighteenth centuries - a topic to be considered in Chapter Two. Here, the focus is on how and how far suits proceeded during the early seventeenth and later eighteenth centuries.

One marked element of continuity, as remarked above, is that many suits never got beyond the filing of a bill. Presumably, the act of initiating legal proceedings by filing a bill (coupled, usually, with the service of the subpoena to appear and to answer) sufficed to bring the two parties together and led to some sort of informal settlement of the quarrel. Out-of-court settlements are, indeed, a familiar feature of the litigation process both in the twentieth and in earlier centuries. But just how often the abandonment by the plaintiff of his suit before the defendant even answered was the result of an agreement is impossible to calculate; usually, out-of-court settlements at this early stage were not reported to the Court and hence do not appear in its records.

Nonetheless, for 1627 (as for much of the seventeenth century), the mere absence of an answer in the surviving records is not conclusive evidence that the defendant did not appear and answer, for the answer may have been lost by failures in the Six Clerks' recordkeeping system. In the eighteenth century, fortunately, it is possible to differentiate more definitely between lost answers and suits in which answers were never filed, since the cause books (which record the actual pleadings filed by the parties and were kept by each Six Clerk) survive intact for over seven decades; for this reason, the analysis begins with the 1785 sample.

Of the 140 files in the 1785 sample, thirty-five would appear from the present PRO class list for C 12 to be 'bill-only' files - that is, to have no answers attached to the bills in question. However, in at least two of these instances an answer was filed: one survives as a stray elsewhere in C 12; another is listed in the appropriate cause book as having been filed, but cannot now be found.

By comparison, some 78 of the 285 files in the 1627 sample are 'bill-only' files. However, even without cause books, it is possible to identity at least 16 of these 78 in which an answer (or other response) was made. In some of these instances, the books of orders record actions which either involve answers or involve stages of a suit necessarily subsequent to the submission of an answer (eg, the issuance of process to depose witnesses); in others, it has proved possible to locate further pleadings in the suits in question which somehow became separated from the bills.[47]

---

46 The objective at the outset was to trace through the record the cases from the first and last sets of sample bills. The cases traced from the 1685 sample set of pleadings constitute those in the first half of the alphabet (A-K). For further discussion of the samples, see Appendix Two.
47 Of the 37 bill-only files in the 1685 sample, only 3 appear to be the result of misfiling or loss.

It is clear, then, that a 'bill-only' file does not necessarily mean that no answer was filed. The Six Clerks' recordkeeping was far from impeccable. Nonetheless, it is also apparent that many, probably most, such files stem from situations in which the defendant never answered *and the plaintiff never exhausted available judicial process* to compel the defendant to answer. Further, it would appear that the proportion of such bill-only suits did not alter markedly from the early seventeenth to the later eighteenth century: from the evidence of the 1785 and 1627 samples, it can be estimated that one in five bills of the period went without an answer, and this estimate is reinforced by the finding that 34 of the 146 traced suits of 1685 went no further than the bill of complaint.

Yet it was not only at this early stage that suits were abandoned. Counting all suits in which there were pleadings (bills, answers, replications, etc) but no further proceedings, the total of such 'pleadings-only' suits (a category including bill-only suits) comes to 221 out of 285 (77.5%) in 1627, 110 of 146 (75.3%) in 1685, and 92 of 140 (65.7%) in 1785. Of these very sizeable totals, only a small number (22 in 1627, 10 in 1685, 9 in 1785) were ever formally terminated by the Court by a dismissal without hearing (an outcome usually indicative of a persistent failure by the plaintiff to proceed); rather, the great majority simply disappear from the record.

Only a minority of suits, then, ever got to the stage of a hearing on the main question in dispute and hence to the issuance of a decree. Often, but by no means invariably, a hearing was preceded by the taking of testimony from the opposing parties' witnesses. Evidence of process for deposing witnesses or the depositions themselves survive for 45 cases in the 1627 sample and 26 cases in the 1785 sample.[48] (Conversely, there were some instances in which suits were dropped after depositions had been taken.) Yet, of the 30 decrees issued in the 285 suits in the 1627 sample, only 16 were preceded by the taking of witnesses' testimony; of the 36 decrees issued in the 140 suits of the 1785 sample, only 21 were preceded by the taking of witnesses' testimony.[49]

In many ways, and despite substantial fluctuations in the volume of business, the course of suits in the early 1600s appears to resemble their course 150 years later. The common characteristics would appear to be: (1) a substantial minority never proceeded beyond the plaintiff's filing of his bill; (2) a considerable majority never proceeded beyond the pleadings; and (3) depositions were taken and/or a decree issued in only a distinct minority of instances.

II Some changes over time

So far in this discussion of practice, the emphasis has been on continuity. But some changes are also worth recording. The first consists of indications of the elaboration of process and documentation. The 285 bills of the 1627 sample are virtually all original bills: only two are bills of revivor while a third is a bill of review seeking the reconsideration of an enrolled

---

48 Excluded from this count are a small number of depositions taken from the parties themselves in contempt proceedings and process for examinations by the Masters in references after hearings. For the survival rate of depositions, see Chapter Three. For 1685, depositions or deposition process occur in 21 of the 146 suits that were traced.

49 Of the 26 decrees issued in the 146 suits in the 1685 sample, 12 were preceded by the taking of witnesses' testimony. It was common for collusive suits to be decided solely on the pleadings.

decree. By contrast, the 140 files of the 1785 sample include five bills of revivor, ten amended bills, and three supplemental bills.[50] And just as plaintiffs in the 1785 sample were more likely to be reviving abated suits and more likely to alter their bills to take account of changing circumstances (or of aspects of defendants' answers), so defendants in 1785 were also more likely to back up their answers with a species of proof. This was the schedule, attached to the answer, and giving a detailed response (usually in pounds, shillings, and pence) to the plaintiff's allegations. Twenty-eight answers from the 1785 sample of 140 suits include such schedules (for example, an executor's accounts, a household inventory, a listing of partnership debits and credits); by comparison, only four are included in the 1627 sample of 285 suits.[51]

In another important respect, the documentation for a later eighteenth-century case may also be fuller. Whereas references to the Masters in Ordinary by the Court were mainly to consider the sufficiency of pleadings (primarily the defendant's response) in the early seventeenth century, by the later eighteenth century references were, for the most part, utilized to sift through the parties' factual claims after the Court had heard the suit on its merits. Thus, in the 1627 sample, no less than 66 of the 89 references to a Master concerned the sufficiency of the pleadings, and other interlocutory matters such as recommendations as to the grant or dissolution of injunctions. But in the 1785 sample, only 13 of the 78 references to a Master concerned the pleadings or interlocutory remedies; rather, the bulk of the Masters' work for the Court was now reviewing matters of fact, supervising the implementation of decrees, and reckoning the costs of the litigation.[52] Thus, Masters' reports over the period grow considerably more informative about the substance of the matter in controversy.

Not all the change in the Court's procedures and in the documents generated in litigation was in the direction of greater elaboration. For one thing, thanks to the statute of 1706, duplicate copies of bills, formerly sent down to the commissioners in the provinces who were to take the answers of defendants, were abolished on the grounds that their only real use was to generate extra income for the officials responsible for drawing them up. And for a second, as noted earlier, the frequency with which decrees were enrolled dropped very sharply. Just how common enrolment was in the early seventeenth century is difficult to calculate. On the one hand, a count of all surviving decrees enrolled between 1627 and 1636 indicates an annual average of around 180. On the other hand, of the thirty-six substantive outcomes from the 1627 sample of 285 suits only five appear to have been enrolled.[53] It would appear, then, that even in the first half of the seventeenth century enrolments were hardly the inevitable accompaniments of decrees. In a way, the situation is much clearer by 1785. None of the decrees in the sample set is enrolled, and only about ten enrolled decrees per annum survive for 1785-1794.

---

50 To some extent, the growth of amended and supplemental bills may be a function of the decline of pleas and demurrers. There were pleas and/or demurrers in 24 of the 1627 suits but only in 3 of the 1785 suits. See also Yale, *Manual*, pp 56-57: the 'comparative neglect' of pleas and demurrers during the 1700s may 'be attributed perhaps to their tendency to terminate litigation in an abrupt manner ... which did not altogether accord with a procedure modelled to explore all the merits of a case.'
51 The 1685 sample falls roughly midway between the 1627 and 1785 ones, with 16 attachments in 146 suits.
52 Again, the 1685 sample seems to fall roughly midway between the other two; of 28 references, 16 concerned matters of substance and/or costs.
53 This count includes both C 78 and C 79. Enrolments are discussed in detail in Chapter Three.

The pronounced fall in the numbers of enrolled decrees seems to have been mainly an eighteenth-century phenomenon. As late as the decade 1685-1694, the average number of enrolled decrees per annum was 170 or so out of a case load roughly comparable to the 1620s.[54] By the decade 1735-1744, the annual average had fallen to slightly under fifty, a more than threefold decline that exceeded the sharp downturn in the overall volume of business in Chancery, and thereafter the decline accelerated.

The third way in which the Court's conduct of its business altered over time was the speed with which suits advanced. Here, the broad pattern of change can be illustrated in tabular form using samples drawn from four years across two centuries.

TABLE ONE: DURATION OF SUITS IN CHANCERY*

	1627(n=285)	1685(n=146)	1785(n=140)	1818-1819(n=149)
under one year (of these, bills only)	212 74.4% (65)	113 77.4% (33)	88 62.9% (35)	67 45.0% (33)
one to two years	46 16.1	17 12.3	19 13.5	18 12.1
two to five years	24 8.4	11 7.5	19 13.5	38 25.5
over five years	3 1.1	5 2.7	14 10.0	26 17.4

* Calculations are based on the last recorded date of any procedural or substantive action in each case as derived from the Court's books of orders, supplemented in some instances by Masters' Reports. Thanks to Dr Patrick Polden for supplying the 1818-1819 data.

As Table One indicates, the speed with which cases in Chancery were disposed of markedly slowed over the two centuries in view. This slowdown reflects a number of features of Chancery litigation in the period, evident in part in the results of the tracing of the sample bills. One is that the proportion of suits pursued to a decree rose substantially - from 34 of 285 (11.9%) in the 1627 sample to 26 of 146 (17.8%) in the 1685 sample and to 36 of 140 (25.7%) in the 1785 sample.

A second, and concomitant feature of the situation, was the parties' greater readiness in the second half of the period to take advantage of the opportunities for delay that certain Court procedures in effect allowed - especially the more frequent employment of motions and petitions on ancillary matters. It is not easy to gauge the precise effects of this tendency, but its existence is well attested in eighteenth-century manuals for practitioners in Chancery and quite evident in the cases. The result (often intended) of the recourse to such tactics, which meant summons to the opposing side and often hearings, was to postpone term after term the implementation of the Court's deadlines for proceeding on to subsequent stages of the litigation. Thus, for

---

54 Again, of the 26 suits reaching a determination of the 146 traced from the 1685 sample, enrolments of the decree have been located in only 3 instances.

instance, one manual of the late eighteenth century explains, though with expressions of disapproval, how a plaintiff, in danger of having his suit dismissed for want of failure to proceed, could stall for term after term to prevent dismissal and thereby delay his liability to pay the defendant the costs of the suit to which he would otherwise owe. And so long as the Court gave such procedural opportunities without effectively curbing the associated abuses, so long would such tactics be employed.

The third dimension to the slowdown in the disposition of litigation in Chancery was the increasing predominance of suits which, by their nature, tended to remain before the Court for long periods of time. This is a topic to be examined in detail in Chapter Two. But the clearest instance of this trend is the growing proportion of estate-related matters brought before the Court - especially those involving the administration of an estate of a deceased with minor beneficiaries, for the Court would often maintain a watching brief until each and every minor came of age and was paid off.

As a consequence, then, both of shifts in the subject-matter of suits before the Court and the seemingly more-determined conduct of suitors once in Court, the speed with which suits were dispatched slowed markedly. All but one-tenth of the suits in the 1627 and 1685 samples were disposed of within two years, but over one-fifth of the 1785 sample and two-fifths in the 1818-1819 sample were still in process after two years. Moreover, these totals are reckoned without taking into account abated suits which were then revived (ie, bills of revivor of earlier suits among the samples).

In a variety of dimensions, then, the Court of Chancery's operation by the later eighteenth and early nineteenth centuries differed quite significantly from its patterns two centuries earlier. And as will become clear in Chapter Two, so did the subject matter of Chancery suits and the identity of Chancery litigants.

CHAPTER TWO:
The Jurisdiction of the Court of Chancery Between the Early Seventeenth and the Early Nineteenth Centuries

A. Introduction

By the beginning of the seventeenth century, the Court of Chancery - despite its relatively late arrival on the scene - was well-established as one of the four leading central royal courts. It had no criminal jurisdiction per se (although on occasion suits before it were linked to criminal cases before other courts), but otherwise its range within England was not significantly constrained save by its own rules (1) that it would not entertain suits with less at stake than ten pounds or land worth less than forty shillings per annum, and (2) that it would not entertain suits de novo for which an appropriate common law action or canon law proceeding existed (provided, that is, that the defendant in his 'plea' made out a persuasive case for this bar to proceeding in equity).[1] To be sure, there was still controversy in the early seventeenth century over the boundaries among jurisdictions, not least between equity and common law. But in practice there was ample business for every jurisdiction in a time of still-rapidly expanding civil litigation, and Chancery's principal problem was how to deal expeditiously with its own case load.

However, the patterns of the early seventeenth century were far from immutable. Even before the Civil War, the Court had its critics, including some of its own office-holders, and in the spring of 1610 the Commons committed a bill to limit references to Masters and to restrain 'excessive fees' to the Six Clerks.[2] After the abolition of the Court of Star Chamber in 1641 (and the demise of the Court of Requests), there were also calls in print and in the ad hoc parliamentary assemblies of the Interregnum for drastic change in Chancery's ways of doing business, and some even sought its abolition as part of a larger revamping of the traditional legal order. Abolition was formally resolved upon by the Nominated Parliament, but - given the Court's central role in the existing judicial system - this was rejected as too radical a

---

1   For the situation of Welsh litigants, and for Chancery's relations with the equity jurisdiction of the Council in the Marches of Wales before its abolition in 1689, see Jones, *Chancery*, pp 348-355. In general, the Court of Chancery would not take cognizance of disputes in which the property at stake lay outside the realm of England and Wales but this did not preclude Scottish and non-British litigants from seeking relief in Chancery for disputes which centred on England (or Wales) nor did it preclude Chancery from dealing with properties of a deceased in the English overseas colonies. Thus, the well-known mid-eighteenth century case, Penn v Baltimore, centred on the boundary line between the two proprietary colonies of the parties. However, the proportion of non-English litigants did not exceed 5% in any of the four samples, and within this category the single largest group both before and after the abolition of the Council of Wales was the Welsh.
2   The best known internal criticism was that of George Norbury, a one-time clerk in Chancery; his 'The Abuses and Remedies of Chancerie' is printed in *A Collection of Tracts relative to the Law of England* (1787), ed Francis Hargrave, pp 425-448. For the 1610 bill, see *Proceedings in Parliament 1610, ed Elizabeth R Foster, vol 2 The House of Commons* (1966), p 71; C 173/2, bundle 1, a letter from N Roberts (an officer in the Examiners' Office) to Sir John Leveson of 23 March 1609 [-10] invoking his assistance in the Commons against the bill. See also *supra*, Introduction, note 6 for the 1621 bill.

solution. However, Chancery did have to operate between 1654 and 1658 under the terms of a reforming ordinance laid down by Lord Protector Cromwell and his council.[3] Whether the changes called for under the 1654 provisions would have achieved their framers' objectives of reducing delay and expense is unclear; they hardly had time to be put into operation. Indeed, the old Chancery officers and the old ways were restored two years before Charles II regained his crown.

However, rejection of the Cromwellian reforms meant that after 1660 dissatisfaction with Chancery's ways was not long in resurfacing. The later 1600s and early 1700s saw renewed calls for streamlining and cheapening Chancery process, and a few changes of marginal significance were actually enacted by parliament.[4] But 'root and branch' reform of the Court had to await the mid-nineteenth century.

Although external pressures for reform had only limited effects on the way Chancery operated in the 1600s and 1700s, there were changes of some significance, though not in the direction the reformers advocated. One such development was the slowdown in the rate at which the Court processed its case load, as evidenced in Table One (*supra* p 28). Other changes - including shifts in the nature of the suits brought before Chancery and in the identity of the suitors - will be discussed (in conjunction with the slowdown) in this chapter by way of an overview of the matters litigated in Chancery and of the identity of the parties in these suits.

B. The Broader Context

Between 1600 and 1800, England's population roughly doubled with the most rapid periods of growth coming in the early 1600s and the late 1700s, interrupted by some periods of stagnation, perhaps even decline as in the later 1600s. Moreover, over the period as a whole this growing population was increasingly urbanized, first chiefly due to the continuation of London's spectacular sixteenth-century expansion, later thanks to the rapid increase in the numbers and proportion of those residing in the larger and middling provincial towns, both established centres and newly-developing ones. And although precise figures are lacking, it is also clear that over these two centuries, agriculture's predominance in the economy was being eroded by the expansion of trade and industry. Insofar, then, as Chancery's case load reflected these changing features of English society, it might be anticipated that the overall volume of litigation would grow substantially, that disputes arising out of the holding of rural land would diminish while controversies involving non-agrarian business transactions would rise, and that the proportion of urban litigants would also be on the increase.

---

3   For an overview, see B Shapiro, 'Law Reform in Seventeenth Century England', *American Journal of Legal History* 19 (1975), 280-312. See also Allan J Busch, jr, 'Bulstrode Whitelocke and Early Interregnum Chancery Reform', *Albion* 10 (1979), 317-330. The ordinance is printed in Sanders, *Orders*, pp 254-272.
4   In addition to Shapiro, cited in *supra* note 3, see Wilfrid Prest, 'Law Reform in Eighteenth-Century England', *The Life of the Law* (1993), ed Peter Birks, pp 113-123. And in general, see Joseph Parkes, *A History of the Court of Chancery* (1828), especially valuable for his extensive citation of the pamphlet literature.

C. The Volume of Chancery Business

However, the volume and mix of civil litigation coming before Chancery, as well as the other central courts, between the early seventeenth and early nineteenth centuries by no means fits neatly with the demographic and economic trends just outlined. Instead, the evidence is that the sixteenth-century expansion in business in the central courts (both common law and equity), while continuing up to the Civil War, thereafter began to run out of steam. The later 1600s were marked by relative stagnation, admittedly at the high levels of the pre-Civil War decades. Moreover, the turn of the seventeenth century saw the beginnings of a decline that would continue through much of the next one hundred years, with the nadir being reached - depending upon the individual court concerned - between the 1760s and 1780s. All told, it has been computed that the volume of civil business in the central courts fell as much as two-thirds between 1640 and 1780. And as yet, a wholly convincing explanation for this phenomenon is lacking.[5]

The volume of business in the Court of Chancery can be estimated by using two related, but distinct, gauges. One is the number of new bills exhibited annually, calculated for select years from the Six Clerks' bill books. Unfortunately, no bill books survive before the early 1670s.[6] Even so, the available data, as summarized in Table Two, clearly indicate a general downward trend quite visible already by the legal year 1720-1721, deepening over the course of the eighteenth century, and showing only a limited recovery in the early nineteenth century.

TABLE TWO: BILLS OF COMPLAINT EXHIBITED IN CHANCERY[7]

1673/74	4717	1734/35	3240
1685/86	5660	1750-54	1706 (annual average)
1700/01	5707	1785	1544
1720/21	3423	1818/19	2335

A second way of calculating the volume of business before the Court is to count the number of 'active' cases (those on which some action was proposed and/or taken during the course of a

---

5   For the overall volume of litigation, see C W Brooks, *Pettyfoggers and Vipers of the Commonwealth* (1986), esp pp 52-55; *idem*, 'Interpersonal conflict and social tension: civil litigation in England, 1640-1830' in *The First Modern Society* (1989), ed A L Beier *et al*, pp 357-399; *idem*, 'Litigation and Society in England 1200-1996', in his *Lawyers, Litigation and English Society* (forthcoming).

6   C 173/10, large vol compiled by Bladen, f 100, refers, in the course of a discussion of the alphabetical filing of pleadings during Charles I's reign, to bill books of that day.

7   Compare Table 1 at p 30 of H Horwitz and P Polden, 'Continuity or Change in the Court of Chancery in the Seventeenth and Eighteenth Centuries?', *Journal of British Studies* 35 (1996), 24-57.

single year) that are recorded in the books of orders; the C 33 volumes survive for the whole of the period and the count yields a somewhat different picture.[8]

TABLE THREE: 'ACTIVE' CASES IN CHANCERY

1609/10	4929	1734/35	4840
1629/30	6198	1759/60	3138
1684/85	5817	1784/85	3612
1709/10	4848	1819/20	6014

The count of 'active' cases qualifies the pattern suggested by the count of bills in two important respects. First, it indicates that the fall in *ongoing* business, at most one-half between 1629/30 and 1759/60, was not as catastrophic as the decline in new bills. Second, it suggests a much stronger recovery between 1759/60 and 1819/20 as the number of active cases rebounded virtually to the level of 1629/30. Furthermore, the differences revealed between these two gauges of business reinforce the evidence of Table One for a marked slowdown in the rate of determination of suits from the later seventeenth century onward as the gap widened between the number of new bills submitted and the number of cases in process. This is illustrated in Table Four by computing the ratio between the number of new bills introduced and the number of ongoing cases during the same years.

TABLE FOUR: NEW VERSUS ONGOING BUSINESS IN CHANCERY

	new bills	active cases	new bills as % of active cases
1684/85	5660	5817	97.3
1734/35	3240	4840	64.8
1785	1544	3612	42.7
1818-1819	2335	6014	38.8

8 The procedure followed for each year computed was to (1) count all entries in the relevant C 33 volume, (2) for an individual letter (P) count all individual cases included in the total of entries under that letter, (3) establish a ratio for that letter of total entries divided by individual cases under that letter, and (4) divide the total under the first count for all entries by that ratio. Eg, for the legal year 1609/10, there are 7887 total entries and of that total there are 458 entries for 286 individual P cases; the ratio of 458 over 286 = 1.6; 1.6 divided into 7887 yields a total of 4929 active cases for the year. Cf Jones, *Chancery*, p 305.

But was the pace at which Chancery appears to be moving in the 1680s characteristic of the 1620s? In the absence of bill books for the pre-1673 years, it is necessary to fall back once more upon the sample data with respect to duration, as laid out in Table One. These show that only one-tenth of the suits in the 1627 and 1685 samples were still active two years after the complainant exhibited his bill, as compared to significantly higher fractions for subsequent sample years.

Presuming, then, that the Court's pace in handling cases in the 1680s can be projected backwards to the early seventeenth century, it is possible to offer some rough estimates for the number of new suits commenced in those years. Applying the 1685 ratio of 97.3% of new bills to active cases to the figures for active cases for 1609/10 and 1629/30 (Table Three) yields rough estimates for new suits of 4800 in 1609/10 and 6000 in 1629/30.[9]

This exercise in estimation also makes it possible to compute a total of all Chancery suits between 1600 and 1800 by extrapolating from the figures for the numbers of bills exhibited for select years over these two centuries. This procedure yields a grand total of approximately 750,000 suits between 1600 and 1800, with the bulk (500,000 - 550,000) in the 1600s. Of this very sizeable total, the data from the samples would indicate that somewhat over one-fifth never proceeded beyond the filing of a bill (a proportion relatively constant over time) and that about one-tenth of the seventeenth-century cases lasted beyond two years. However, perhaps as many as three-tenths of the eighteenth-century cases lasted beyond two years and one-tenth of them beyond five years. To put it slightly differently, as seventeenth-century cases were more commonly dealt with relative expedition, so they were less likely to generate continuing series of entries in the books of orders.

But why should a slowdown in the transaction of Chancery litigation have occurred at roughly the same time that the volume of new cases was beginning to fall noticeably? To some extent, the operation of official self-interest may help to explain the phenomenon. Certainly, one well-informed early eighteenth-century critic of the Court was convinced that many of the ills of Chancery could be put down to the fact that so many of the under-officers of the Court had to purchase their places; under such circumstances, they might well respond to a diminishing volume of cases by trying to drag out what litigation there was so as to maintain their incomes.[10]

Yet, it would be misleading to explain the problem by laying all at the door of the self-interest of the Chancery officers (and/or legal practitioners). For one thing, for some segments of the Court bureaucracy there were other possible responses to the decline in business. As early as the first quarter of the eighteenth century, the Sworn Clerks took collective action to counteract the effects of declining business upon their incomes, petitioning the Master of the Rolls not to reappoint to places that fell vacant by death; the result of these and other measures was that by the last two decades of the century their numbers had fallen by well over fifty per cent from their peak in the later 1600s.[11] For a second, changes in the mix of Chancery suits

---

9   The procedure is to multiply 4929 (1609/10) and 6198 (1629/30) by 97.3%, and then round the results to the nearest 100.

10   *Observations on the Dilatory and Expensive Proceedings in the Court of Chancery* (1701), pp 13-14. On the same logic, lawyers (especially barristers) might well seek to proliferate motions to generate additional fee income in an era of limited litigation..

11   In 1688 each Six Clerk's quota of Sworn Clerks was raised from 12 to 15 for a total of ninety; by the mid-1780s the total number of Sworn Clerks was down to 37.

may, as suggested in Chapter One, have had a very considerable effect on the prolongation of litigation before the Court in the eighteenth and early nineteenth centuries.

D. The Subject Matter of Chancery Suits

Five main subject-groupings have been employed in categorizing the sample suits: estate [testamentary and intestacy] matters, landholding and land transactions, *inter vivos* trusts, debts and bonds, and business transactions.[12] These are 'artificial' in the sense that Chancery knew no forms of action and had no need to classify its business. And their artificiality may be exaggerated by employing them to make comparisons across two centuries.

In broad terms, suits classed as estate matters concern issues arising out of wills and intestacies - above all, claims for payment of legacies and for performance of other provisions of wills (including testamentary trusts). Other significant subcategories under the estate rubric include suits brought to secure the assets of a deceased, suits disputing the validity of testaments, and suits concerning charitable bequests (with the Attorney General often a plaintiff in such cases, usually acting 'at the relation', *ex rel*, of the designated beneficiaries).

Suits categorized as related to landholding and other real property issues include, most prominently, demands for specific performance of agreements to convey, mortgage foreclosures and redemptions, and (especially in 1627) claims to land with requests for remedies for defective transfers (ie, the claim of hidden encumbrances, and the like). In addition, the landholding category embraces disputes over the performance of leases as well as suits involving waste, boundaries, manorial rights, tithes and advowsons.

The principal type of *inter vivos* trust litigated relates to marriage settlements; no other type figured frequently.

The single largest subcategory of suits under the heading of debts and bonds, at least for the seventeenth century, involves complainants seeking relief from the enforcement of conditioned bonds and other debt instruments. However, when such credit relationships derive from a sale of goods or other business transaction, the suits have been counted under the heading of business. In other words, the debt/bond category is something of a residual one, including both clear-cut cases of financial obligations arising out of personal relationships and also those suits in which the documents simply do not spell out the underlying circumstances. Also included in this category are suits brought by creditors of deceased individuals seeking repayment from their legal representatives, and disputes over arrangements involving the transfer of realty or personalty for the benefit of non-business creditors.

Finally, the grouping labelled business embraces a motley array of situations, among them matters of account between partners or between employers and employees, the sale of

---

12 The sample suits total 1118 (1627, 1685, 1735, 1785, and 1818-1819); in those cases where litigation never proceeded beyond the bill of complaint, knowledge of the substance of the dispute depends solely upon the plaintiff's allegations.

goods and services, the collection of business debts (with some plaintiffs in the 1700s assignees in bankruptcy), and occasional insurance and copyright cases.[13]

The results of this classification of the sample suits are summed up in Table Five.[14]

TABLE FIVE: SUBJECT MATTER OF CHANCERY SAMPLE SUITS*

	1627 (291)		1685 (251)		1735 (299)		1785 (143)		1818-1819 (152)	
Business	18	6.2%	45	17.9%	36	12.0%	25	17.5%	25	16.4%
Debts/bonds	84	28.8	45	17.9	47	15.7	18	12.6	14	9.2
Trusts	21	7.2	6	2.4	9	3.0	9	6.3	16	10.5
Land	114	39.2	84	33.5	109	36.4	29	20.3	47	30.9
Estate	54	18.6	70	27.9	94	31.4	61	42.7	49	32.2
Miscellaneous	0	0.0	1	0.4	4	1.3	1	0.7	1	0.7

* The nos for some years include suits classified under two categories: 1627 (285 suits + 6 in two categories), 1685 (250 suits + 1), 1735 (294 suits + 5), 1785 (140 suits + 3), 1818/19 (149 suits + 3).

In considering shifts in the distribution of the subject matter of the sample bills, it is well to keep in mind the sharp decline in business that the Court suffered over the course of the eighteenth century, with active cases falling off by roughly one-half and new bills diminishing

---

13   It should be noted that in carrying out the process of categorization, some subsets of suits might have been handled in several different ways: cases involving mortgages (a substantial number) are classed as land disputes but might have been treated as involving bonds; cases brought by representatives of the deceased (executors or administrators) seeking to bring in assets are classed as estate disputes but might have been treated as involving debts; suits brought by creditors of the deceased might have been classed as estate cases but have been treated as involving debts. Thus, it seemed appropriate to preserve the more prominent subcategories (eg, mortgage cases) in order, when relevant, to consider them in isolation. In a limited number of instances in which suits seem to straddle or overlap two main categories, they have been counted under both.

14   Somewhat different results would have been obtained by analysing the subjects of decrees in decided cases or those printed in law reports. By comparison to bills, both decrees and reports tend to over-represent trust and estate cases as compared to debt/bond and business cases, in part because the formal authority of Chancery was more likely to be needed in trust and estate matters, in part because these matters were apparently also judged by the legal reporters to be of greater interest to practitioners. Thus, for example, while estate cases comprise 42.7% of the 1785 sample of bills, they comprise 51.6% of all 1785 decrees (n=268) and 56.9% of all 1785-1787 reported cases (n=188); conversely, business cases comprise 17.5% of the 1785 bill sample but only 5.3% and 5.8% of the decrees and reports respectively. Again, of the 194 estate and trust cases traced from the 1627, 1685 and 1785 samples, over one quarter (40 of 161 estate cases, 10 of 33 trust cases) proceeded to the pronouncement of a decree; of the 196 land cases less than one sixth (30); and of the 189 business and debt cases only a shade more than one eighth (24).

to roughly one-quarter of their seventeenth-century levels, for these phenomena were accompanied by marked changes in the type of suits coming before the Court. Most noticeable are the nearly threefold *rise* in proportion of business cases and the more than threefold *decrease* in the proportion of suits involving debts and bonds. Given the uncertain boundary line between these two categories, these trends may be somewhat exaggerated, but their existence is hardly in doubt. In addition, the proportion of estate cases (wills and intestacies) came close to doubling while suits involving land fell by almost one-quarter. And over the same period, cases involving trusts rose by almost one-half.

What do these changes in the type of suits drawn in the samples add up to in a strictly quantitative sense? If, using a somewhat rough and ready procedure of estimation, the figures for active cases for 1629/30 and 1819/20 (Table Three, each rounded to 6,000) are multiplied by the percentages per category for new bills in the samples for 1627 and 1818-1819 (from Table Five), the results are summed up in Table Six.

TABLE SIX: ESTIMATES OF TYPES OF ACTIVE CASES

	1627 %	(n=6,000) no	1818-1819 %	(n=6,000) no
Business	6.2	372	16.5	990
Debts/bonds	28.8	1728	9.2	552
Trusts	7.2	432	10.6	636
Land	39.2	2552	30.9	1848
Estate	18.6	1116	32.2	1932
Miscellaneous	0.0	-	0.7	42

It is relatively easy to count, but to account for the numbers so generated is more problematic. To begin with, by no means all the trends observed are continuous. In some respects, the figures in Table Five for 1818-1819 look more like those for 1735 than for 1785; again, there are especially sharp departures between 1627 and 1685.

Second, the data suggest that the broad economic developments of the 1600s and 1700s had only a very qualified effect on the changing mix of Chancery cases. Certainly, by the end of the second decade of the nineteenth century the Court was handling a good many more cases involving business matters than two centuries earlier (see row 1 of Table Six). But given the undoubted expansion of trade and industry, what is striking is how many land cases Chancery was still dealing with by this time (row 4) - more or less double the number of business cases. Granted, the simple category of landholding does not locate the realty in question; whereas in 1627 virtually all real property suits in that sample involved rural land, by 1818-1819 at least one-third of the somewhat diminished total involved urban realty.

Third, there is also the possibility that some of the shifts reflected in the tables stem not from broader developments in the larger society but from more specific changes in the law and in the boundaries among the courts. The clearest case is the legal treatment of conditioned or penal bonds. It had long been Chancery's practice to relieve those obliged under penal bonds (the penalty, a kind of self-enforcement mechanism, was double the amount borrowed or owed if that sum were not repaid on time) under a variety of circumstances which the common law courts traditionally declined to take into account when dealing with sealed instruments - eg, that a plaintiff had in fact paid the debt in question but failed to receive back from the defendant the penal bond itself. However, parliament, by statutes of 1696/97 and 1705, authorized the courts of common law to provide analogous relief in such situations, thereby sanctioning innovations made by the common law courts, especially Common Pleas, at least a generation before. Indeed, in the early 1670s, Lord Chancellor Nottingham remarked, without any indication of novelty, that the common law courts had adopted an equitable approach in such situations, in effect allowing defendants to save the costs of bringing suit in Chancery for relief and also enhancing their own business.[15] This judicial departure is clearly reflected in the results of the 1627 and 1685 samples. Overall, debt-related cases fell from 28.8% of the 1627 total to 17.9% of the 1685 total (Table Five), while the fall in the subcategory of cases involving conditioned bonds was even more pronounced - from 57 such cases in 1627 (or 17.6% of the 1627 total) to only 18 in 1685 (or 7.2.% of the 1685 total).

Another illustration of the influence of changes in legal boundaries concerns estate cases - 18.6% of the 1627 sample and no less than 42.7% of the 1785 sample, though falling back to 32.2% of the 1818-1819 sample (Table Five). To be sure, the church courts did maintain their exclusive right to grant probates. Yet they do appear to have steadily lost ground to courts of equity, and especially Chancery, with respect to contentious and administrative matters relating to wills. The crux of the matter would seem to be that only the courts of equity could provide adequate remedies for a variety of estate-related complications - among them, the capacity to make ongoing provision for the maintenance of minor legatees until they came of age, the authority to enforce sureties on legatees (for repayment, if required), and the readiness to safeguard legacies made to married women against their husbands. And at the same time, executors may well have become increasingly cautious about administering any sizeable estate without Chancery's involvement.[16]

Fourth, in seeking to gauge the effect of legal changes upon Chancery's business, the posture and activity of a wide range of other courts, especially other equity jurisdictions,

---

15   Yale, *Manual*, p 203; M Macnair, 'Common law and statutory imitations of equitable relief under the later Stuarts', *Communities and Courts in Britain 1150-1900* (1997), ed C W Brooks and M Lobban, 115-131. Among Sir Mathew Hale's papers (the Fairhurst MSS) now in the Lambeth Palace Library, there is an interesting draft bill, probably prepared as part of the Hale Commission's proceedings in the early 1650s, which would have instituted similar changes, including giving the common law courts the power to examine under oath a plaintiff in litigation over a penal bond with respect to the underlying facts: Lambeth Palace MS 3475, ff 240-243.

16   George Spence, *The Equitable Jurisdiction of the Court of Chancery* (2 vols, 1846), I, 580. Failure to invoke the Court's assistance by an executor might bring a harsh response: note the treatment meted out to one litigant by the Irish Court of Chancery under Lord Redesdale (author, as John Mitford, of the standard manual on English Chancery pleading) who made a systematic effort to import English equity practice into Ireland; *Doyle v Blake* (1804), 2 Sch & Lef 231 at 243.

needs to be taken into account. Three clusters of other equity jurisdictions impinged on Chancery.

In the first place, there were a number of local jurisdictions, among them those covering the old palatine counties of Chester, Durham, and Lancashire and also such other special areas as the Duchy of Lancaster and Dover and the Cinque Ports.[17] None can be regarded as typical, but at least that of Durham has well-preserved records and has been carefully studied. The Durham Court of Chancery handled 173 cases per annum in the mid-1630s; during the same years, the Court of Chancery at Westminster handled about one-tenth that number of suits emanating from the county. The advantages, apparently, of the local jurisdiction were convenience and cheapness, with costs at that time of a suit at Durham being no more than one-seventh of the costs of a suit at Westminster (excluding travel expenses). Despite these advantages, the number of suitors at Durham after 1660 fell sooner and faster than the number of suitors overall at Westminster. In the light of this evidence from Durham (confirming Jones's findings for Chester), it is impossible to explain the falling off in Chancery's business in the eighteenth century by any greater recourse by litigants to local equity courts, even in those relatively few areas in which they operated.[18]

The second group of equity jurisdictions were those exercised by the two regional councils, the Council in the Marches of Wales and the Council in the North. Jones suggests that the regional councils were 'inundated with business' in the early Stuart period, with the former alone hearing between 1,200 and 1,500 suits annually in the 1630s.[19] But both were abolished by the Long Parliament, and while the Council in the Marches had a brief afterlife under the later Stuarts, its heyday had clearly passed. Thus, what were flourishing equity jurisdictions in the early seventeenth century provided no competition for Chancery after the Civil War.

It is possible, then, that the maintenance of Chancery's case load in the generation after the Restoration was, at least in part, the result of diminished competition from local and regional jurisdictions. At the centre, too, the array of potential rivals was thinned, albeit marginally, by the demise of the Court of Requests in the early 1640s, for if Chancery had mainly treated Requests as an ancillary to deal with cases in which either the parties or the cause seemed relatively trivial, Requests had also handled a significant minority of suits in which the plaintiffs were royal officials with the privilege of litigating there. But while Chancery may have gained by the demise of some alternative tribunals and the decline of others, the growth of the equity business of the Court of Exchequer accelerated during the mid-seventeenth century.[20]

Already in the late sixteenth century, Exchequer had established itself 'as an equity court of true significance'; then, in the late 1640s it expanded its activities by a new, or at least greater, willingness to accept a fictitious allegation by the complainant that he was a debtor to the crown (being a debtor or an accountant to the Crown had been a requirement to invoke the

---

17   For an overview, focussing on the pre-1640 period, see W J Jones, 'Palatine performance in the seventeenth century', in *The English Commonwealth 1547-1640* (1979), ed Peter Clark *et al*.

18   Kenneth Emsley and C M Fraser, *The Courts of the County Palatine of Durham* (1984), 72-84; Marcus Knight, 'Litigants and Litigation in the Seventeenth Century Palatinate of Durham', Cambridge University PhD, 1990, esp pp 107-109, 114.

19   Jones, 'Palatine performance', p 192.

20   A handbook now in preparation by the author will treat Exchequer equity proceedings and records.

Court's jurisdiction).[21] Granted, the equity business of Exchequer, like that of Chancery, suffered a sharp fall during George II's reign, but its subsequent revival appears to have antedated Chancery's. Whereas for each bill of complaint submitted to Exchequer in 1685 there were more than eight submitted to Chancery (c 650 to 5660), a century later the ratio of bills submitted in the two Courts had shifted to one in fewer than four (c 450-1544). However, Chancery's revival - once finally underway - did outpace Exchequer's and by 1818-1819 the gap had begun to widen again to roughly one in six (374 to 2335).[22] The shifting balance between the two courts might be read as evidence of competition for business, but there is no direct evidence to suggest that the two courts viewed one another as rivals.[23] Although the two post-1660 central equity tribunals specialized to some degree, Exchequer in tithes and Chancery in trust cases, they followed quite similar procedures and offered like remedies.[24] Indeed, there was a considerable overlap in their business, and Exchequer, too, saw a significant fall in debt-related suits and a considerable increase in estate cases.[25]

This brief look at the equity jurisdiction of the Court of Exchequer underlines conclusions already reached with respect to Chancery itself. On the one hand, the drastic drop in new Chancery business over the eighteenth century was part of a general malaise afflicting the courts of equity and, indeed, the courts of common law as well, not attributable primarily either to the emergence of new rivals nor to poaching by other established jurisdictions. On the other hand, there was a partial convergence in the character of the declining volume of suits brought before the two central courts of equity. Hence, with respect both to Chancery and to Exchequer, it is easier to pinpoint specific areas where boundary movements among the common law, church, and equity courts were significant than it is to see how changes in the larger society affected the mix of subjects coming before them. However, the effects of broader economic and social development become easier to discern in examining the changing profile of litigants in Chancery.

---

21   W H Bryson, *The Equity Side of the Exchequer* (1975), pp 24-27, 33, followed by R M Ball, 'Tobias Eden, Change and Conflict in the Exchequer Office, 1672-1698', *Journal of Legal History* 11 (1990), 70. Suggestions that the Court's emergence as a general court of equity (ie, that it had ceased to enforce the requirement that the plaintiff be a debtor to the crown) came some decades earlier are not confirmed by a review of the Court's decrees for 1627 (E 126/142): in over two-thirds the plaintiff was the Attorney-General, and of the remaining a substantial proportion involved lands in which the crown had some kind of interest.

22   Figures on Exchequer bills are derived from Bryson, *The Equity Side of the Exchequer*, p 168; from *Parliamentary Papers* 1836 (32) xliii, 7 ff; and also from independent calculations from the Court's bill books, IND 1/16842-16847. Figures on decrees are derived from E 126. In the 1820s and 1830s, the level of Exchequer bills fell off sharply.

23   That each - at a party's request - would enjoin proceedings relating to the same matter in the other when the matter had been initiated in the court issuing the injunction is an indication not of competition but comity.

24   The author of the *The Compleat Solicitor Performing his Duty* (1672) observed that while practice in Exchequer was 'in effect one and the same with the Chancery', it was 'a little more chargeable'; p 61. Few later practice manuals went beyond the observation that procedure in the two courts was more or less the same. And see David Burton Fowler, *The Practice of the Court of Exchequer* (1795), I, ix, and II, 2, 193.

25   To judge from Exchequer decrees extracted from E 126, estate cases rose from 13.2% of 1685 decrees (n=68) to 24.5% of 1818-1819 decrees (n=105). There was also a fall in debt/bond cases from 23.5% in 1685 to 12.3% in 1818-1819.

E. The Identity of the Litigants

Because Chancery required plaintiffs to give some indication of status and/or occupation as well as place of residence in their bills of complaint, relatively full information about their identity (or, in the case of women parties, the identity of their husbands or fathers) is available. Information concerning these characteristics is also available for the substantial majority of defendants, sometimes supplied by the plaintiff in his bill and more usually by the defendant in his answer. Occasionally, the pleadings disclose the fluidity of self-ascriptions, as when a plaintiff describes himself as a maltster and the defendant characterizes him as an innkeeper. Nor was the plaintiff always accurate in his statement of a defendant's residence, as subsequent affidavits relating to the service of subpoenas attest.[26]

While differences in characterization of status or occupation, or errors in specifying places of residence for defendants, pose no serious problem for this analysis, more troubling is the lengthy period of time covered, especially in the light of the increasingly common tendency in the eighteenth and early nineteenth centuries to expand the definition of gentility. Sometimes, it is possible from the pleadings themselves to take account of this phenomenon: the lawyer who describes himself as A B esq, barrister of the Middle Temple, has been categorized here not as an esquire but as a professional. Such additional information is not always available, and in those instances in which the documents suggest, but do not state directly, that the 'gent' or 'esq' is a professional or a man of business that individual has been categorized in accordance with his self-description. Yet as Table Seven indicates, even the steady enlargement of the ranks of the 'genteel' over time can only have qualified, rather than concealed, the growth in the proportion of non-gentlemen parties.

---

26   In addition, there is the issue of how to treat parties who were representing the interests of others - most often, an executor/administrator of an estate, but also trustees, guardians, and the like. There are 32 representative plaintiffs in the 1627 sample, nine in that of 1818-1819. Here, the representative party has been treated as the individual whose identity is to be tabulated chiefly because in a substantial number of instances full information is lacking either about the deceased or about the real party in interest. When the status (and also residence) of the deceased or other represented party is actually given, residence frequently corresponds to that of the representative party. For instance, the first five representative parties (and the deceased, or real party in interest) encountered in the 1785 sample are a provincial trader representing a provincial gentleman; a London merchant representing a London trader; a metropolitan gentleman representing his late wife, a separate trader; a provincial grazier representing a provincial carrier; and a metropolitan esquire representing a metropolitan esquire.

TABLE SEVEN: STATUS/OCCUPATION OF ALL-NAMED PLAINTIFFS

[85 sets of multiple plaintiffs in 1627; 84 sets in 1818-1819; average no. of plaintiffs per suit, 1.57 in 1627 and 1.81 in 1818-1819.]

	1627 (n=446)		**1818-1819** (n=269)	
Gentlemen and above	140	31.4%	50	18.5%
Farmers*	58	13.0	17	6.3
Commercial and artisanal	62	13.9	44	16.4
Professional	21	4.8	18	6.7
Minors	67	15.0	51	19.0
Widows	23	5.2	19	7.1
Wives	38	8.3	27	10.0
Spinsters	4	0.9	11	4.1
Miscellaneous - men	9	2.0	1	0.4
No designation - men	24	5.4	31	11.5

* predominantly yeomen in the 1627 sample, but also includes husbandman, copyholder, farmer, and rural labourer

What immediately catches the eye in Table Seven is the sharp decline over the intervening centuries in the categories of 'gentlemen' and 'farmers'. Also evident is the sizeable increase in the proportions of women plaintiffs, up from 14.4% to 21.2%, with the principal source of increase the rising proportions of widows and spinsters. The category of professionals also shows a considerable increase. But despite the growth of trade and industry over these two centuries, the proportion of commercial and artisanal plaintiffs shows only a limited rise.

To some extent, of course, the degree of change in any of these categories is muted by the presence in Table Seven of minors and of men (and occasionally corporate bodies) who have not been and often cannot be placed in those categories, and so appear as miscellaneous or undesignated. Indeed, when minors, miscellaneous and undesignated men are removed from the computations, women figure as no less than 30.6% of all-named plaintiffs in the 1818-1819 sample.

In succeeding tables on the status/occupation of litigants, the focus will be on the males in the first four categories and on first-named plaintiffs (and, subsequently, on first-named defendants). Several considerations have shaped this choice. In the first place, minors (male and female) and undesignated and miscellaneous males cannot be easily assigned status/

occupation labels. In the second place, married women, with the exception of the few spinsters, derived their status chiefly from their husbands (whether alive or not), and were predominantly involved in estate and land suits. In the third place, when there are multiple plaintiffs, they often come in sizeable numbers - eg, groups of minor children in testamentary cases and groups of assignees in bankruptcy in business-related matters - and their inclusion would tend to skew a status/occupational analysis.[27]

The results of this paring down of categories appear in Table Eight.

TABLE EIGHT: STATUS/OCCUPATION OF FIRST-NAMED MALE PLAINTIFFS

	1627 (232) (A-Z)	**1685** (105) (A-K)	**1735** (122) (A-K)	**1785** (99) (A-Z)	**1818-1819** (118) (M)
Gent & above	50.0%	39.0%	43.4%	32.3%	38.1%
Farmers	21.9	15.2	14.8	12.2	6.8
Comm/artisanal	20.3	39.0	32.8	49.5	44.1
Professional	7.8	6.7	9.0	6.1	11.0

* for the 1685 and 1735 samples, the count is limited to plaintiffs whose names fall in the first half of the alphabet.

The data on *first-named* male plaintiffs' status/occupation prompt a number of observations, partly by way of comparison with the figures in Table Seven. The first is that as in Table Seven, so in Table Eight there appears a considerable increase over the period as a whole of professionals and a considerable decrease in gentlemen and farmers. However, the increase in commercial and artisanal plaintiffs in Table Eight is much more pronounced than that recorded in Table Seven - a result of the exclusion of women, minors, and non-designated males.

The second observation is that the decline in the proportions of gentlemen and farmers as well as the rise in the proportion of commercial and artisanal plaintiffs was by no means steady over the time span covered by the five samples: compare, for instance, in Table Eight the entries for 1735 with those for 1685. There is also a marked resurgence in 1735 in the proportion of gentlemen among the plaintiffs which parallels the revival in the proportion of land-related cases in that sample; similarly, the decline from 1685 to 1735 in the proportion of commercial and artisanal types parallels the fall in the percentage of business cases. It is also noteworthy that the decline from 1785 to 1818-1819 in the proportion of commercial and artisanal plaintiffs is accompanied by a partial revival in the percentage of land cases.

Third, it should be observed that the principal conclusion to be derived from Tables Seven and Eight is that in large part the changing mix of Chancery complainants over the five sample years trails behind the broad socio-economic trends of the era, above all the growth of

---

27   In one 1627 estate suit, there were no less than 46 named plaintiffs.

trade and industry. But despite Chancery's reputation as *the* forum of the landed gentry, the fall in Chancery plaintiffs with styles of gentleman or higher between 1627 and 1818-1819 (evident in both tables) was substantially more pronounced than the decline in the percentage of suits involving land over the same period (39.2% to 30.3% in Table Five).[28] In any event, it would be rash to link too closely the fall in the proportion of gentlemen plaintiffs with the downturn in land litigation, or, conversely, to tie the increase in the proportion of commercial and artisanal plaintiffs to the rise in business suits. On the one hand, not all gentlemen plaintiffs were litigating over land-related matters, and neither were all traders and craftsmen pursuing business disputes.[29] And on the other, as remarked earlier, a substantial fraction of the realty at issue in Chancery by the later 1700s and early 1800s was urban property, in sharp contrast to the land disputes of 1627.

What, then, of the socio-economic identity of the defendants in the sample suits? Here, similar trends are visible. In 1627, gentlemen and those of higher status comprised 52.1% of first-named male defendants; but in 1818-1819, only 28.3% (Table Nine) - that is, the fall in this category of first-named male defendants exceeded that among first-named male plaintiffs.[30] Again, the proportion of farmers as defendants also fell, but not so sharply as among the plaintiffs. Meanwhile, the proportions of commercial and artisanal sorts and of professionals grew at almost the same rate among defendants as among first-named male plaintiffs.

TABLE NINE: STATUS/OCCUPATION OF FIRST-NAMED MALE DEFENDANTS

	1627 (184)		1818-1819 (120)	
Gent & above	94	51.1%	34	28.3%
Farmers	41	22.3	18	15.0
Commercial/artisanal	35	19.0	55	45.8
Professional	14	7.6	13	10.8

The results, then, of combining first-named male plaintiffs and defendants offer no surprises.

---

28   Brooks, 'Interpersonal conflict', p 385; also p 397; for the comparison with Common Pleas, see *ibid*, p 384.
29   Of the 58 suits in the 1785 sample begun by litigants who were residents of London and the metropolis (33 of them businessmen, or the widows or children of businessmen), 13 related to commercial transactions, 15 to matters of realty (mostly metropolitan and some commercial property), while 20 more involved estate-related matters.
30   In the 1627 sample, of the 100 complainants styling themselves 'gentlemen' or of higher rank only 9 resided in London or its environs; in the 1818-1819 sample, of the 43 English complainants styling themselves gentlemen only 26 resided in the provinces.

TABLE TEN: STATUS/OCCUPATION OF FIRST-NAMED MALE PARTIES

	1627 (n=403)	**1818-1819** (n=238)
Gent & above	50.6%	33.2%
Farmers	22.3	10.9
Commercial/Artisanal	20.1	45.0
Professional	6.9	10.9

But what do these shifts in the array of plaintiffs and defendants mean? When we encounter a 'yeoman' of Bloomsbury among the 1818-1819 parties, his anomalous self-ascription is a reminder of the fragility of contemporary socio-occupational categories. Indeed, there can be little doubt that many who styled themselves 'gent' or 'esq' in 1818-1819 would hardly have done so two centuries before. For this reason, an analysis of the places of residence of the litigants (both male and female) may add meaning and depth to this examination of the litigants. The data are in Tables Eleven through Thirteen.

TABLE ELEVEN: PLACE OF RESIDENCE OF ALL FIRST-NAMED PLAINTIFFS

	1627 (n=285)	1818-1819 (n=149)		1627 (n=285)	1818-1819 (n=149)
North: Yorks, Lancs, Durham, Northumb, Cumb, Westmor.	22	10	City of London.	27	9
Midlands: Derb, Cheshire, Heref, Hunts, Northants, Oxon, Leics, Lincs, Notts, Staffs, Worcs, Warw, Rutland, Salop.	64	17	Metropolitan: Westminster, metropol Middlesex and Surrey.**	13	47
South-west: Corn, Devon, Dorset, Dorset, Somerset, Glos, Wilts.	52	23	Other British Isles.	9	12
East Anglia: Norfolk, Suffolk, Cambs.	22	5	Overseas: Continent and colonies.	2	3
South: Surrey, Sussex, Hants, Kent.	27	11	Other.	1	-
Home Counties: Herts, Berks, Beds, Bucks, Essex, rural Middlesex.	20	12	No locale.	26	-

* to facilitate comparison with figures generated for the common law courts, we have followed Brooks in grouping places of residence by the assize circuits.

** 'metropolitan Surrey' is essentially Southwark.

TABLE TWELVE: PLACE OF RESIDENCE OF ALL FIRST-NAMED DEFENDANTS

	1627 (n=285)	1818-1819 (n=149)		1627 (n=285)	1818-1819 (n=149)
North: Yorks, Lancs, Durham, Northumb, Cumb, Westmor.	19	13	City of London.	17	21
Midlands: Derb, Cheshire, Heref, Hunts, Northants, Oxon, Leics, Lincs, Notts, Staffs, Worcs, Warw, Rutland, Salop.	46	17	Metropolitan: Westminster, metropol Middlesex and Surrey.	8	33
South-west: Corn, Devon, Dorset, Somerset, Glos, Wilts.	37	19	Other British Isles.	5	6
East Anglia: Norfolk, Suffolk, Cambs.	17	3	Overseas: Continent and colonies.	1	3
South: Surrey, Sussex, Hants, Kent.	16	14	No locale.	104	6
Home Counties: Herts, Berks, Beds, Bucks, Essex, rural Middlesex.	15	14			

TABLE THIRTEEN: PLACE OF RESIDENCE OF ALL FIRST-NAMED PARTIES

	1627 (n=440)		1685 (n=237)		1785 (n=240)		1818-1819 (n=292)	
London metropolis	65	14.8%	58	24.5%	111	46.2%	110	37.7%
English provinces	357	81.1	169	71.3	113	47.1	158	54.1
Other	18	4.1	10	4.2	16	6.7	24	8.2
(No locale	130		55		40		6	)

As Tables Eleven through Thirteen indicate, James I's lament that soon London would become all England seems to have been an apt prediction, at least so far as Chancery parties are concerned. While 357 of the 440 (81.1%) of the identifiable first-named litigants in the four main categories of the 1627 sample came from the English provinces outside the metropolis, by 1818-1819 only 158 of 292 (54.1%) did so. Concomitantly, the number from the metropolis (the City, Westminster, Southwark, and their environs) rose from 65 (14.8%) to 110 (37.7%) over the same period. In the meantime, the total population of the metropolis (though not of the City) expanded substantially; even so, there was a striking disproportion by 1818-1819 between the percentage of Chancery litigants from the metropolis and the metropolitan share of the total population of England.[31] London and Middlesex accounted for roughly one-tenth of the total English population in the first quarter of the nineteenth century, yet the City and metropolitan area together accounted for three-eighths of the Chancery litigants in the 1818-1819 sample, and an even larger share of the 1785 one.[32] The sharp decline in litigants in Chancery from the provinces is not easy to explain. While local courts of equity are known to have been less important after 1660 than before 1640, the added expense involved in conducting a lawsuit at a distance does not seem to have diminished significantly.[33] Moreover, distance does not account for the varying patterns of activity of individuals from particular regions. In fact, the fall in the proportion of plaintiffs between 1627 and 1818-1819 was sharpest for relatively proximate East Anglia (from 8.5% to 3.4%) and almost as marked for the Midlands (from 24.7% to 11.4%). But if relative distance does not account for the differing trends among litigants from the individual circuits, proximity cannot be discounted in helping to explain the very substantial gain made by the metropolitan region, especially the expanding urban area outside the City walls. *Excluding* the City, the metropolitan share of first-named plaintiffs rose from 7.4% in 1627 to 31.5% in 1818-1819, with the only other circuit registering even a small increase over the period being the Home Circuit (from 7.7% to 8.1%).

Like the fall in the numbers of higher status litigants, the growth in the proportion of metropolitan parties was not unique to Chancery; it was also apparent on the equity side of Exchequer and in the common law courts. Between 1606 and 1750 the proportion of cases litigated in Common Pleas and King's Bench at the London and Middlesex sittings rose, respectively for the two courts, from 16% to 19% and from 21% to 32%.[34] Even so, over roughly the same period, Chancery experienced a substantially greater proportionate expansion of litigants from London and metropolitan Middlesex and Surrey - 14.8% in 1627, 24.5% in 1685, and already 36.3% in 1735.[35]

The paradox, then, is evident. At the very time that regular and lengthy parliamentary sessions were bringing the landed gentry from every part of the kingdom to Westminster, their readiness to sue in the central courts was declining (and declining most markedly in equity matters which, unlike common law ones, could not be litigated in most of their counties on *nisi prius*). Yet if country gentlemen were less prone to launch suits in Chancery, the same

31 In categorizing parties' locales, we have taken into account the very considerable expansion of the metropolis's boundaries over the two centuries in view. Overall, the City contributed 44 of the first-named parties in 1627 and 30 in 1818-1819; the *rest of* the metropolitan area contributed 21 in 1627 and no fewer than 80 in 1818-1819.

32 For regional breakdowns of the English and British population in the eighteenth and early nineteenth centuries, see Phyllis Deane and W A Cole, *British Economic Growth 1688-1919* (2nd edn, 1967), p 178 (Table 27) and C H Lee, *The British Economy since 1700: A Macro-economic perspective* (1986), p 127 (table 7.1).

33 Examination of the pleadings for the Duchy of Lancaster discloses the same sharp drop in suits begun between the later seventeenth and later eighteenth centuries as in Chancery: DL 1/444, 492, 502. For similar findings for Durham, see K Emsley and C M Fraser, *The Courts of the County Palatine of Durham* (1984), 81-85; Marcus Knight, 'Litigants and Litigation in the Seventeenth Century Palatinate of Durham', Cambridge University PhD, 1990, esp pp 101, 109.

34 Brooks, 'Interpersonal conflict', p 370. It is also noteworthy that the sharpest downturns in King's Bench were registered by litigants from the Midlands and Norfolk circuits.

35 Exchequer bills from London and Middlesex underwent a similar proportional increase between the later seventeenth and later eighteenth centuries.

cannot be said of their metropolitan counterparts. In fact, metropolitan plaintiffs (like their provincial counterparts) were a medley of the fashionable and the workaday. To instance only the first fifteen of the sixty-one such plaintiffs in the 1735 sample, they include three West End esquires (one the brother of Lord Whitworth, another 'late of Ravensworth Castle, Durham', and the third a descendant of John Locke's friend Popple), three widows of men of unspecified status (from Westminster, Holborn, and Marylebone), three gentlemen (from Holborn, Southampton Row, and Lincoln's Inn), a surgeon and a victualler from Southwark, a mercer from St Clement Dane's, an innholder from St Giles, a cordwainer from Clerkenwell, and, lastly, a shipjoiner from Wapping.

While the fall in provincial suitors to Chancery (and to the other central courts) remains to be explained, it may be worth noting that those Chancery plaintiffs of the eighteenth and early nineteenth centuries who did come from outside the metropolis were, rather more frequently than metropolitan suitors, aiming to resolve estate-related issues. As late as the 1780s, to judge by the sample data, provincial plaintiffs suing with respect to wills and intestacies still outnumbered their metropolitan counterparts by a ratio of seven to four. At first glance, this may appear surprising since estate suits tended to be prolonged by comparison to most other types of cases, and hence all the more expensive to carry through. Indeed, of the 13 suits which lasted beyond five years in the 1785 sample, all involved estates, as did 14 of the 26 suits of the 1818-1819 sample which went beyond five years.[36] But for those involved in the administration of complicated estates, not least executors wishing to safeguard themselves against subsequent charges of laxity or corruption, supervision of their proceedings by Chancery might well seem a necessary evil - a choice eased by Chancery's usual practice of allowing the costs of such administration to be paid out of the assets of the deceased.[37]

F. Conclusions

Although the Court of Chancery escaped reform from without in the seventeenth and eighteenth centuries, its jurisdiction gradually altered in character. These alterations were, in part, linked to developments elsewhere in the legal system, especially the common law courts' adoption of a more flexible approach to the conditioned bond and the church courts' difficulties with some of the complexities of estate administration. But the common law courts, along with Chancery, were themselves sufferers by the marked decline in new business coming into the central courts during the eighteenth century despite the overall growth in population, industry and commerce, and urban living. Paradoxically, however, in Chancery this pronounced decline in new cases over the course of the eighteenth century went hand in hand with a slowdown in the processing of the business that remained to it. This slowdown may have been due in part to the delays in process that self-interested court office-holders (and/or the parties' own legal representatives) threw up in the way of suitors in Chancery. But at the same time it reflected the changing mix of cases coming to Chancery, above all the growing proportion of estate cases, often very prolonged affairs and especially if there were minors involved. Surely, it was

---

36 By contrast, only 10 of the 39 suits lasting beyond 2 years in the 1627 and 1685 samples are estate cases.
37 *Supra*, note 16.

no accident that Dickens chose an estate case to mount his attack upon the Court in *Bleak House*!

Along with changing patterns in the substance of cases coming before Chancery were shifts in the identity of the litigants. In the first place, there is the declining proportion as plaintiffs of gentlemen (especially landed gentlemen) and of farmers, coupled with the rise of professionals and of artisanal and commercial types. Yet, these shifts did not make for a marked decline in cases involving realty nor preclude a marked rise in estate cases - and the rising proportion of women plaintiffs clearly contributed to both the relative persistence of the former and the increase in the latter. In the second place, there is the quite startling fall in the number and proportion of provincial parties. Whereas close to 85% of first-named parties in the 1627 sample were from the English provinces, only 47% were in the 1785 sample when the Court was handling less than 60% of its earlier caseload (and receiving barely 25% of the number of new bills per annum).

In turn, the partial revival of the Court's activity by the end of the second decade of the nineteenth century was accompanied by interesting shifts by comparison to 1785 in the identity and locale of parties, in the mix of cases, and in the duration of suits. These may be summed up as

(1) a downturn in the proportion of commercial and artisanal plaintiffs coupled with a corresponding recovery in those styling themselves gentlemen (or above) and a limited reappearance of parties from the provinces (up to 54%);
(2) a marked downturn in estate cases from over 42% in 1785 to just above 32%; and
(3) a sizeable increase in the number of suits lasting five years or longer.

These developments are worth remarking for two reasons. First, because it would appear that a significant part of the impetus for the Court's revival came from the revival in proportion (amid an overall rise in business) of provincial litigants. Second, because it underlines the need to consider other possible causes for the Court's enhanced exposure in the early nineteenth century to criticisms of its delays and the lack of finality in its determinations. Among the other factors contributing to Chancery's increased vulnerability in the early 1800s, it may be suggested, was the very revival in the Court's business; after a half-century or more of stagnation its creaking machinery was now under heavy strain. And, in turn, this strain was magnified by the distinctive character of Lord Chancellor Eldon (holder of the Great Seal for all but a few months from 1803 to 1827). On the one hand, Eldon seems to have preoccupied himself with time-consuming but more profitable bankruptcy proceedings.[38] On the other, his notorious 'cunctative habit' in pursuit of the absolutely correct decision meant that not even the institution by statute in 1813 of a Vice Chancellor to help cases to a conclusion could compensate for his very deliberate pace.[39]

---

38 For the rise in bankruptcy (and lunacy) petitions, see *Parliamentary Papers* 1826 (143) xvi, app B6 (bankruptcy doubling and lunacy more than doubling between 1800 and 1820).
39 Baker, *Introduction*, pp 130-131.

The moral of this tale should, then, be clear. The searcher, and particularly one intent on formulating a subject search, needs to bear in mind

(1) the marked fluctuations in the overall volume of Chancery business between the early 1600s and the early 1800s;
(2) the substantial shifts in the kinds of cases brought before the Court over these two hundred years; and
(3) the marked transformation in the identity of the parties - above all, the long-term decline in litigants from the provinces.

CHAPTER THREE:
The Records and the Finding Aids

A. Introduction: the Survival of the Records

Despite the enormous mass of extant materials in the PRO relating to the equity proceedings of the Court of Chancery during the seventeenth and eighteenth centuries, it is possible that a significant number of the records generated in the course of litigation have not survived. If so, it is probable that the losses were incurred before the records were transferred, at various times during the middle decades of the nineteenth century, from the repositories and offices where they had hitherto been held - principally the Tower, the Chapel of the Rolls, the Six Clerks' and other offices of the Court, and lastly the Masters' offices - to the PRO.

In part, the risk of loss was a function of the physical character of the records themselves. Very heavy and sizeable volumes, such as the books of orders, were much less likely to go astray or be damaged extensively than were smaller, more fragile items - save perhaps by fire. It was fortunate, then, that the fire of 1621, which certainly resulted in the loss of some pleadings, was confined to the Six Clerks' offices.[1] But besides the sudden destruction wrought by fire, there was the insidious damage caused by rot from damp and by the gnawing of rodents; thus, attached to a copy of a 1627 Master's report is a note that 'the original [report] which this is a true copy was eaten by the Rats.'[2]

Furthermore, on one occasion at least, there seems to have been a theft of a sizeable quantity of records.[3]

Much, then, depended on the actual care and attention given the records. But the risks of fire, decay and theft cannot wholly be separated from the ways in which various types of records were generated and used. This is especially evident with respect to the pleading classes for the 1600s and 1700s, C 2 through C 12.

In these classes, there is ample evidence of both misfiling and loss. Take the filing of answers. Answers, of course, were never made if a bill of complaint had not first been exhibited; they were then to be physically attached to the original bill. Yet, between five and ten per cent of all the items now listed in C 2 through C 12 are answers (or other responses) without bills.

---

1 Thus, William Chapman noted in his bill of complaint of 21 Nov 1627 that an earlier bill in this dispute, filed in 1619, was destroyed, along with the associated pleadings, in the 1621 fire: C 2/C15/53. See also the 1627 order re procedure on depositions destroyed in the fire: Sanders, *Orders*, 155. The offices were rebuilt in brick, but in 1701 Martin Bladen, in his treatise on 'the antiquity and constitution of the Six Clerks and their office', reflected that the reconstructed office 'stands to this day crowded and environed with taverns and dwelling houses ... so that it is still exposed to suffer by the like calamity of fire'; C 173/10.
2 C 38/57, Dec 1627.
3 This incident is discussed below at pp 54-55.

Sometimes, it is possible to locate the bills elsewhere in the same or another pleadings class (eg, C 2 answers with C 3 bills), but in many instances the bills cannot now be found.[4]

The filing of bills, answers and other pleadings in a specific case (including depositions from examinations taken by commission in the country) was the responsibility of the plaintiff's Six Clerk.[5] But there were inherent problems in carrying out this duty. For one thing, two Six Clerks - at a minimum - had to be involved, since the complainant and defendant as a matter of course had different Six Clerks (and if there were co-defendants, additional Six Clerks might be involved). For a second, since the real work of the Court in the pleadings stage was largely carried out, even in the early seventeenth century, by the 'under-clerks' (later the Sworn Clerks) in each Six Clerk's division, it was the Sworn Clerks who received the bill and other documents from litigants (or their solicitors), who oversaw the copying of such documents for a variety of purposes, and who often kept the originals by them as the suit proceeded. Thus, the Six Clerks were, in effect, dependent upon the efficiency and conscientiousness of the Sworn Clerks to carry out their own record-keeping responsibility (by the seventeenth century, their principal remaining function), and their incentive to do so was chiefly to obtain their allotted share of the copying fees. The results of these divisions of responsibility - among the respective Six Clerks and, even more importantly, between the individual Six Clerks and the various Sworn Clerks of their 'divisions' - was late filing, misfiling, and sometimes loss.

It is not easy to gauge the gravity of the problem, particularly since the Six Clerks and Sworn Clerks, often at odds over fees during the later 1600s and the 1700s, recurrently traded accusations of misconduct which centred on misfiling and loss of the pleadings.[6] Nonetheless, there are several significant indicators. First, there is the fact that the Six Clerks by the 1660s (and probably earlier) were bundling the files in their studies in at least two different categories. The first consisted of 'pleadings'; the second of so-called 'study matters'.[7] In brief, 'study matters' were documents filed according to the rules (bills, with any subsequent pleadings attached) while 'pleadings' were documents brought in (or returned) by Sworn Clerks out of the normal sequence - documents which the Six Clerks did not try to attach or to reattach to the original files.

Another indicator of the gravity of the problem concerns the finding aids supposed to be kept by the Six Clerks so that, if need be, they could certify to the Court the actual state of the pleadings and also so that the relevant records of dormant suits that might be subject to revival or useful as evidence could be located. The principal finding aids were the bill books

---

4   A case in point is Turpin v Tyson. First encountered as a single bill of 26 Oct 1685 at C 7/333/59, on further searching there was found at C 6/282/93 (dated 1686 in the new C 6 'alphabet' but 1689 in the older 'alphabet' for the class) the joint answer of two of the defendants with the copy bill of 30 Oct 1685 which had been sent down with the commission into the country to take the answer (itself dated 9 Oct 1686). In turn, the surviving cause book for the year, IND 1/4191, shows two bills, one of 26 Oct, the other an amended bill of five days later (omitting one of the four original defendants). The bill(s) and the joint answer, moreover, tell remarkably different stories.

5   The rules, and some of their problems, were set out by Samuel Reynardson in a memorandum reproduced in Appendix One.

6   See also H Horwitz, 'Recordkeepers in the Court of Chancery and their "record" of accomplishment', *Historical Research* 70 (1997), 34-51.

7   See, for example, the old 'alphabet' to C 6.

and the cause books, both taking the form of 'alphabets' (ie, listing by first letter of the surname or title of the first-named plaintiff). Both were to be kept by each Six Clerk, and in addition a composite bill book was to be kept for all six divisions. It is, then, a measure of the losses incurred that no composite bill book survives before 1673-1674 and a continuous run only begins in 1715. Similarly, while a cause book for one division survives from the 1620s, and a considerable number survive for individual divisions for the later seventeenth and early eighteenth centuries, cause books for all six divisions for a single year do not survive prior to 1700. Furthermore, a continuous run of cause books only survives from 1729 onwards.

Without adequate finding aids, locating records could be very difficult, whether the searcher was looking in the studies of the Six Clerks (where current records were kept, in principle, for six terms), in the Six Clerks' record rooms (whence bundles were supposed to be transferred after six terms and kept for consultation and search), or in the Court's long-term repositories - the Chapel of the Rolls, and from the 1670s onwards (at least for the pleadings) the Tower. And, indeed, there were recurrent complaints that searchers were encountering difficulties. For example, in one Master's proceeding of 1695, it is recorded that one of the parties had been searching 'diligently' in the Tower for three days, looking for the materials in a 1630 suit listed 'in a book which from comes from Mr Wilkinson's [a former Six Clerk] office', but yet failing to find them.[8] More generally, Master of the Rolls Trevor - reporting in 1704 to the House of Lords on the preservation of Chancery records - observed that when he 'first came to be Master ... these records were very ill kept, and in confusion, so that the search to find out any record was difficult.' However, Trevor did go on, in a more positive vein, to note considerable improvements in the intervening years so that now in each division 'every record keeper has alphabetical books to find out the records upon any search, though some, I conceive, are more perfect than others.'[9]

Others in Trevor's day took a less sanguine view than he of the effectiveness of the Six Clerks as record-keepers, and there was a move afoot in Anne's reign to get rid of them altogether (though with generous compensation) and entrust their recordkeeping responsibilities to newly-chosen specialists. But this project perished, and subsequent Six Clerks did not seem to take the warning seriously.[10] Thus, Harry Charles Bateman, deputy record-keeper to the Six Clerks, recalled in 1766 that during his predecessor Benjamin Collison's tenure 'complaints had often been made by the solicitors and suitors of this Court' about the difficulties of locating records. Part of the problem was the failure of the Sworn Clerks to return documents to their Six Clerks, but Collison had also left 'a great arrear of records unsorted' in the record room, with 'bundles lying heaped on the floor and in other places', while also failing to provide adequate finding aids. Bateman went on to observe that since Collison's demise in the late 1750s much had been done, at no little expense, to put matters right. Even so, there were still problems, including the retention of large numbers of bundles of older records by various Sworn Clerks.[11]

Moving forward to the early nineteenth century - a time of renewed parliamentary concern with the preservation of records - much the same mixed picture can be painted. On the one

---

8   C 38/263, proceedings in West v Hart before Master Franklin - report of 5 Dec 1695.
9   *The Manuscripts of the House of Lords, 1704-1706* (House of Lords MSS, new series VI), pp 47-48.
10 C 173/5, unnumbered bundle of draft bills with a 1706 proposal that seems to lie behind them.
11 C 173/36, bundle re the records, Bateman memorandum to the Six Clerks, 27/11/1766.

hand, when Six Clerk William Turton was examined in 1836 by the House of Commons committee on the records, he had no hesitation in returning an *omnia bene*. Speaking of the records still in the Six Clerks' possession (ie, the pleadings since 1758), he asserted that they were in a 'very good' state of arrangement, with 'good indexes', stored in 'dry and very airy' conditions, and that there was no difficulty 'at all' in searchers locating 'anything which may be wanted'. On the other hand, when Vice-Chancellor Sir Lancelot Shadwell was asked about conditions in the Rolls Chapel, he told a tale of disorder, coupled with damp and rot, a situation that had prevailed until the present Master of the Rolls had taken up his post.[12]

Also suggestive is the episode alluded to by Six Clerk Francis Vesey in his testimony of 1824 to a parliamentary inquiry into the Court of Chancery. This involved the theft of 'some very considerable quantity' of pleadings (bills and answers, but not depositions) in the not-very-distant past, apparently shortly before Vesey had become a Six Clerk in 1811. Granted, the culprits (apparently, copyists or other employees of a Sworn Clerk) had been apprehended, prosecuted, and transported; even so, they had managed to find a market for their takings - for 'waste paper' according to *The Times*, for 'drumheads' according to a subsequent version of the episode![13] To be sure, Vesey as a Six Clerk may have been willing to defend his colleagues' care by casting the blame on employees of the Sworn Clerks. Yet given the procedures for handling the pleadings, it was in fact the employees of the Sworn Clerks who were the most likely to be in a position to carry off such a theft; indeed, as far back as 1647 there is record of two of the under-clerks 'taking out of the six clerks office diverse decrees and records of the Court and disposing them to other uses.'[14]

In these instances, at least, there is direct evidence of embezzlement of Chancery records. But how much was lost, whether by theft, material damage, or other causes? This question can be answered, at least for those years for which the bill books are available in virtually continuous runs, by counting in the bill books the number of original bills of complaint exhibited and then by counting the number of original bills that are recorded in the present class lists for the years 1714-1800 (C 11 and C 12).[15]

The bill books list some 2073 original bills for the letter 'N' for the years 1714-1758; the present class lists of C 11 and C 12 list only 1877 (90.5%).[16] Perhaps surprisingly, the loss ratio for pleadings for the 1758-1800 period is somewhat higher. For 1770, the survival ratio is 89.3%, for 1785 it is 84.7%, for 1800 it is only 52.6%.[17]

12 *Parliamentary Papers* 1836 (4225, 565) xvi, app, columns 6672-6674, 6654-6655.
13 *Parliamentary Papers* 1826 (143), xvi, A(9) 139. *The Times*, leader of 27 Dec 1826, reprinted in Joseph Parkes, *A History of Chancery* (1828), pp 575-584; John D Cantwell, *The Public Record Office 1838-1858* (1991), pp 65-66 mentioning a brief reference of 1841 to the theft in which 'the bills and answers had been converted into drumheads'.
14 Sanders, *Orders*, p 218 (and see p 219). For another theft, again involving 'agents in the office', see *The English Reports* 21, 293-294.
15 In other words, in order to avoid double-counting it is necessary to eliminate from the billbook tabulation both amended and supplementary bills and to do likewise (where possible) from the C 11 and C 12 lists. Bills of revivor have also been eliminated in both counts. Given the limitations of the C 11 list, particularly, it is not always possible to identify such 'duplicate' bills so that the C 11 count has a built-in bias minimizing the extent of loss.
16 If all listings in the bill books were included, the percentage of survival would fall to 78.7%.
17 Again, 'duplicate bills' have been eliminated. For 1770 and 1800, four letters have been counted; for 1785, the entire alphabet has been used.

The extraordinary level of loss for 1800 raises the possibility that it was at that time that the theft alluded to by Vesey occurred, but the apparent connexion becomes somewhat more tenuous when Vesey's account is examined in detail. To be sure, the loss of which he spoke was of bills and answers. But he also indicated that the pleadings had been taken from the Six Clerks' offices, not from the record room - ie, the stolen documents were of quite recent vintage when the theft occurred. It is, thus, all the more frustrating that it is virtually impossible to replicate for earlier classes of pleadings the kind of quantitative analysis carried out for C 11 and C 12.

Nonetheless, it is possible to extend this analysis of loss beyond the pleadings records by drawing upon the data concerning depositions and Masters' reports from the 1627, 1685, and 1785 samples.

All told, there are 92 suits (of the total of 571 traced cases) in which there are entries in the books of orders for the taking of depositions or for their publication. However, depositions have been located in the relevant classes (C 21 - C 22, C 24, and C 11 - C 12) in only 62 of these instances. This suggests a loss of one set of depositions in every three. The actual loss may have been somewhat smaller as in some instances parties may not have taken advantage of the authorization to examine witnesses. Nonetheless, in 19 of the 30 suits in which depositions were authorized but do not survive, the litigation had proceeded at least as far as the making of an order for the publication of depositions *already taken*. Taking these orders into account, it may be concluded that the likelihood of loss was, at a minimum, one in approximately four cases (ie, 19 of 81).[18]

An even larger loss of Masters' reports has been suggested by the historian of the Masters in Ordinary, Edmund Heward. Citing the findings of a Privy Council inquiry of late 1724 (prompted by the discovery of defalcations in suitors' funds in the 'safekeeping' of individual Masters), Heward draws the conclusion that only about one quarter of all the reports made by the Masters were ever filed - ie, that the 847 volumes of Masters' reports now in C 38 for the seventeenth and eighteenth centuries contain only a small fraction of the total number of reports prepared. He grounds this conclusion on the explanation given by the officers of the Report Office of their fee income given to the commissioners of inquiry: that is, that as it was up to the parties to file a report, a process involving the payment of fees, there was little incentive to file when both parties in a given case were prepared to accept the report. Hence, only if at least one party aimed to enforce the report (or was simply playing safe) would the office fees be paid and the report be preserved.[19]

In fact, Heward's conclusion is unduly pessimistic. In the first place, the report of the 1724 inquiry has been misread; instead, it suggests that only one-quarter of Masters' reports

---

18 This is to assume, for purposes of making a minimum estimate, that in all other cases in which there are entries in the books of orders for the taking of depositions those depositions were *never* taken and hence were not subject to loss.

19 Edmund Heward, 'The Early History of the Court Funds Office', *Journal of Legal History* 4 (1983), 49, repeated *idem*, *Masters in Ordinary* (1990), 50, citing SP 35/54, no 24 (four ms copies of the report dated 16 Dec 1724).

made were *not* filed.[20] In the second place, crosschecking Court references of matters to the Masters (as found in the books of orders) for the suits included in the 1627, 1685 and 1785 samples against the actual reports preserved in the relevant volumes of C 38 indicates that a substantial majority of reports ordered by the Court were made by the Masters and *filed* (163 of 192 or 84.9%).[21] It would appear, then, most Masters' reports that were ordered were actually made and filed for the record, and that the record of the Report Office, at least from the later seventeenth century, was substantially better than that of the Six Clerks in the preservation of the documents which fell to them to keep and to safeguard.

It should be clear, then, that the present body of Chancery equity records is incomplete, and the realization of substantial losses in certain important categories of the Court's records, and especially the pleadings, is discouraging. Even so, the remaining records are massive, and the searcher's most common difficulty will probably be in locating records that are still extant. To facilitate that task, there follows an analysis of the organization of the records and a description of the individual classes and their associated finding aids.

B. The Organization of the Records

There are, in fact, sixty-three separate 'C' classes in the PRO containing material relating to Chancery equity proceedings of the seventeenth and eighteenth centuries; in addition, hundreds of volumes of listings (and related material) prepared by the Six Clerks and other officials of the Court are now located in the IND 1 class. Even so, there is no single or comprehensive index to the Chancery equity classes, or even to the main groupings - the pleadings classes (C 2 through C 12), the deposition classes (C 21 through C 25), the Masters' reports and certificates (C 38, C 39, C 40), affidavits (C 31 and C 41), and Masters' Exhibits and Papers (C 101 through C 129, and also C 171).[22] And the point to be underlined is that the materials for any particular suit will be scattered across a half dozen or more of the individual classes, and for the most part must be searched for by the use of the finding aid(s) specific to each class.

I The Finding Aids

1. The 'Standard List' (hereafter, SL)

At present, most of the individual classes are listed in SL, class by class, with the very important exception of the great majority of the pleadings classes. The class lists for Chancery equity records in SL all carry the prefix 'C' followed by a number - eg, C 33 - and these class lists are held in binders volumes accessible on the open shelves in the two reference rooms at Kew.

---

20 *The Reports of the Commissioners appointed to Inspect the Accounts of the Masters in Chancery* (1725), p 4: 'one fourth part of the Reports are never filed, the Sollicitors keeping them in their own Hands, to save Expence', checked against SP 35/54, #24. This publication may have been unauthorized; see SP 35/55, examination of Nathaniel Mist, 23/1/1725. The pamphlet can be found on reel 3500 #6 of the Resource Publications microfilm series 'The Eighteenth Century Short Title Catalogue'.

21 It is also worth noting that the bulk of the losses found in the traced suits (23 of the 29 missing reports) come from the 1627 sample; that is to say, for the 1685 and 1785 cases combined, the survival ratio is 94.3%.

22 Stray items are also located in other 'C' classes, including C 18 and C 98.

The Records and the Finding Aids

Virtually all class lists are preceded by an introduction to the specific class of records, and followed by a listing which gives the date-range (or other indication of contents) of each box (eg C 33/201); the introductions often refer to related classes and to other relevant finding aids for the given class. Some of these introductory notes, in turn, draw on the first edition of this handbook. It is anticipated that the printed version of the SL will be superseded over the next few years by an online version, searchable either at Kew or via the PRO's website.

(a) Chancery equity record classes in SL: C 4 (in part), C 24 - C 26, C 28, C 31, C 33, C 36 - C 42, C 48, C 78, C 102 - C 116, C 127 - C 129, C 171, C 173, C 240.
(b) Introductions to classes in the SL (but not class lists): C 2, C 3, C 5 - C 12, C 21, C 22, C 79.

2. Non-standard listings and finding aids

The bulk of these are older lists, some printed, some typescript, and some manuscript. Many are the working records of the officials of the Court themselves, others are the subsequent compilations of officers of the PRO, genealogists, and scholars. Many of these, especially for classes without lists in SL, are at present shelved by class number in the 'medieval and early modern record' reference and reading room on the second floor at Kew. (This is the only open-shelf location for the great bulk of the non-standard listings.) Those not available on the open shelves are kept in the repository and must be called for as documents (the great majority of these are to be found in the class IND 1 and the handbook gives the document references to such finding aids, class by class, below). Any difficulties encountered in locating Chancery finding aids should be put to those of the staff on duty in the second floor reading room; the PRO maintains a computerized list of finding aids in the database known as 'Moris'. Non-standard finding aids are listed and described below under the relevant record classes - C 2, C 3, C 5- C 12, C 21, C 22, C 78 (part), C 117 - C 126. Many of these non-standard finding aids, especially but not exclusively those compiled by officers of the Court, share a number of features.

(a) Most are listings by name. The Chancery clerical staff located materials almost wholly by the names of the parties; they did not make index entries of subject matter or of the locales either of the parties' residences or the matter in dispute.
(b) These older listings were generally compiled using the surnames of the first plaintiff and of the first defendant. This habit can complicate life for the researcher if the case(s) being searched involved multiple parties on one or both sides, or if the names of the parties changed during the course of the litigation (by death, marriage, or the addition of parties) or if a party could be described by more than one surname (eg, in the long-running controversy of the mid-1700s between the proprietors of the Maryland and Pennsylvania colonies, the Maryland proprietor is variously identified as 'Calvert' and as 'Baltimore').
(c) The compilers of these listings often employed a number of conventions. In particular, persons with titles (familial or official) and corporate bodies will usually be listed under their *Latin* title - eg, the Earl of Warwick will be listed under the

57

letter 'C' for *Comes Warwick*, the Bishop of Worcester under the letter 'E' for *Episcopus Wigorn*, the inhabitants of a given parish under the letter 'P' for *Parochiae* ..., and so on. (In the later 1700s, the use of Latin began to wane, but the keying of entries to titles persisted, eg, the *Duchess of Portland*.)

(d) For the most part, these listings are organized either on an annual basis or on a term-by-term basis (the four legal terms of Michaelmas, Hilary, Easter and Trinity). The volumes are generally organized by year, and often are subdivided by the four legal terms.

(e) These listings are only partly alphabetical: that is, while suits are grouped by the letter of the alphabet with which the first plaintiff's surname begins, within each letter there is no alphabetizing. So, for example, if the first plaintiff's surname in the suit to be traced begins with the letter 'A', the searcher must scan *all* the entries for that letter. Nor can the searcher expect to find, if there is more than one entry for the suit in question in that term, those multiple entries grouped together; rather, the suits tended to be entered by the sequence of proceedings (though each letter may contain a number of different sequences as well as a few items not in any discernible sequence).

Given the distinctive character of these non-standard listings, they have throughout this *Guide* been referred to as 'alphabets', reserving the term 'index' to identify modern fully-alphabetized listings (whether by name, locale, or subject). Many of the alphabets (some on the open shelves, and others needing to be ordered) are part of the class 'IND 1'; there is a partial list of this class in volume 232 of the 'List and Index Society' but since that volume was issued some IND 1's have been re-classed (see class list) so that recourse to the computerized list of finding aids is advised. The IND 1 listing is, in turn, organized by class numbers - ie, all the finding aids in IND 1 for the Chancery classes are to be found under their respective Chancery numbers (eg, the bill books and cause books that survive for the pleadings are listed under the heading C 5 to C 12, and so on).

3. Classes lacking lists

C 23 (sealed depositions, not used in Court), C 96 (docquets for enrolments of decrees), C 101 (Masters' Accounts - the PRO now has a leaflet advising readers to search this class).

II The Individual Classes of Records and Their Finding Aids

To some extent, though with significant limitations, the entries in the books of orders (C 33) help to link the various stages of the suits. So C 33 will serve as the point of departure in reviewing the individual classes and the finding aids available to help in searching them.

(A) The Books of Orders: C 33 and C 37

1. C 33 - Books of Orders, 1544-1875: 1219 boxes (SL)

The books of orders, compiled by the Register (or, rather, by his deputies and their staffs), begin in 1544. These volumes were the Court's official record, and they contain *verbatim* texts of all orders and decrees.

For years up to Michaelmas 1629, there are two volumes per annum ('A' and 'B') - near, but not exact, duplicates of the other. Most entries in one volume will be found in the other (though not necessarily on the same-numbered folio) but on occasion an entry will only be found in one. Thereafter, there continue to be two volumes per legal year (ie, starting with Michaelmas term and covering the succeeding Hilary, Easter, and Trinity terms), but from this date forward they cover, respectively, suits for the first and last halves of the alphabet (A-K, L-Z) respectively. From Michaelmas 1629 onwards, then, there is usually (although not invariably) only one entry for any order, decree, or item of process.

The C 33 volumes are nominally divided into chronological sections - term by term - and most entries have calendar dates. But it is possible to find items dated, for instance, in Easter term yet entered under Trinity term, and so on. Often, but not invariably, such late-appearing entries are the texts of decrees, which - especially in complicated cases - required time for drafting and checking by one of the deputy registers before they were ready to be entered.

Within each term, it is difficult to discern any overall pattern to the array of entries, whether by date or by type of action or process. A batch of subpoenas and other such process entries may be followed by some proceedings on petitions and motions, then by several decrees, and then by more process entries, and so on. This seeming lack of order is probably a function of the fact that a variety of officials were responsible for generating the materials entered in these volumes, with the clerks of the deputy registers who made the entries simply working their way through the material as it was submitted to them. Thus, there is little sense in paging through these volumes, each of which - in busy years - can number over one thousand folios. Generally, the way to approach the C 33 volumes is through the separate volumes containing term-by-term listings of suit titles which constitute the 'alphabets' for this class. The class list for C 33 gives the appropriate IND 1 reference to the alphabet for each C 33 volume; unfortunately, that number does not correspond to the date of the volume (though at first glance the IND 1 number does appear to be a date!). These IND volumes are presently shelved in the second floor reference and reading room; the C 33 volumes themselves must be called for from the repository.

To use the alphabets, and hence the books of orders, it is necessary to know (or to be able to make a good guess as to) the surname of the *first* plaintiff and, if possible, of the *first* defendant as well. In this regard, it is all the more ironic that the books of orders do not normally include entries for the exhibition of a bill or the submission of an answer. The reason is simple: the pleadings were the domain of the Six Clerks, not of the Register.

In general, the alphabets to C 33, while not without the occasional error and inconsistency, are full and accurate (bearing in mind the entry of some parties by title [eg *domina* Wharton, under the letter D], and other features of these contemporary listings). There are, however, occasions when suits are listed under a different title (for either plaintiff or defendant) than is used in the records of the pleadings (as in the specimen search described in Chapter Four below for 'DaCosta v Dubois').

What, then, are the types of entries to be found in the C 33 volumes? First, in order of importance, are the decrees, along with cognate matters including hearings and rehearings, consideration of parties' petitions and motions, and orders of reference to the Masters. These are interspersed within each term by entries for a wide variety of procedural matters - among them, the issuance of subpoenas and related process to secure a defendant's appearance and answer, arrangements for commissions to take defendants' answers in the country, permission for parties to revive earlier suits or to amend their bills of complaint, proceedings on preliminary injunctions, arrangements for the taking and publication of depositions, process to enforce orders and decrees, and so on. Given, then, the problems involved in the use of these volumes, it makes sense for the searcher in most circumstances to have recourse to them *only after* tracing the case at least through the pleadings classes.

2. C 37 - Minute Books, 1639-1875: 4776 boxes (SL)

Behind the C 33 volumes lie the minute books compiled by the deputy registers who supplied many, though by no means all, of the entries in the books of orders. A list of the deputy registers is given in the Introduction to C 37. The earliest extant C 37 minute book comes from Michaelmas 1639, and by the 1660s they survive in substantial numbers, with each minute book bearing the name of the deputy register who compiled it. In turn, the work of individual deputy registers in the preparation of C 33 can be identified by the initials appended to the C 33 entries they submitted, chief among them the decrees. Save, however, for brief notes on the identity of counsel at hearings, the C 37 volumes (usually, sixteen to eighteen yearly in the eighteenth century) do not add significantly to the C 33 entries; they can, however, be searched relatively quickly as each is in date order. Judging from those volumes examined in the preparation of this handbook, most entries are crossed out (though legible), apparently indicating that the appropriate entry had been made in the corresponding C 33 volume.

(B) The Pleadings Classes: C 2 through C 12, and related material in IND 1 and C 173

Collectively, C 2 through C 12 hold the surviving bills, answers, and other pleadings in Chancery suits from the later sixteenth century to 1800. In certain instances (C 11 and C 12), country depositions are also included (reflecting the Six Clerks' claim that such documents should be filed with them, and not with the Examiners' Office).[23] Note, too, that while many of the classes purport to be chronological in scope, there may be a substantial number of items from earlier or later years included (eg, the many pre-1649 items to be found in C 5 through C 10).

Usually, the items listed in the pleading classes (with the partial exception of C 4) are bills, either bills with defendants' responses (answers, predominantly) or 'single bills' as the Six Clerks styled them - that is, bills to which responses were never filed. For items up to 1706 (when this requirement was abolished by statute), it is quite common to encounter 'copy' bills

---

[23] See the petition of the Six Clerks on this score to Master of the Rolls Sir Joseph Jekyll early in George I's reign at C 18/6/5; one may speculate that the Six Clerks' pressure accounts for the filing of country depositions with the pleadings of C 11 - C 12, by contrast to the practice of the seventeenth century as represented by C 2 - C 10.

(normally, but not always, filed with the original bill); such copies were made when the defendant was answering by commission in the country. Nonetheless, the pleading classes (as is apparent from the lists of some of these classes) do contain a minority of pieces, at a minimum over five per cent, which are files of answers (or other responses) without bills. Such 'answers-only' files are listed under the name of the first plaintiff - eg, in the suit of P v W, W's answer-only will be listed under P v W. Sometimes, the class will contain the bill to which the answer is being made either in the same or a different box. Occasionally, separated bills and answers are found in different classes (eg, C 2 and C 3). And occasionally, no bill can now be located. It should be noted, however, that even an answer lacking a bill may be a valuable source since the defendant normally proceeded by reciting the plaintiff's accusations (at least in summary fashion) before giving his own account.

The only finding aid that covers a wide range of the pleadings is the so-called Bernau Index, the work of the genealogist C A Bernau. Copies of the Index are available on microfilm at the Society of Genealogists' Library in London and (by prior order) at any Family History Centre of the Genealogical Society of Utah. The Index, though important by reason of its broad scope, is not easy to use for a variety of partly-interrelated reasons:

(1) the microfilmed slips are compiled partly from published sources, partly from the original documents themselves, and some of the deficiencies of the Index mirror the limitations of the published sources;
(2) the slips within each surname are not sorted by first names, and the difficulties this poses are compounded by the failure to standardize the spelling of surnames;
(3) only rarely are identifiers other than the individual's name and date of the suit (eg, residence, save for C 21 deponents) provided, thus making the Index virtually unusable for very common names (save those with very unusual first names);
(4) the slips often give only abbreviated document references, omitting the class numbers; *these omissions have been supplied below where relevant*;
(5) the Index is not confined to Chancery records; it also includes a minority of slips compiled from other judicial records in the PRO, from pollbooks, and from a number of other types of unrelated materials;
(6) Finally, the slips themselves, at least on the microfilm, are sometimes not easy to read.

For all these limitations, the Index can be an invaluable aid, but prospective users are advised that a fee for its use will be charged by the Society of Genealogists' Library in London (unless the searcher is already a member of the Society) and also by the Family History Centres of the Genealogical Society of Utah (which will have to order specific reels for the searcher's use). The best published guide to the use of the Index (and to the Bernau notebooks to C 11 discussed below) is the series of articles by Guy Lawton, 'Using Bernau's Index', *Family Tree Magazine* VIII (3 parts, Dec-Feb, 1991-1992).[24]

---

24 See also his 'Using Bernau's Notebooks' in *Family Tree Magazine* X (3 parts, Dec-Feb 1993-1994) and the discussion below of C 11.

Notes of the Bernau Index's coverage (relying primarily on Lawton's work) are provided below in conjunction with the discussion of finding aids for individual classes. Suffice it to say here that in searching that Index, and indeed many of the alphabets in the PRO, it is clearly advantageous to be looking for individuals with unusual surnames (or unusual first names if the surname is a relatively common one).

1. C 2 - 1558-1649: 2240 boxes (introduction only in SL)

This class is organized into regnal series - ie, C 2/Eliz I, C 2/Jas I, and C 2/Chas I - and documents must be called for accordingly. Within each reign, the materials are organized by the letters of the alphabet. So, for example, a suit of Nalson v Smith of 1630 would be called for by C 2/Chas I/N + box number + piece number. Unfortunately, a substantial number of items have been boxed out of chronological order - eg, box 14 for the letter O for Charles I's reign (C 2/Chas I/O/14) contains, of a total of 61 items, 8 from James I's reign and 1 from Elizabeth I's.

For C 2/Jas I, there are several useful listings and indexes. Pleadings for which the first plaintiff's name begins with the letters A - K are listed in box by box order in vol 47 of the PRO's printed *List and Index* series (to be found on the open shelves). Entries include

(1) the full names of the first plaintiff and first defendant, and of additional parties;
(2) a description of the subject matter of the suit (sometimes quite specific); and
(3) an indication of the county in which the property, if tangible, was sited.

This printed index is continued through the rest of the alphabet in four manuscript volumes; they are similarly structured and contain entries in the same form. In addition, there is a one volume alphabet of names to C 2/Jas I and a one volume index of places (both also on the open shelves). The former was compiled in the early eighteenth century when these records were sorted and deposited in the Tower of London; it is organized in the same way as the modern volumes already noted (though omitting subject matter and locale) and contains no information not found in them. The 'Index Locorum', in three ms volumes, is more useful. It is fully alphabetical, and offers an alternative route into C 2/Jas I if the search is by place.

For C 2/Chas I, the situation varies. On the one hand, the four volumes covering these records which were published by the 'Index Library' (*Calendar of Chancery Proceedings, Bills and Answers, Charles I*, ed W P W Phillimore and E A Fry, presently on the open shelves) late in the nineteenth century replicate the structure of contemporary alphabets. Pleadings are listed box by box, without alphabetization within letters, and *without any dates*. Only the first parties are listed, and there is no indication of subject matter or locale. On the other hand, there are two additional volumes, based on the 'Index Library' volumes but giving all (first) plaintiffs in alphabetical order and all (first) defendants in alphabetical order. These two volumes, compiled by the genealogist Peter Wilson Coldham from the 'Index Library' volumes (and on the open shelves), can - within the limits of the original entries from which they were compiled - be very helpful. A searcher can quickly make a list of all the suits in which his or her subject(s) or their namesakes were involved, either as (first) plaintiff or as (first) defendant, in this segment of C 2. And in addition, the volume for defendants contains at the very end an index to places in that limited number of cases in which one of the parties was a 'place' (eg, a borough).

Bill (only) of complaint (undated, but addressed to Francis Bacon as Lord Verulam, Lord Chancellor: hence between 7/1618 and 1/1621) of Alice ap William widow against Thomas ap William Lloyd. (C 2/Chas 1/W102/23)

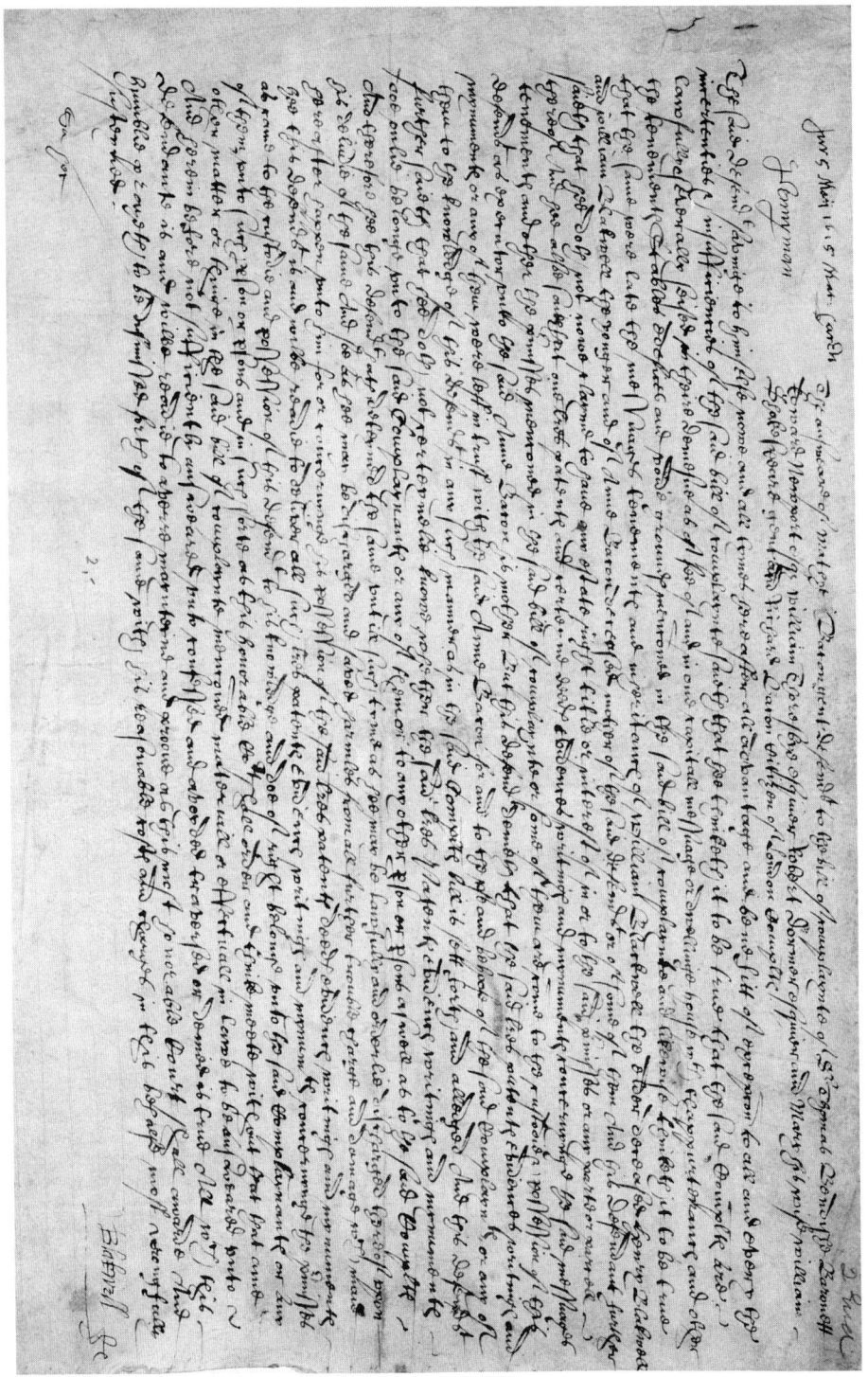

Answer (with bill) sworn 5 May 1615 of Mathew Bacon gent to the bill of Sir Thomas Bendysh bart et al. (C 2/James 1/B11/9/2)

A portion of the accounts submitted with the answer sworn 12 Sept 1787 of James Hayling to the bill of William Taylor esq 'proprietor of the King's Theatre or Opera House in the Haymarket'. (C 12/2147/14)

Deposition of James Collee of the Middle Temple, gent, aged 40 years or thereabouts, sworn 15 April 1736, in the suit of Ketelbey v Ketelbey. (C 22/951/13)

A single sheet of the 'B' order book for 1619. (C 33/138)

For C 2, the Bernau Index purports to cover the printed volume (A-K) for James I's reign.[25] Bernau's slips of surnames for this segment of C 2 are labelled 'Chancery Proceedings Jas I'; to call up the documents, it is necessary to have recourse to the printed volume for the PRO reference. In addition, the Index includes first defendants' names for Charles I's reign, and the slips are labelled 'Chancery Proceedings Chas I'; they do not give the precise PRO reference but they incorporate the document reference - for instance 'L26/20'. The actual PRO reference, then, is C 2/Chas I/L26/20.

Some 441 suits from C 2/Chas I are calendared in 'A Genealogist's Kalendar of Chancery Suits at the time of Charles I', published in *The Ancestor* 1-12 (1902-1905): this calendar covers all of C 2/Chas I/A1, B1, C1, D1, and E1, as well as selections from C 2/Chas I/F1, G1, H1, L1, and M1.

2. C 3 - 1558-1660: 485 boxes (introduction only in SL)

A much higher proportion of the items in C 3 than C 2 are single bills, along with some stray answers, replications, and rejoinders. It is likely, indeed, that this is a residual class, reflecting the Six Clerks' procedure for separating out single bills from files which were fuller (ie, containing at least bill and answer). At the same time, it should be noted that C 2 and C 3 are not wholly separate classes; answers and other pleadings that should be filed with apparently single bills in C 3 can be located in C 2. C 3 is organized chronologically by Lord Chancellor, beginning for the seventeenth century with the twenty-year tenure of Lord Ellesmere (1596-1616) and then continuing 1617-1621, 1621-1625, 1626-1639, 1639-1640, 1640-1642 and 1642-1660. This means that the items in any given box may be from any one of the years in the grouping. The boxes, organized by letter of the alphabet for each Chancellorship, are numbered consecutively so that it is not necessary to use an additional designation beyond C 3/box no/piece no in ordering items. For example, C 3/403 contains 177 pleadings, with the first plaintiff's surname in every case beginning with G. By contrast to C 2 there are many fewer items out of date sequence.

The principal finding aid for this class consists of two volumes, 24 and 30, of the printed *Lists and Indexes* (presently on the open shelves); they cover the entire class save for boxes 470-485 (transferred to C 3 from C 4 in the mid-1950s). The two volumes, like their predecessors for C 2/Jas I, give the names of the parties, a brief indication of subject matter, and a locale for tangible property in dispute. The listings in these volumes for James I's reign are structured as alphabets; the listings for 1626 onwards (ie, from box 393 onwards) are fully alphabetized. However, neither gives yearly dates for the individual items. By contrast, the present list for boxes 470-485 is a series of indexes by the first letter of the first plaintiff's surname: boxes 479-481 contain alphabetically-arranged documents from James I's and Charles I's reigns; box 482, similarly-arranged documents from 1649-1660; and boxes 483-485, similarly-arranged undated documents.

These C 3 listings (except for boxes 470-485) have been included in the Bernau Index so that first defendants' surnames are arranged there in alphabetical order. However, for these

---

25 Doubts about whether Bernau's Index does cover the letters A-K for C 2/Jas I are voiced by Guy Lawton in 'Using Bernau's Index', *Family Tree Magazine* VIII no 3 (Jan 1992), 43. Until this issue is resolved, it seems safer simply to rely directly on *List and Index* vol 47.

slips - labelled 'Chancery Proceedings series II' - it is necessary to consult *List and Index* vols 24 and 30 in order to locate the PRO document reference in question.

3. C 4: 173 boxes (partial list in SL)

This class of strays and fragments spans the time period from the fifteenth to the mid-seventeenth centuries, and many of the items are undated. There is a modern index incorporated in SL for plaintiffs and defendants but it covers only boxes 1-47 (omitting box 35); this gives the type of document (bill, answer, commission, inventory, etc) and a date or estimated date where possible. The copy in the reference room indicates that this index is not wholly trustworthy. There is no finding aid for the remaining boxes of C 4. A number of items originally in C 4 were transferred to C 3 in the 1950s and organized as boxes C 3/470-485.

4. C 5 through C 10 - '1649-1714': 3618 boxes (only introductions in SL)

For some purposes, these six classes may be considered together as each emanates from an individual Six Clerk's division ostensibly from the period between Charles I's execution and the accession of George I (1649-1714). Thus, C 5 is referred to as Bridges division (640 boxes), C 6 as Collins (611 boxes), C 7 as Hamilton (671 boxes), C 8 as Mitford (658 boxes), C 9 as Reynardson (491 boxes), and C 10 as Whittington (547 boxes). In fact, the covering dates for these six classes are somewhat misleading, for while there are few post-1714 items, there are many pre-1649 items, in some instances going back to Elizabeth I's reign. Usually, but not invariably, these pre-1649 items are bunched together in the lower-numbered boxes of each of these classes; in C 8, for instance, boxes 1-35 are mainly Elizabethan and Jacobean pleadings and boxes 36-64 mainly date from the 1620s.

Overall, no clear pattern of organization is discernible in the boxes of C 5 through C 10. Some boxes within each of the classes are bunched by letters of the alphabet and represent a narrow span of years; others are grouped by letter but cover a considerable time-frame (eg, C 7/51, all pleadings with the surname of the plaintiff beginning with the letter B: 27 are pre-1640, 19 from the 1640s and 1650s, 16 from the 1660s, 1 from the 1670s, 11 from the 1680s, and 38 from 1690 to 1713, and of these 112 files 25 are answer-only). Still others appear to have been kept or been sorted by type and date - eg, C 9/415 consists of 321 'single bills' covering the letters A-H and spanning the years 1676-1685, while C 9/489 consists of 106 'single bills', all from 1685.

Equally disparate is the quality of the finding aids (most available on the open shelves) to these classes. To begin with, it should be noted that the list for C 9 edited by Fry (see below), though deficient in a number of respects, is a fully alphabetical listing of suit titles (first-named plaintiff and defendant). So if the searcher does not know where to begin in these six classes and is looking for a particular party's suit, it makes sense to check first in C 9 - a check that can be quickly made and may yield some reward.

If the C 9 index yields nothing *and* if the searcher is after a testamentary cause, the next step should be to consult the modern indexes to personal estate cases in C 7, C 8, and C 10 (compiled by P W Coldham from the existing alphabets). The indexes to personal estate cases are available in the second floor reference room (filed by class number), along with an earlier index to personal estate cases for C 6 (only to box 269). While these personal estate indexes include only a fraction of all the cases in the classes concerned (and their completeness is dependent on the completeness of the alphabets from which they were derived), they are especially useful as they are organized alphabetically by the surname of the *deceased*, which may not be the surname of any of the parties to the litigation. The Coldham indexes for estate cases in C 8 and C 10 also contain topographical indexes at the back of the respective volumes. In addition, an index prepared by S van Dulken in 1992 provides alphabetical listings for Pembrokeshire suits by the names of individual parties (and at least some deponents) and of the suits by their titles; this 'Index of Chancery proceedings of Pembrokeshire interest' covers classes C 5 - C 10 and a copy of this index is at present available on the open shelves next to the C 5 alphabets.

More generally, for all of C 5, C 7, C 8, C 10, and part of C 6 (two separate alphabets, the first through box 269, the second through box 360) and for the first 43 boxes of C 9, there are alphabets compiled since the documents came into the PRO. These alphabets (all presently kept on the open shelves), some in longhand, some in typescript, and those for C 5 printed as *Index of Chancery Proceedings, Bridges Division, 1613-1714 (Lists and Indexes*, vols 39, 42, 44 and 45) provide:

(1) the names (surname and first name) of at least one party on each side;
(2) the year of the document;
(3) 'place or subject';
(4) the county (missing for some suits); and
(5) an indication of files not containing bills - eg, 'answer', 'replication'.

Suits are listed by first letter of the first plaintiff's surname (for the most part not alphabetized within the individual letters) and box by box - that is, the alphabets begin with all the A's in box 1, then proceed to all the A's in box 2, continuing until the last box in the class containing such plaintiffs is reached, and then starting through the B's, etc. Searchers should bear in mind that since the boxes in each class consist of three or more roughly chronological series, A's (or any other letter) for a given year or range of years may be quite widely dispersed within the class. The place and county entries for the items in these volumes are specific. However, the subject entries are, for the most part, very general, with the most common being 'money'. There, are however, a few more specific subject categories more or less consistently employed - among them, 'personal estate' of a named person (these entries would appear to be the sources for the 'personal estate' listings noted above), 'marriage contract' (or agreement or settlement), and (less consistently) 'mortgage'. There are no indexes to these volumes, and the only way to search them at present, bearing in mind their organization, is page by page and volume by volume.

What of the remainder of C 5 - C 10? For C 6, other than the two alphabets covering up to box 360 described in the previous paragraph, there are three contemporary volumes, also presently on the open shelves. These are the original Six Clerk's listing, now keyed to the present box and piece numbers. The first and second volumes cover boxes presently numbered 1-572. Through box 508, the suits are listed by the first plaintiff's surname, with the defendant's surname, and, in some boxes, the date of the document. However, the entries for boxes 509-569 give only the first plaintiff's surname *and first name*. In addition, in some boxes the contents of each piece are noted by abbreviation, with 'b' for bill, 'r' for answer, 'sch' for schedule or attachment, 'cert.' for certificate, and so on. The third volume covers the remaining boxes of the class, 573-611; the listings parallel those for boxes 1-508, save for 611 (listed like 509-569).

Three points may be noted concerning this C 6 contemporary alphabet. First, for the time being at least it provides the only entry into C 6/360-610, no matter how inadequate. Second, it is worth consulting even for C 6/1-359 should the searcher wish to know the contents of an individual file, though reference will still have to be made to the newer alphabets in order to obtain a piece number for any given suit of interest found in the old alphabet for most boxes from 1 to 268. Third, the organization and headings of this older alphabet illustrate the overall structure of C 5 through C 10, especially the chronological structure of boxes 101-362 and the heading 'single bills' for boxes 573-610.

Finally, C 9 is, in some ways, the most inadequately served of these six classes even though, as noted above, the principal finding aid is fully alphabetized. A two volume set edited by E A Fry ('Index Library' of the British Record Society) and entitled *Index of Chancery Proceedings, Reynardson's Division, 1649-1714* is all that is available at present.. There is, shelved with this set, part of a more recent alphabet covering boxes 1-43 of C 9; for those boxes which it lists, it is more informative than the Fry volumes. The limitations of Fry's listings are:

(1) generally, only first plaintiffs and first defendants are indicated;
(2) first names are lacking; and
(3) no other information about the suit save the date of the document is given.

Fry's listing by first plaintiff's surname can be supplemented by the Bernau Index in which defendants' surnames (extracted from the Fry volumes) labelled 'Chancery Proceedings Reynardson' are also listed alphabetically. Apart from these entries from C 9, the Bernau index includes only C 5 suits: these entries, labelled 'Chancery Proceedings Brydges', are extracted from the printed listings of C 5 in the four *List and Index* volumes. In addition, the Dwelly index at the Society of Genealogists' Library includes parties for the first part of C 6 (up to box 269).

Given the tediousness of conducting a nominal search in C 5 - C 10, searchers should be able to save considerable time when the current 'inputting' of extant PRO lists for these classes into the 'data equity base' has been completed. Nonetheless, the database will be of little assistance for subject-matter searches for these classes until the original documents themselves are relisted.

5. C 11 - '1714-1758': 2793 boxes (introduction only in SL)

There is a significant overlap between C 11 and C 12, as there are many pre-1759 items in C 12 (see below under C 12 for listings of these items).[26] In addition, there are a small number of items pre-dating George I's accession.

---

26 A count of one letter ('N') suggests that well over 15% of the total surviving bills for 1714-1758 are now to be found in C 12.

As C 11 is composed of the records of all Six Clerks, the list (on the open shelves) contains six separate subsections, though the class is numbered consecutively (first division 'Sewell', boxes 1-460; second division 'Winter', boxes 461-955, etc). Unlike earlier pleadings classes, C 11 also includes (largely in separate boxes) all surviving interrogatories and depositions taken in the country by commission (eg, in 'Sewell' for the letter 'A', boxes 386-387, 448, and 458). (For partial indexes of these depositions, see below under C 22.)

The list for C 11 has the same basic structure as the alphabets for C 5 - C 10, but provides somewhat different information. The nature of each file is indicated ('b', 'br', 'r', 'dep', etc) but no information is given about place or subject matter. Also lacking are the first names of the parties. The C 11 list also suffers from another major deficiency. Although years are given for roughly two-thirds of the pieces, the dates of the remainder are concealed under a number of headings. These headings include clumps of years such as '1714 to 1720' and '1752 to 1757', regnal designations such as 'Geo 1st', 'Geo 1st and 2nd', 'Geo 2nd', and even a few nominally single years - especially '1737' and '1739'. (Such groups of '1737' and '1739' boxes, as distinguished from those pieces actually so dated, are normally encountered in the lists for the six divisions in conjunction with other semi-dated boxes listed only as 'Geo I', 'Geo II', etc)

To a limited extent, a logic of sorts can be discerned in the use of these headings. First, those for sequences of years (eg '1714 to 1720') appear to be reasonably accurate descriptions. Second, those for single years such as '1739' do not seem to contain any pieces later than the year designated (ie, 1739), and take as their starting point the latter years of Anne's reign (1710-1714). Third, those for 'Geo 1st' do not appear to contain any pieces later than 1727. Fourth, those for 'Geo 2nd' do not contain any pieces later than the 1740s, though in some instances they contain material as early as 1714. Fifth, those for 'Geo 1st and Geo 2nd' span the widest range of these groupings with some boxes containing pieces as early as 1700 and as late as 1745. Overall, and with the exception of a few post-1740 groupings such as '1752-1757', the bulk of this material dates from c 1714 to 1739, with a few outliers both earlier and later.

Why the maker(s) of the C 11 listings fell back upon such unhelpful practices in dating is unclear, particularly since virtually all the documents are dated! More germane is how to overcome this obstacle. Since the Bernau Index includes the names of *all* parties to C 11 suits (along with the names of all deponents of the country depositions in C 11), it is an especially important resource for searching this class; these slips are labelled 'Chancery Proceedings 1714-58'. In addition, the notebooks from which Bernau made up the slips for C 11 may be of help. (Like the Bernau Index, one set of these notebooks is held on microfilm at the Society of Genealogists' Library; another microfilm copy is held by the Genealogical Society of Utah and can be ordered at any Family History Centre. In addition, a third microfilm copy is now held by the PRO and is available in the second floor reference room.)

The Bernau C 11 notebooks contain a piece by piece listing of all 2793 boxes in the class beginning with C 11/box 1/piece 1. In addition to providing years (though not months and days) for each file in C 11, the compilers of the notebooks normally entered:

(1) all the parties' surnames;
(2) all the parties' first names; and
(3) in most instances, the status/occupation and residence of at least the plaintiffs and, with some frequency, of the defendants as well.

Thus, these notebooks constitute a valuable finding aid in and of themselves, in part as a topographical listing, in part as to subject matter as suggested by occupation (especially when parties on either side have similar or linked occupations) or by relationship to a named deceased individual. Unfortunately, only the parties' (and deponents') names as taken from the notebooks are included in the main Bernau Index; hence, access to the other information entered in the notebooks requires reading through them reel by reel: a key to the contents of individual reels - organized in the sequence of C 11 references but with some overlap among reels - is supplied by Guy Lawton, 'Using Bernau's Notebooks', Part III *Family Tree Magazine* X no 4 (Feb 1994), p 15. Thus, for instance, reel two (film number 0385285) begins with the second part of box 60 (box 60 piece 20) and continues to box 109 piece 6 *but with some omissions*, only to double back to box 100 piece 22, and then to continue forward again until box 164 piece 17. In turn reel 3 (film number 0395286) begins with box 159 piece 5 and goes up to box 221 piece 6, and then doubles back to box 213 piece 15 with the last item on the reel being box 254 piece 68.

One other partial analysis of C 11 is available: R J Goulden's *Some Chancery Lawsuits: An Analytical List* (1982-1983). This brief work focuses on one hundred or so lawsuits relating to the printing trade, and contains three lists: a list of principal plaintiffs; a list of all the parties involved; and a list of particular books involved in the lawsuits.

One further point about the PRO listing for C 11. The first half of the eighteenth century is a time when amended bills were becoming much more common, but the compilers of the C 11 list do not seem to have adopted a consistent position as to which of the two possible dates to use - the earlier date (when the bill was filed) or the later date (when it was amended). So, some amended bills are listed by the earlier date, some by the later date. Thus, even if a case was initiated in, say 1735, there could have been an amended bill and hence a later date (usually one to two years but sometimes even longer after the first date of filing) may be used in the C 11 list - that is, if any real date at all is provided!

6. C 12 - '1758-1800': 2434 boxes (Introduction only in SL)

Like C 11, the list for C 12 (available in the second floor reference room) is divided in six separate subsections, but consecutively numbered. The C 12 list is, however, considerably easier to use than most of the others available for the pleading classes as it is fully alphabetized within each subsection. (Thus, country depositions are intermingled with the main pleadings, by contrast to C 11.) Virtually all items are dated. Only the surnames of the first plaintiff and defendant are given, along with an indication (as in the C 11 list) of the nature of the file ('b', 'r', etc) and also a notation of amended bills.

For four of the six subsections, there are separate listings, abstracted from the main list, of pre-1759 items (mostly 1714-1758 but a few earlier). These listings cover the divisions 'Whittington and Sewell', 'Purcas and Winter', 'Woodford and Kipling', and 'Zincke and Ford'. To locate pre-1759 items in the other two divisions, the searcher must resort to the main listings for those divisions.

The Bernau Index covers only the deponents in those country depositions included in the first two divisions of C 12 (Whittington and Sewell, Purcas and Winter); these slips are labelled as 'C 12'.

7. Contemporary records and lists of the pleadings and related matters: IND 1, and C 173

On a number of occasions, the bill books and cause books compiled by the Six Clerks have been mentioned. Though only a limited number are extant for the seventeenth century, for the next century most have survived, and they can be of considerable use.

(a) the bill books (IND 1/2136-2151, 14416-14500).
One bill book yearly was kept to record the bills filed in all of the Six Clerks' offices. The earliest surviving bill book runs from Easter 1673 through Hilary 1673/74 (after 1760 they were kept on the new style year beginning January 1). There is a continuous series from 1715 onwards. Each volume is divided into the four legal terms and within each term is subdivided by letter - the first letter of the first plaintiff's surname (but not alphabetized within each letter). The information they contain, then, is the term in which a bill was filed and the surnames of first plaintiff and first defendant. Most volumes distinguish between original bills, amended bills, supplemental bills, and bills of revivor. Bill books for the period 1714-1800 are listed in the introductions in SL to C 11 - C 12.

(b) the divisional cause books (IND 1/4105-4207).
Individual cause books were kept for each of the Six Clerks' offices. The earliest surviving cause book covers the years 1620-1626, but not until 1729 is there a continuous run of cause books for each and every Six Clerks' office. While the absence of even one cause book may affect the conclusions that can be drawn from a search of the other five for a given year or group of years, even pre-1729 volumes can be of considerable use since they provide an account of the course of individual suits through the pleadings stage. Commonly, the cause books for a given year will provide information on the date a bill was filed with a listing of all the plaintiffs' names, and any subsequent pleadings associated with it (eg, defendants' answers [all names] and other responses, amended and supplemental bills, and revivors). Lists of the divisional cause books may be found in the introductions in SL to C 5 - C 10 and in those to C 11 - C 12, accompanied by listings of the holders of the Six Clerkships from 1660 onwards.

(c) individual Sworn Clerks' cause books (IND 1/7388-7525 and 20314-20318).
Behind the cause books for the individual divisions are many similar compilations made by various Clerks in Court (that is, the Sworn Clerks and Waiting Clerks) who were actually acting on behalf of individual clients in conjunction with the clients' solicitors. The earliest of these extant date from 1714. In all likelihood, the principal incentive for keeping two sets of cause books was that both the Six Clerks and the Clerks in Court derived fee income from the pleadings and from copies made by the parties from the originals. The Clerks in Court's books contain, unlike the cause books, the dates of appearance and other proceedings in suits with which they were concerned; they also list the names of the solicitors for those parties whom the individual Clerk in Court represented and the names of the Clerks in Court for the opposing parties. The surviving Sworn Clerks' cause books are listed in the introductions in SL to C 11 - C 12.

(d) the rule books in C 173 (SL).
There survive runs of 'rule books' spanning the years 1725-1790 for each Six Clerks' division (eg, 11 volumes for 'Reynardson' in C 173/38): the 'rules' in question relate to process for the deposition of witnesses (pre-hearing) and the scheduling of 'publication' of their depositions. They do not appear to add anything to C 33 entries relating to commissions for depositions and rules for publication. Six further such volumes, labelled 'cost and rule books', can be found in C 173/11.

(e) miscellaneous contemporary lists of pleadings and depositions (C 173/12, 15-30, 32-34, 44-47 and C 18/10/22) (SL for C 173 and C 18).
These are fragmentary listings which suggest how the Six Clerks kept the pleadings records, coupled with listings of depositions for limited time periods, but they appear to have little independent value.

Summary: to conclude this account of the internal records of the Six Clerks and the Sworn Clerks, we should emphasize that some can be of considerable utility. First, the bill books may be used to find the term of the filing of a suit the searcher believes was filed but has no precise date or reference (including the first defendant's name); it takes very little time to scan the relevant letter in each term for a run of years. A variant of this procedure would be to use the bill books to try to identify the names of a suit the searcher has some knowledge of but cannot trace back to its earlier stages because the names of one or both of the first plaintiff and first defendant had changed over the course of the suit. (The cause books can also be used for similar purposes, though their organization by division suggests that the bill books might be searched first. For examples, see Chapter Four on specimen searches.)

Second, the cause books are of especial value because they provide a full listing of the pleadings and may also signal special characteristics of individual suits (changes of parties' names, in particular). In addition, the cause books routinely designate those bills which are bills of revivor and direct one back to earlier proceedings by giving a reference to the term in which the original bill was exhibited; they also routinely signal the submission of amended bills and sometimes the filing of supplemental bills. In turn, once the searcher has located the *main* entry (ie, in the plaintiff's Six Clerk's cause book) in one or another of the six cause books covering a given time period, it may be worthwhile to continue the search for the secondary entry (ie, in the defendant(s)' Six Clerk's cause book(s)) which, on occasion, contains additional information. Note, however, that for stages of the litigation subsequent to the pleadings, the searcher must look elsewhere, especially to the books of orders, since the Six Clerks were concerned primarily with the pleadings.

(C) Interrogatories and Depositions: C 21 through C 25, and Country Depositions filed in C 11 and C 12

The principal forms of 'proof' - ie, evidence - in a Chancery cause were the sworn statements of the opposing sides' witnesses and documents submitted by the parties (or at the Court's request). The documents submitted by the parties were normally returned to them at the end of the litigation (though, see below, under the classes of Masters' Exhibits for some left behind);

the interrogatories and depositions remained in Court. But in which office these materials remained chiefly depended upon whether they had been taken in and around London or in the provinces. In the former case, they were taken by and kept by the Examiners' Office; in the latter, they were taken by specially-appointed commissioners and were, at least in the view of the Six Clerks, to be returned to the respective Six Clerks and kept with the pleadings in the suit (in fact, they were only kept with the pleadings after 1714). (In either case, these depositions, taken at the individual parties' initiative to support their cases at hearing, are to be distinguished from depositions taken by the Masters when issues were referred to them for purposes of investigation and report; depositions taken as part of a Master's reference usually are to be found in the Masters' classes and will be discussed below.)

It was common form for depositions to give the deponent's name, address, age and occupation at the head of the document. The deponents in some of these classes are included in the Bernau Index, as indicated below.

1. C 21 - Country Depositions (and Interrogatories), Elizabeth I - Charles I: 767 boxes (only introduction in SL)

The two manuscript volumes which constitute the finding aid to C 21 (presently available on the open shelves) are organized as alphabets and the entries are undated. The only clue the searcher is given is the suit title (ie, Knyvett v Leveson). Since the alphabets reflect the organization of the boxes themselves, this is a class in which the unusual surname factor works at a premium, especially since the documents in this class must be called for piece by piece. Given the difficulties involved, it may be worth searching the relevant C 33 alphabets and volumes to ascertain whether a commission to examine witnesses in the country was approved before the searcher attempts to locate any country depositions in the cause.

The Bernau Index includes the names of all deponents in the documents in this class (see above, C 2 and C 3). The slips are in the form: 'Chancery Deponents' (sometimes adding 'Eliz.-Chas I'); followed by the name and place of residence and age of the deponent, the date of the deposition, the county (by a group number), and finally a reference such as M18/8. To call up this deposition, the PRO reference would be C 21/M18/8.

2. C 22 - Country Depositions (and Interrogatories), 1649-1714: 1052 boxes (only introduction in SL)

The finding aids to these depositions are in six manuscript volumes, a product of the Six Clerks' offices, and are presently available on the open shelves. These volumes are organized as alphabets, and reflect the division of pleadings for this era into six classes (though in C 22 the bundles are numbered consecutively across the six divisions). A minority are dated, but for the most part C 22 poses the same obstacles to the searcher as does C 21; usually, the only clue one is given is the suit title. Again, in light of these difficulties, it is probably worth searching the relevant C 33 indexes and volumes to ascertain whether a commission to examine witnesses in the country was approved before trying to locate any country depositions in the cause.

The Bernau Index includes the names of deponents in the first 75 boxes of this class. The Bernau slips usually are labelled as 'Chan Deps before 1714'; they provide the case name, and also give box and piece number - eg, 36/24. In this example, then, the PRO reference for the document is C 22/36/24.

A much smaller selection of deposition materials from C 22 (some 495 cases, all with first plaintiffs' surnames beginning with the letter A) was calendared by F S Snell as a supplement to *The British Archivist* (1913-1920).[27] The Society of Genealogists' Library also holds:

(1) a manuscript calendar of the last 110 suits in the class; and
(2) a copy of a topographical index to depositions taken by commission in Norfolk, identified as 'Norfolk Deponents'. This typescript topographical index covers boxes 76 to 373 and provides the names, ages, and usually occupation/status of all litigants and deponents from Norfolk among the cases included.

3. Country Depositions (and Interrogatories), 1714-1800

These are kept and listed with C 11 and C 12 (*supra*). The Society of Genealogists' Library holds an index, 1714-1744, of the places at which depositions in C 11 were taken ('A Topographical Index to Chancery Depositions taken by Commission, 1714-44', compiled from the Bernau notebooks by members of the Norwich Record Society). See also J H Mann, *Chancery Depositions taken by Commission A Complete List of All Such Depositions for the County of Devonshire as are Filed among 'Chancery Proceedings 1714-1758' at the Public Record Office, London* (1950): this is a box by box listing of deponents in over 500 causes (the great majority of George I's reign); it also gives the full names and status of the parties in the litigation though not, at least directly, the subject matter of the suit.

4. C 24 - Town Depositions (and Interrogatories), 1534 to 1853: 2509 boxes (SL)

This class includes all surviving depositions taken in and around London by the Examiners. The class list indicates the organization of the boxes by year and term (though in some instances the designation by term is inaccurate). There is an index covering the period 1558-1714 in IND 1/9115-9121, but although it is fully alphabetical it is also seriously incomplete.[28] The PRO supplies these documents by box, not by piece.

The Bernau Index is said to contain slips for all deponents up to 1800. The slips are headed 'Town Depositions', and they give the year, box number, and 'initial letter of suit' - eg '1571. Bundle no. 96 suit C'. Thus, the PRO reference for this box is C 24/96.

Because the searcher can call for the entire box, C 24 is rather easier to search than C 21 or C 22. However, since in any given year of the seventeenth century there may be 15 or more boxes, each containing a substantial number of documents, it may be worth using the C 33 alphabets and entries to attempt to narrow down the time period to be searched.

---

27 Snell supplies a listing of the parties to the suit, the deponents, and a brief summary of the issue in controversy. Copies of the supplement are held, *inter alia*, by the Society of Genealogists and by the Guildhall Library. The latter has a typescript title page giving Bernau as the author (he was the publisher of *The British Archivist*), and includes also a typescript index.

28 Of 25 depositions from C 24 located for the 1627 sample, the index contains entries for only 7; of 12 depositions from C 24 located for the 1685 sample, the index lists only 6.

In addition, the last sixty boxes of C 24 contain (1) unpublished depositions 1755-1853 (see below, C 23), and (2) a mixture of miscellaneous interrogatories and depositions, mostly of the nineteenth century. A contemporary manuscript list of unpublished depositions from 1755 up to the mid-nineteenth century (by term, up to 1808) is presently included in C 98/2.

5. C 25 - Interrogatories, 1598-1852: 107 boxes (SL)

Although the searcher can usually deduce the questions posed to witnesses from the depositions themselves even if the interrogatories have become separated from the depositions, in some instances it is possible that interrogatories have survived although the depositions have not. C 25 consists of separated or solely-surviving interrogatories, most apparently originating from town examinations. The class is organized chronologically; there is a summary class list in SL for boxes 1-106 which is followed by a piece-by-piece listing of the items in box 107 (all of them coming from the year 1667). There are many interrogatories as well in C 21, C 22, and C 24.

6. C 23 - Sealed depositions, Elizabeth I - 1778: 391 boxes

These are depositions collected by the parties and submitted to the Court but never used, in some instances because the depositions had been taken *de bene esse* (ie, provisionally, with their use subject to the Court's approval), more usually because the litigation was settled or otherwise discontinued before 'publication' was ordered. These depositions were listed at the time the Six Clerks moved to their new building in 1778-1779 (IND 1/10779 - must be called for as a document); however, because they were rearranged subsequently, the drawer numbers given in the older list are no longer valid and no new class list has yet been prepared. So all that the older list does is to give an indication of the causes for which such depositions (still sealed) survive. As noted above, C 24 contains sealed depositions of the later eighteenth and the early nineteenth centuries.

(D) Affidavits: C 31 and C 41

Affidavits were sworn statements made for a variety of purposes. Those who swore them were not doing so in the capacity of witnesses chosen by the parties but rather fulfilling the Court's requirements for sworn statements on a wide range of matters. Most concern procedural questions - especially service of documents (eg, subpoenas) and notice by a party of the intent to make a motion, but also including a diversity of other matters such as eligibility to be admitted *in forma pauperis*, illness of a party, and so on. Many of the original affidavits survive in C 31; their texts and the text of other original affidavits which have not survived are recorded in the registers (C 41) kept by the Affidavit Office.

Occasionally, the contents of an affidavit may shed light on the position of the parties or the substance of a suit. Thus, for instance, an affidavit in a 1685 suit, Coates v Myers, states that the plaintiff has, besides the lands in question, a customary estate of 14 pounds per annum (C 41/25, Hilary term 1686, no 344). However, such titbits of information are few and far between (for another example, see below Chapter Four). In searching for affidavits, it is probably easiest to begin with the alphabets which can be used to find individual affidavits either in the volumes of the registers (C 41) or in the boxes of the originals (C 31). For the years for which registers exist, they are significantly fuller than the extant originals.

1. C 41 - Register of Affidavits, 1615-1747: 53 boxes (SL)

The registers are full transcriptions of the originals. For the years for which they exist, they contain copies of many originals that have not survived, and are also easier to use than the surviving originals in C 31. Individual entries are numbered, and the alphabets to C 31 (below) are also finding aids to the registers. There is a summary class list.

2. C 31 - Affidavits, 1607-1875: 3036 boxes (SL)

The affidavits are organized chronologically, by term, up to 1819. Alphabets exist at IND 1/7245-7293 (these cover some, but not all individual years from 1607 to 1755). In addition, there are modern compilations for the years 1611-1699 at IND 1/14545-14552 and for 1700-1800 at IND 1/14553-14567. These modern compilations are both fuller and easier to use, but IND 1/7245-7246 remain the only available finding aids for the years 1607-1610. There is a summary class list.

(E) Petitions: C 28 and C 36

Petitions were one of two ways (the other being motions in Court) by which litigants might request the Court to schedule certain kinds of hearings, to authorize the payment of funds in Court, and to initiate a range of other actions or steps in the course of a suit. Petitions were also required to begin proceedings for the rehearing or appeal of a decree. The searcher is unlikely to encounter in ordinary petitions any substantive information or, indeed, any information on the course of litigation not already discernible from the entries in the books of orders. However, appeal petitions did normally summarize the substance of the controversy and the course of the previous litigation.

1. C 28 - Lord Chancellor's petition books, 1774-1794, 1801-1869: 43 boxes (SL)

These petitions cover all matters for which litigants might petition the Court, save for rehearing or appeal. The volumes in C 28 are transcriptions of the original petitions, usually with some indication of the action taken on them by the Court. The volumes are chronologically organized and come two by two - a volume for plaintiffs' petitions, another for defendants'. Thus, volume 26, spanning the years 1785-1788, is a defendant's volume; volume 27, spanning the years 1786-1789, is a plaintiff's volume. There is a gap in the volumes between 1794 and 1800. There is a summary class list, but no index.

2. C 36 - Ordinary and appeal petitions, 1774-1878: 1584 boxes (SL)

Boxes 1-53 of C 36 contain appeal petitions from 1774 to 1869. The rest of the class consists of ordinary petitions from 1834 to 1878. Appeal petitions were petitions for rehearing or appeal of a decree; ordinary petitions, like those in C 28, were petitions made in the course of the original suit.

Boxes 1-53 are structured as a fully alphabetized series across the nine decades covered, with each letter of the alphabet taking up one or more boxes. Thus, appeals spanning the years 1774-1869 from parties whose surname begins with the letter 'A' are to be found in boxes 1 through 5, and so on. In addition to the summary class list, there is an index (by suit title) at IND 1/15029 ff (repository).

(F) Masters' Reports and other Masters' materials: C38 through C 40, C 101 through C 129, and C 171

As the Masters were increasingly relied on by the Court during the later seventeenth and eighteenth centuries to inquire into and report back on a wide variety of substantive questions referred to them after the parties were heard on the main issues, it should not be surprising that the volume of paper generated by the Masters and their staffs increased greatly.[29] Unfortunately, only the Masters' reports were systematically filed (provided that the parties paid the requisite fees); for the rest, their survival was chancier and their present arrangements more chaotic. Against this must be weighed the fact that the Masters' papers include a large volume of material (correspondence, accounts, etc) laid before the Masters in the course of their inquiries and never reclaimed by the parties themselves. These Masters' 'Exhibits' (C 103 through C 116, and also C 171) have proved a treasure trove for researchers, not least in economic history, and often they can be married to the Court's records of proceedings in the suit in question. An almost equally rich source, the Masters' Accounts (C 101), has as yet gone relatively unexplored for lack of adequate listing.

Many of the Chancery Masters' classes (apart from C 38 - C 40) bear the names of individual Masters - those Masters who were serving in the various divisions of the Masterships when they were abolished in the mid-nineteenth century.[30] Hence, in searching for documents generated by a reference (or submitted by a party), the first step is to identify in the division in which the presiding Master served. Lists of the Masters, in alphabetical order and also chronological order within the individual divisions, are provided in the SL under C 103. For example, if the searcher has identified a particular Master's proceedings either from a C 33 entry or from a C 38 - C 39 document, use of the Masters' lists in SL at C 103 will lead to the pertinent Masters' 'Exhibits', 'Documents' and 'Interrogatories' classes: eg, material stemming from a reference to Peter Bonner (Master 1757-1765) should be looked for, at least initially, in C 108 and C 122. Note, however, that interrogatories and depositions generated by references to many of the Masters are scattered through the 'Exhibits' and 'Documents' classes (see below). Also, while there are eleven named 'Exhibits' classes, there are only ten named 'Documents' classes; 'documents' from Master Lynch's division are to be found, rather, in C 123 and C 124.

---

29 On occasion, the Court also had recourse to Masters Extraordinary, appointed because of the pressure of business or to handle inquiries best pursued in the localities.

30 Up to the creation of the Accountant-General's post in the mid-1720s, there were eleven ordinary Masters and hence eleven divisions; between that date and the abolition of the equity side of Exchequer in 1841 there were ten divisions plus the Accountant-General. Between 1841 and the termination of the Masterships, Master Richards (formerly of the Exchequer) served as the eleventh ordinary Master.

(I) Masters' Reports and related materials

1. C 38 - Masters' Reports and Certificates, 1544-1875: 3330 boxes (SL)

This class is organized chronologically and within each year by letter of the alphabet (eg, if there are six boxes for 1785, the first box will contain reports arising out of suits in which the first plaintiff's surname begins with a letter from the early part of the alphabet). Alphabets of suit names (last names of first plaintiff and defendant, along with the name of the Master) exist at IND 1/1878-2028 (1606-1759), IND 1/10700/1-41 (1760-1800), and IND 1/14919 ff (1801 ff); at present, these volumes must be called for from the repository as documents. These alphabets, which also cover C 39 documents, are organized on a year by year basis, with a separate alphabet for each term.

    The reports themselves may be as specific or as wide-ranging as the Court's reference to the Master in the suit in question dictated. In the earlier part of the period, the bulk of the references concerned matters of pleading (most often, whether a defendant's answer was 'sufficient') and the issuance of injunctions when the grant of an injunction was not a matter of course (eg, when a defendant was not answering by commission). However, from the later seventeenth century onward the majority of references came after an initial hearing and decree in the suit and charged the Master with inquiries into matters of fact (chiefly matters of account but also such other questions as whether a party had good title to convey) and, with respect to the property of a deceased, to oversee the property's administration while the suit was under consideration or even until minor beneficiaries came of age. Thus, on occasion, Masters' reports incorporate detailed schedules of property. Moreover, since the Masters were empowered to take, on the parties' behalf, further examinations of witnesses (and could also examine the parties themselves, if need be), there may survive both interrogatories and depositions from such Masters' examinations. In turn, the parties to the suit were allowed to review, and dispute, the Master's findings and recommendations before they were submitted to the Court.

    Generally, post-hearing Masters' reports (including determinations of costs) were reviewed by the Court, with counsel for both sides present if they chose. At this stage, too, parties might put in exceptions to the report, and the Court might, on hearing such exceptions, refer the matter back to the Master. Once approved, the substance of a report would often be incorporated in a supplementary decree.

    Also to be found in the boxes of Masters' reports, after the office of Accountant-General was created in the mid-1720s, are certificates for the payment of various sums, usually payments to minor beneficiaries of estates under Court administration.

2. C 39 - Additional Masters' Reports and Certificates, 1703-1882: 25 boxes (SL)

This small class consists of oversize Masters' Reports and Certificates. Their contents figure in the alphabets to C 38, being listed with a marginal note as 'not bundled'. The boxes are organized chronologically, and the first report in C 39/1 dates from 1703.

3. C 40 - Exceptions to Reports, 1756-1859: 44 boxes (SL)

These materials, arranged in chronological order, are statements of exceptions by parties to Masters' reports. At the end of the later eighteenth-century alphabets to C 38 there appear to be listings (year by year) of exceptions to reports.

(II) Other Masters' papers: 'Accounts', 'Exhibits', 'Interrogatories', and 'Documents'

Most of the rest of the voluminous mass of Masters' papers are at present to be found in C 101 ('Accounts'); C 103 through C 116, and C 171 ('Exhibits'); C 117 through C 126 ('Documents'); and C 127 through C 129, and C 102 ('Interrogatories'). As indicated above, the bulk of the these Masters' papers have been organized into named classes, which are in turn grouped by the types of material involved; however, a certain amount of rearrangement continues to occur as individual groups of documents are listed in more detail (including the items in C 171 which originally formed part of the body of Masters' papers). Hence, the old (and only) finding aids to the 'Documents' classes also contain references to materials now in the 'Exhibits' classes, and some of the 'Exhibits' classes contain material which logically should be part of the 'Interrogatories' classes. By and large, the underlying logic of rearrangement has been that the 'Exhibits' classes should consist of documents (including deeds and court rolls, as well as account books, etc) submitted by the parties and not reclaimed by them for one reason or another, that the 'Interrogatories' classes should consist of interrogatories and depositions stemming from examinations taken in Masters' proceedings, and that the 'Documents' classes should constitute the residue of the larger mass.

1. C 101 - Masters' Accounts, c 1700-1850s: 6755 volumes

This class consists of Receivers' yearly accounts and cognate material concerning realty and other property in the administration of the Court; the accounts have been copied out in notebooks for submission to the Master to whom the suit had been referred. Far and away the largest proportion consist of rentals of land. But there are also some accounts for mining, trading, and other enterprises, as well as some household inventories for deceased individuals whose estates were in Chancery. The suit(s) to which the accounts relate are almost always specified at the beginning of the accounts, and in some instances the date of hearing is given as well.

This class is at present unlisted, and the notebooks themselves are not organized either chronologically or alphabetically. Hence, the only way to locate material in this class is via the alphabetical index to the first plaintiff's surname (which also gives the surname of the first defendant) at IND 1/10702/1-4; unfortunately, this index (repository) does not give dates. A PRO leaflet providing guidance for searching C 101 has recently been prepared.

The bulk of the accounts would appear to be post-1800, but there is a considerable volume which derive from eighteenth-century litigation.[31]

---

31 Of 100 items examined, 44 pre-dated 1800, with the earliest 1705.

2. The 'Exhibits' classes: C 103 through C 116, and C 171(all listed in SL)

The suits from which the materials in each of these classes stem span a wide range of time (early seventeenth to the mid-nineteenth centuries, with some documents of title pre-dating 1600 - see especially C 116). For the most part, the boxes are not organized either chronologically or alphabetically so that classes have little unity or coherence save in their common source - ie, the Master's Office or division in which materials in a given class originated. Each of these classes is listed box by box; the usual format is the title of the suit, with some indication of subject matter and with date or date range. In addition, the SL contains a modern index to parties for C 103 - C 114 and C 171 as well as a brief subject index to business, trade, and professional papers in these classes. The introductory notes to C 103 - C 116 also contain lists of the succession to the respective Masters' offices.[32]

C 103 (Blunt):	205 boxes.
C 104 (Tinney):	269 boxes. The SL also contains a recent index of persons and places for bundles 195-269; this overlaps with the C 103 - C 114 and C 171 index of parties noted above.
C 105 (Lynch):	58 boxes (and see below 'Interrogatories').
C 106 (Richards):	239 boxes. Included are some analogous Court of Exchequer materials transferred to Chancery from ongoing cases when Exchequer's equity jurisdiction was abolished in 1841 and when Richards became a Master in Ordinary in Chancery (see also, below, C 121).
C 107 (Senior):	224 boxes (and see below, 'Interrogatories').
C 108 (Farrer):	424 boxes.
C 109 (Humphry):	442 boxes.
C 110 (Horne):	189 boxes.
C 111 (Brougham):	230 boxes. The SL for C 111 includes a recently-completed index of persons to persons and place names for boxes 162-230 which overlaps with but is more inclusive than the index to parties for C 103 - C 114 and C 171.
C 112 (Rose):	247 boxes.
C 113 (Kindersley):	295 boxes.
C 114 (unknown):	208 boxes.
C 115 (Harvey: Duchess of Norfolk deeds):	132 boxes. SL contains an index to the court rolls in this class.
C 116 (Manor Court Rolls):	326 rolls, 1294-1808. SL contains an index by place name.
C 171 (Six Clerks):	54 boxes. Mainly later seventeenth century to mid-nineteenth century. List in SL.

---

32 It should be noted that the class J 90 contains exhibit material submitted to the Court of Chancery and to its successor, the Chancery Division of the High Court of Justice, in numerous nineteenth and early-twentieth century suits: some of this material, as indicated by the date range given in the SL for individual J 90 items, consists of title deeds and other records pre-dating 1800.

3. Masters' 'Interrogatories' (and depositions): parts of C 102, C 105, C 107, C 112, and all of C 127 through C 129

Scattered among the various classes of Masters' papers are a number of sets of materials relating to examinations conducted by the Masters in the course of their inquiries into matters referred to them for administration and report. Generally, these have been listed, if at all, in only sketchy fashion.

C 102/1-5:	These five boxes consist of transcriptions of testimony taken in one Master's office for the years 1722-1728, 1738-1747, and 1774-1799, in chronological order. SL for C 102.
C 105/40-58:	Boxes 40-50 date mainly from the early 1720s to the late 1750s; boxes 51-58 date mainly from the 1810s-1840s. SL for C 105.
C 107/189-223:	These boxes are organized and listed alphabetically by title of suit (with date) in SL for C 107. The bulk of them are eighteenth century; they range from the 1680s to the 1840s.
C 112/212-247:	Predominantly interrogatories ranging in date from the 1690s to the 1840s. The boxes are not arranged in either alphabetical or chronological order. SL for C 112.
C 127 (Kindersley):	85 boxes. SL. Organized by letter of the alphabet; no dates are given for these materials in the class list, but they range from the very early eighteenth century to the mid-nineteenth century.
C 128 (Farrer):	25 boxes. SL. Organized by letter of the alphabet; they appear in the class list with dates, 1730s-1840s.
C 129 (Legard):	1 box. SL. Organized alphabetically and listed with dates, virtually all early eighteenth century.

4. Masters' 'Documents': C 117 through C 126

These classes lack anything but the most primitive alphabets, IND 1/6616-6627 (*some* at present on the open shelves as indicated below), almost always without dates. Nor are the references always clear, especially to C 123 through C 125 in which the marking system for the boxes in those classes is a mixture of at least two different arrangements (one numerical, the other alphanumeric). This may be, at least in part, the result of the inclusion in C 123 and C 124 of material from Master Lynch's division. The result, so one searcher has reported, is that 'on a trial investigation of a dozen or so references ... rather more than half the bundles could not be found.'[33] The principal exception is for C 120/981-985, a much later addition to these mid-nineteenth century listings, and the dates for the items in these five boxes range from the mid-seventeenth to mid-nineteenth centuries. It would appear, however, that most of the material in these classes comes from the eighteenth and the first half of the nineteenth centuries, and consists of a melange of papers submitted by the parties and documents produced by the respective Masters and their clerks (including copies of reports in some boxes).[34] The existing

---

33 P W Coldham, 'Genealogical Resources in Chancery Records - 2: Documents of Masters in Chancery', *Genealogical Magazine* 20 (1980-1982) 257-260. The PRO now has a leaflet explaining how to proceed in ordering documents from C 123-125.

34 Examination of sixty boxes, spread relatively evenly across these ten classes, suggests that the bulk of the material is post-1820, with a scattering of eighteenth-century items; the earliest material located comes from the 1690s.

indexes also include references to much of the material, listed under each letter by the designation 'box' or 'chest', now in the 'Exhibits' classes.

C 117 (Brougham):	425 boxes (c 5% missing). IND 1/6625 (repository).
C 118 (Horne):	774 boxes. IND 1 /6620-6621 (two separate alphabets - repository).
C 119 (Rose):	810 boxes. IND 1/6619 (repository).
C 120 (Tinney):	985 boxes. IND 1/6617 (repository).
C 121 (Richards):	456 boxes. IND 1/6626-6627 (two separate alphabets - repository). As with C 106, this class contains some materials from like proceedings in the Court of Exchequer transferred to Chancery in 1841.
C 122 (Farrer):	600 boxes. IND 1/6624 (repository).
C 123 (Humphry):	IND 1/6618 (on open shelves). The class comprises c 935 alphanumeric boxes (eg, A4, B7) and a small number of additional unnumbered boxes (16).
C 124 (Blunt):	IND 1/6616 (on open shelves) - a fully alphabetical list but without dates. The class itself comprises c 475 alphanumeric boxes plus another 500 boxes indicated simply by letter and the designation 'bundle' (eg, B 'bundle').
C 125 (Senior):	IND 1/6623 (on open shelves). The class itself consists of a mixture of predominantly alphanumeric boxes (705, but missing c 25), several unnumbered boxes, and a few wrapped bundles.
C 126 (Kindersley):	106 boxes. IND 1/6622 (on open shelves) - fully alphabetized but without dates.

(G) The enrolled decrees and docquets: C 78, C 79, and C 96

Only a distinct minority of Chancery suits ever reached the stage of the entry of a formal decree or decretal order, resolving or at least going some way towards resolving the original controversy. Moreover, only a fraction of that distinct minority was ever enrolled on parchment; as explained in Chapter One, enrolment was a discretionary process undertaken at the initiative of one or other of the parties and involved the payment of fees. Ordinarily, an enrolment had to be set in motion within six months after the date of the decree - a rule complicated by the delays in entering decrees in the books of orders. The Court could, however, and did grant permission for enrolment after the six-month period had expired. As enrolment became less common, so the interval between the date of the decree and the enrolment tended to lengthen: in one (admittedly extreme) instance, a decree of 1731 was not enrolled until 1764, and then as part of an appeal to the House of Lords.[35] Such diversity in practice, coupled with the fact that the responsibility for preparing enrolments was divided among the offices of the Six Clerks, may help to account for the fact that it is rare for all the decrees on a single roll to come from a single year; rather, a single roll will often include decrees spanning a substantial number of years - in some instances twenty-five years or more.

The text of an enrolment was prepared on paper in the form of a so-called docquet, setting out the decree verbatim. In turn, this docquet, after it was checked on behalf of the initiating party by his Six Clerk (or by the Six Clerk's deputy), would be signed by the Lord Chancellor. In other words, the process generated two documents, the enrolment on parchment and the signed docquet on paper.

---

35 *The English Reports*, I, 684 (Smythe v Lomax: House of Lords appeal, 1770).

As enrolment gave the Court's decree an enhanced formality and finality, so the enrolled decree (and also the docquet) provides the searcher with the opportunity to trace cases backwards from their conclusion through the main intermediate stages to their initiation. This is because it was customary in Chancery, and a source of revenue to the staff who prepared the enrolments, to provide extensive summaries of the pleadings and proofs before the recital of the terms of the decree. (Note, however, that less attention was given to providing the status/occupation and place of residence of the parties.) This is, however, a route that can only be followed with difficulty, even in the minority of suits for which an enrolled decree survives.

2605 decree rolls now survive for the entire history of the Court, with the bulk dated between the reigns of Henry VIII and George III. As a given roll may contain anything from a single long decree to 20 or more much shorter ones, these rolls *in toto* may contain in the neighbourhood of 35,000 decrees, with the largest single concentration in the seventeenth century. Thus for the years 1627-1636, there are 180 enrolled decrees per annum; for 1685-1694, 170 per annum; for 1735-1744, 50 per annum; and for 1785-1794, no more than 10 per annum.

This sharp falling off reflects at least two long-term developments: first, the cutback in Court business (by the 1780s, new bills were perhaps twenty-five per cent of the level of the 1620s though a larger proportion of suits filed did reach the decree stage); second, the Court's discouragement of enrolment in the eighteenth century, especially in matters of account, to facilitate relatively minor amendments or modifications of the decree. In addition, there is evidence of laxity among the Six Clerks and Sworn Clerks in actually carrying out the enrolments solicited by clients (see below, under docquets), and there were complaints on this score as early as the 1620s.[36]

The extant rolls are grouped into two classes, C 78 and C 79.

1. C 79, consisting of 348 rolls, is a supplementary class created when an additional set of decree rolls was discovered in no particular order in the Rolls Chapel. For C 79 enrolments there is a list for the first 284 rolls in IND 1/16960B (in repository and entered on the computer as IND 1/16960). IND 1/16960B is an alphabet, and the dates it gives for each suit are the dates of commencement (ie, when the bill was exhibited) - *not* the dates of the decrees. The unlisted rolls from number 285 onwards are from the very late eighteenth century and the first half of the nineteenth century.

2. C 78: the great majority of the decree rolls are in C 78 (with class list in SL) - all told, some 2257 rolls, most of which are included in the topographical index classified as IND 1/16960A (on open shelves). Only the sixteenth and some of the seventeenth century rolls have modern listings in detail. Rolls 1-130 have been listed in detail by the PRO, giving parties' names, subject matter, date and place, and these lists (in SL) are indexed; rolls 131-750 (save for rolls 393 and 663) and a selection of rolls from 751 to 1250 have been listed by Professor Maurice Beresford whose listings provide similar (if not always totally reliable) information;

---

36 E 215/488: 'the enrollments of very many decrees which concern many men's estates are never brought to the Rolls at all whereby the subject is dangerously prejudiced'; and among those that are brought in some come in as late as 7 years after others.

unfortunately, Beresford's listings (incorporated in SL) are not indexed.[37] All rolls from 739 to 2253 are listed in a set of eight contemporary volumes, classified as IND 1 but presently available on the open shelves: note, however, this set excludes rolls 1987-1990. A modern list of rolls 2254-2257 is appended to the SL for this class.

A list by roll number of these various finding aids to C 78 follows:

Rolls 1-130 (16th-early 17th c) - modern official list, indexed, in SL.
Rolls 131-750 (17th-early 18th c) - modern unofficial listing in SL.
Rolls 751-1250 (17th-early 18th c) - modern unofficial listings for some in SL, but most only listed in contemporary lists as follows: Rolls 739-867 - in IND 1/16953 (1st alphabet - on open shelves); Rolls 754-1023 - in IND 1/16957 (1st/2nd alphabets - on open shelves).
Rolls 1025-1299 + 2254 (James I - Anne) - IND 1/16954 (on open shelves).
Rolls 1300-1644 (Charles I - George II) - IND 1/16955 (on open shelves).
Rolls 1645-1890 (1649 - George II) - IND 1/16956 (on open shelves).
Rolls 1891-1940 (1649 - George I) - IND 1/16953 (2nd alphabet - on open shelves).
Rolls 1941-1990 (1720s - 1780s) - IND 1/16959 (on open shelves).
Rolls 1991-2017 (William III - Anne) - IND 1/16958 (1st alphabet - on open shelves).
Rolls 2018-2036 (1649 - Anne) - IND 1/16957 (2nd/3rd alphabets - on open shelves).
Rolls 2037-2079 (Charles II - George II) - IND 1/16958 (2nd alphabet - on open shelves).
Rolls 2080-2253 + 2256 (1791-1903) - IND 1/16961B (on open shelves).
(Also IND 1/16961A, in reverse numerical order, Rolls 2079-1891; on open shelves).
(For rolls 2254-2257, see the last page of SL for this class).

The eight contemporary volumes covering roll numbers 739 forward reflect, in large part, the eight divisions in which the rolls were originally organized. Thus, the alphabets give the 'part' number within a given division; to call up a roll, the searcher must have recourse to a key, relating each 'part' to the current C 78 piece number; such keys are to be found at the beginning of each volume. (Note that IND 1/16953, and 1/169557 and 1/16958 each contains two or more separate alphabets and hence two or more separate keys.) Generally, these alphabets give the date of the decree; most also include a location if there was realty in dispute. A few also provide additional subject information (the first one-third of IND 1/16955, and the bulk of 1/16956 and 1/16959; these volumes cover some of the rolls for the second half of the seventeenth century and for the eighteenth century).[38]

As the above description of the finding aids to C 78 suggests, the rolls are by no means in chronological sequence; thus, for instance, decrees from the decade 1627-1636 can be found scattered through rolls 214 to 712. For this reason, one may well have to search through a good many of the volumes to locate a given decree. Perhaps the best indicator of the state of this class is given in the preface to IND 1/16961A by Alfred Kingston, a PRO officer writing in 1866: 'The set of decree rolls collected together [here] was, I have always understood, got

---

37 One in five for rolls 751-910; all from 915 through 925; one in ten for rolls 930-1190; all from 1200 through 1230; and rolls 1240 and 1250. See M Beresford, 'The Decree Rolls of Chancery as a Source for Economic History, 1547-c.1700', *Economic History Review*, 2nd ser 32 (1979), 1-10.
38 The more recent volume IND 1/16961A covers rolls 2079-1891 (ranging from the mid-seventeenth to the later nineteenth centuries) in that order, but with less full subject entries than those to be found in the parallel older volumes.

together in the following manner: Some years ago a large number of inrolments of docquets were found scattered about in various places in the Rolls Chapel, ... It was found impossible to discover how they had accumulated, from whence they had come, or indeed anything beyond the fact that there they were ... the best course was thought to be to make up a series without regard to chronological sequence in order that the documents in question might be kept together & preserved in some kind of order.'

3. C 96: The principal point to bear in mind about the docquets, reposing in the 152 boxes of C 96, is that these documents lack any internal chronological or alphabetical order. Nineteenth-century material can be found cheek by jowl with seventeenth-century material. And though the second part of IND 1/16960B (repository - called for on the computer as IND 1/16960) is a list of some of the docquets in C 96, it is a list without locations. Thus, until these docquets are sorted and listed, this potentially valuable source is virtually impossible to use even though there would appear to be a significant number of docquets for which enrolments have not survived (or, more likely, were never made). For example, of 38 docquets in C 96/152 in an alphabetical bundle spanning the years 1662-1682, only one-half have been traced in C 78 (spanning roll numbers 555 to 1229!). Again, the alphabet volumes for C 78 also suggest a considerable laxity in practice. Thus, for instance, at the back of IND 1/16958 is a list of 95 docquets (ranging in date from 1661 to 1737) marked as 'a list of the docquets of decrees that was found unenrolled on the seat of Mr Francis Bowyear after his death and brought over by Mr Cremer of the Six Clerks Office' in 1742.

(H) Miscellaneous Chancery equity classes: C 42, C 173 (parts) and C 48, C 27, and C 102

1. C 42 - Agreements and awards: 1694-1844 - 14 boxes (SL)
Parties in Chancery litigation might always compromise the matter in dispute between themselves; if they chose, they might in addition seek a Court decree to record the compromise and put the authority of the Court behind it. Some of the contents of these boxes relate to such agreements brought into Court. On the whole, agreements are very informative but some do not spell out the substance of the compromise.

In addition to such agreements to end a suit, the parties might agree to submit the dispute to the arbitration of a third party or parties. In the sixteenth and early seventeenth centuries, the arbitration might be relatively informal, as in the form of Court instructions to commissioners in the country (then, often JPs and other local notables) to take the initiative in reconciling the parties. Reports of the outcomes of such arbitrations can be found in C 38, along with entries in C 33 respecting such proceedings. In the later seventeenth and eighteenth centuries, arbitration proceedings acquired a greater formality. There are fewer C 33 entries of instructions to commissioners to settle disputes, more C 33 entries of 'rules of court' whereby the parties recorded their decision to submit to arbitration and bound themselves to accept the arbitrator's formal decision, his 'award', and it is with arbitration process and outcomes that the bulk of these documents is concerned. The boxes in C 42 are for the most part organized chronologically (the principal exception is that some of the earliest material is in box 14). There is a summary class list, but no index.

Arbitration documents tend to be more informative than agreements, as the awards usually spell out the nature of the dispute while rules of court sometimes specify the issues to be resolved by the arbitrator(s).[39] Many arbitrations were backed up, as well, by the exchange of penal bonds between the disputants, and the sums to be forfeited for failing to accept an award (bearing in mind that it was normal practice to make such penal bonds for double the amount at stake) are a useful indicator of scale.

2. C 173 (SL)) and C 48 (SL) - Six Clerks' and Register's materials

In addition to those segments of C 173 which relate to the pleadings and have been discussed under that heading, these classes, especially C 173, contain a substantial body of material relating to the Six Clerks' quarrels with other officers and offices of the Court, and especially their long-running feuds with their former under-clerks - the Sworn Clerks of the later seventeenth and eighteenth centuries. The material is partly historical (that is, documentary support of the Six Clerks' origins and rights) and partly the fruits of specific episodes of the quarrel (as in the mid-1630s, the late 1660s, the early 1730s, and the mid-1780s) including appeals to the Master of the Rolls and the Chancellor, lawsuits, and parliamentary lobbying. Related material (emanating from the Register's Office) is to be found in the single box classed as C 48.

3. C 27 - Miscellaneous Books: 28 boxes (SL)

Most of the volumes of this class relate to equity proceedings of the nineteenth century. However, volumes 24 and 26 concern the commission of inquiry of the 1730s into the Court's operation, and volumes 7 through 11 are eighteenth-century precedent books for the Rolls Office, the deputy registrars, and for the taxing of costs.

4. C 102 - Masters Miscellaneous Books: 49 boxes (SL)

In addition to the volumes of copies of eighteenth-century depositions in C 102 (vols 1-5, noted above), volume 8 is the only (early) eighteenth-century admissions book of solicitors to practice in Chancery, and volumes 42-47 are Masters' account books (all dating from the scandal years of 1725-1726 except vol 42).

5. C 240 - Orders to Ushers 1542-1760 - 34 boxes (SL)

Drafts of orders which appear in C 33 relating to the disposition of money, securities, and evidences brought into Court. Some contain annotations (not in C 33) relating to subsequent proceedings in those cases.

---

39 Arbitrators might include neighbours, specialists (eg, merchants in a mercantile dispute), or officers of the Court.

CHAPTER FOUR:
Searching the Chancery Equity Records

Preceding chapters have discussed judicial process in the Court of Chancery, the kinds of cases that figure in the Chancery equity records and the types of litigants involved, and the present organization of these records. This chapter offers some advice on how to go about searching the records. The first section provides a brief account of how some searchers have proceeded and succeeded and discusses three types of searches: searches for information about a particular place, about a particular individual, and about a particular subject. The second section is intended to illustrate, by means of 'specimen' searches (chosen in part to reveal the range of materials that can be found and in part to illustrate the limitations and complexities of the finding aids), how to begin to grapple with the records of Chancery equity proceedings. This section concentrates on searches about particular individuals and specific subjects.

A. Some Successful Searches

I About particular places

Two major historical/topographical collective projects have made extensive use of Chancery materials - 'The Victoria County History of England' and 'The Survey of London'. From the Victoria County History's early days, the practice of its various sections has been to search systematically those lists of Chancery equity records that specify the location of the property (or other matter) in dispute and then, whenever possible, to draw upon the documents so identified. A similar routine was followed by the Survey of London, and analogous procedures have been used by smaller-scale projects such as Dr Alan Macfarlane's investigation of Earls Colne, Essex. For Earls Colne alone, over 70 items were located in Chancery equity records up to 1714.[1] Nor should we suppose that Earls Colne would be unusual in this respect; it has been estimated that were one to divide the number of separate items listed in the Chancery pleadings up to 1800 by the total number of English parishes, one would arrive at a figure of about 80 items per parish.[2]

II About particular persons

Such searches are more common in practice, and usually involve a more limited time-frame. One example in print concerns John Dwight, a late seventeenth-century potter operating in Fulham who sued in Chancery to enforce his rights under a patent granted him by Charles II.

---

1   *Records of an English Village: Earls Colne 1400-1750* (1980), ed Alan Macfarlane, part i, list of items at pp 55-57.
2   Dorian Gerhold, *Courts of Equity A Guide to Chancery and other Legal Records* (1994), p 4. Gerhold uses the term 'items' to count separately those instances in which pleadings in the same suit are now separated.

A number of the defendants were Staffordshire potters, including the Wedgwoods of Burslem. Using the existing lists for C 5 through C 10, and searching by tracing the references to Dwight by name in them, the researchers located a series of suits in C 5, C 6, and C 7, spanning the years 1693-1698. Then, tracing these suits through other classes, they also located interrogatories and depositions (C 24), affidavits (C 31 and C 41), as well as a linked series of orders in the Court's books of orders (C 33).[3]

III About particular subjects

When one thinks of significant finds in Chancery on particular subjects, many of the examples that come to mind have derived from searches of the Masters' Exhibits (C 103 through C 116, and C 171), recently made more user-friendly by partial relisting and by the compilation of indexes to parties and certain subjects (business, commercial, and professional matters). Although the quality of the listings for these classes still is uneven, they have been (and continue to be) an obvious place for subject searches to start, since much of the material consists of documents brought into the Masters' offices by litigants in proceedings on references - eg, account books, rentals, correspondence - which for one reason or another the parties failed to retrieve. Economic historians, in particular, have made some very valuable finds - for example, the business correspondence and papers of the mid-seventeenth century Baltic trader Charles Marescoe, printed in part and edited by Professor Henry Roseveare.[4] But it is not only for matters economic that the materials in these classes have proved valuable - for example, the papers of Lord Ossulston exploited by the political historian Clyve Jones as part of his ongoing investigations on the House of Lords in the eighteenth century.[5] Nor have the riches of these classes yet been fully exploited.

Subject searches have also proved profitable for the determined (and the lucky) in the main body of Chancery equity records. How have such searchers succeeded in the absence of subject indexes to most classes of Chancery equity records? Ordinarily, they have proceeded either by searches keyed to places or persons, or sometimes by a combination of the two. Thus, for example, one recent by-product of The Survey of London's collection of Chancery references has been a detailed study of architectural practice in speculative building of later Stuart London.[6] A somewhat similar route into the records was followed by Dorian Gerhold in his inquiries on road transport. Starting with a list of names of London carriers of the late seventeenth century published in a contemporary work on London, he was able to identify in

---

3   *John Dwight's Fulham Pottery 1672-1978*, eds D Haselgrove and J Murray (comprising *Journal of Ceramic History* 11 [1979]): 44 documents, or extracts from documents, are printed as sec xi of this in-depth study. It was first drawn to my attention by Andrew Federer.
4   *The Marescoe-David Letters 1668-1680*, ed Henry Roseveare (British Academy, Records of Social and Economic History, new series 12 [1987]).
5   C Jones, 'The parliamentary organization of the Whig Junto in the Reign of Queen Anne: the evidence of lord Ossulston's diary', *Parliamentary History* 10 (1991), 164-182. *Idem*, 'The London life of a peer in the reign of Anne: a case study from Lord Ossulston's Diary', *London Journal* 16 (1991), 140-155.
6   Elizabeth McKellar, 'Architectural Practice for Speculative Building in Late Seventeenth Century London', PhD, Royal College of Arts 1992, esp pp 15-16: my thanks to Dr McKellar for lending me a copy of her dissertation and for answering my questions about her uses of the transcripts of Chancery cases very generously made available to her by Mr Frank Kelsall, now of English Heritage.

the existing class lists a number of suits involving these individuals; the documents for those suits, in some instances, furnished the names of others involved in the trade and hence additional names with which to search the available listings of the records, including the Masters' Exhibits. By the time Gerhold had finished, he had located dozens of suits (as well as several rich Masters' exhibits) including twenty suits relating to a single firm spanning the decades from the 1680s to the 1830s.[7] But it is perhaps the theatre and opera historians Professors Judith Milhous and Robert Hume who have mined the main body of Chancery equity records most assiduously, following in the footsteps of Leslie Hotson and other early researchers in their field.[8] For the most part, they have proceeded in Chancery by laborious name searches in C 5 through C 12, and some indication of the range of their finds (and those of their precursors) is given in their *A Register of English Theatrical Documents 1660-1737*.[9]

Besides such indirect subject searches, there have been a few instances of direct subject searches. A recent case in point is Dr Amy Erickson's work on the property rights of middling married women of the seventeenth century. Taking advantage of the fact that several of the class lists for C 5 through C 10 specifically identify suits involving marriage settlements (and contracts), she was able to construct from some seventy sets of pleadings located in C 5 a data base for analysis of contested settlements including many involving middling women.[10]

B. Specimen Searches

I For particular individuals

Although most of the finding aids are to names, the sheer quantity of surviving materials, the lack of a comprehensive nominal index, and the listing of much of the seventeenth and eighteenth century material by the individual Six Clerks' divisions can make the first stage of any search a very laborious process - even when one knows, before one begins, the surnames of the (principal) plaintiff and the (principal) defendant. Here, the aim is to 'walk through' four separate searches from the early 1600s to the later 1700s, partly to illustrate the character of the relevant finding aids and partly to draw attention to the different kinds of material beyond the pleadings that may survive. In most of the examples, the surnames of the principal plaintiff(s) and defendant(s) are assumed to be known at the outset.

---

7 Dorian Gerhold, *Road Transport Before the Railways* (1993), pp 292-294.
8 The earliest guide to the use of Chancery equity records for academic research that I know of (first drawn to my attention by Professor Milhous) was directed to students of literary history in a series on 'Public Record Office Research': Margaret Dowling, 'The Equity Side of Chancery, 1558-1714', *Research in English Studies* 8 (1932), 185-200. See also J Milton French, *Milton in Chancery New Chapters in the Lives of the Poet and His Father* (1939), and his prefatory note of thanks to Leslie Hotson.
9 2 vols, 1991. A copy of the *Register* is available at the PRO. Chancery items listed in the *Register* are mainly pleadings, but there are also entries from most of the main Chancery classes. For an example of their exploitation of their finds, see Curtis Price, Judith Milhous and Robert D Hume, *Italian Opera in Late Eighteenth-Century London*, vol I (1995), *The King's Theatre, Haymarket 1778-1791*, especially App I.
10 Amy L Erickson, *Women and Property in Early Modern England* (1993), chap 7.

1. Eyre v Wortley - mid-1620s: litigation about the will of a London merchant, Christopher Eyre

The parties were the dead man's kin versus his widow Hester, who remarried Sir Francis Wortley. At stake was the validity and interpretation of a deathbed will and codicil, lacking proper witnesses, which could be interpreted as nullifying the legacies which the Eyres were bequeathed under an earlier will.

Since this dispute falls within the chronological scope of both C 2 and C 3, the best starting point is the finding aids for C 2 - primarily the fully alphabetical listings (compiled from an earlier 'alphabet') of plaintiffs' and defendants' surnames. They yield five references to 'Eyre v Wortley': C 2/E4/9, C 2/E6/54, C 2/E18/65, C 2/E21/43 and 44.

Upon calling the documents up, it appears that the C 2/E21/43 reference is erroneous - a typist's slip for C 2/E21/44. The other four documents all relate to the dispute, but involve two different suits.

C 2/E18/65 is a bill of complaint of 13 February 1627 submitted by Thomas Eyre (the father of the minor Christopher), and filed with it are Wortley's and his wife's plea and demurrer (essentially arguing they should not have to answer in Chancery; and that instead the dispute should be heard in the church courts).

The other three documents relate to a subsequent suit. C 2/E21/44 is another bill of complaint of 25 October 1627 filed by Thomas Eyre (and a large array of other kin), and attached are a new plea and demurrer from the Wortleys. C 2/E6/54 is an answer of the Wortleys dated 13 June 1632, but nonetheless stating that it is to the bill of 25 October 1627; C 2/E4/9 is an undated replication by the plaintiffs to this answer.[11] One might deduce that the answer comes so long after the bill because the parties had been disputing the validity of the original plea and demurrer.

In turn, both these bills of complaint refer to an earlier decree of the Court in a related suit, one in which Robert and William Eyre (other brothers of Christopher) had sued the Wortleys for their legacies; Thomas and his co-plaintiffs were seeking to take advantage of that decree in their own proceedings. Thus, there appear to be two threads to follow: first, Thomas Eyre's (second) suit of late 1627; second, the earlier suit of William and Robert Eyre. Both leave extensive traces, as might be expected, in the Court's books of orders - traces which can be followed up via the alphabets (term by term, and year by year) to C 33, searching under 'Eyre v Wortley'.

This search, however, produces almost too much information, for not only does it yield a substantial number of references to the two Thomas Eyre suits and the William & Robert one, but also it suggests that there was another related suit brought by the City of Salisbury. In each instance, the defendants were the Wortleys, sometimes with additional parties.

Here, it may be worth recalling that the various Eyre suits running from the mid-1620s into the 1630s (in the case of Thomas's second) span a major shift in the way the books of orders were kept. In Michaelmas 1629, the deputy registers abandoned their earlier practice of

---

11 The replication does contain a date on it, but that date - put on by a clerk - refers to the starting date of the suit in 1627; it cannot be the date of the replication which, procedurally, comes after and responds to the defendants' answer. And since the Court very shortly after the date of the answer began to record orders for the taking of depositions, which would not have occurred unless and until a replication had been made, it may be assumed that the replication dates from mid-June 1632.

keeping two concurrent and virtually parallel books ('A' and 'B') and started keeping only a single record of entries (though still in two books dividing the alphabet). This is to say that a good many of the references in the pre-1629 books are parallel ones, *but by no means all*. Taking the example of C 33/151 and C 33/152, five of the C 33/151 references to the various Eyre suits are to be found in both books, one only in C 33/151, and three only in C 33/152. Obviously, then, for suits before the changeover in procedure in 1629, the searcher will find it worthwhile to follow up all the C 33 index references, even though a good many will be parallel ones. (Among the parallel ones in this instance are C 33/151, f 471, and C 33/152, f 457 - the texts of the judgment of 28 November 1626 in favour of Robert and William Eyre.)

However, finding C 33 entries for the suits prior to Thomas Eyre's is easier than locating the pleadings and other materials for them. In fact, all that it has been possible to trace of these suits in either C 2 or C 3 is the replication of the plaintiffs in Robert & William Eyre against the Wortleys and Saunders (Elizabeth Saunders was apparently one of those present at the deathbed of Christopher Eyre). More valuable than the replication are, however, the depositions taken in the earlier case. The likely existence of these depositions is signalled by the process entries in the books of orders for this case and also for the later case of Thomas (for the depositions from the earlier proceedings were allowed to be used in the later one). A searcher resorting to the 'alphabets' for C 21 (country depositions: indicated by the C 33 entries for the allowance of a commission to take depositions outside London), under 'Eyre v Wortley', will find two sets of depositions taken in 1625-1626 listed at C 21/E8/7 and C 21/E8/12.

Coming back now to Thomas Eyre's suits and reviewing the C 33 references for them, there are thirteen in all - two from 1627, one from 1628, one from 1629, and the rest from 1632. Calling up the relevant C 33 volumes brings to light the following information. The first two references relate to the bill of February 1627 and indicate that it was dismissed as legally insufficient - ie, that the plea and demurrer were upheld (C 33/151, ff 1274 and 1224, respectively 7 and 19 June). (Note that the two C 33 references are in reverse date order: given the way the books of orders were compiled, this is a common occurrence.)

The remainder of the C 33 references relate to the bill of October 1627, a refiling in light of the failure of Thomas's previous attempt. The first of these entries (C 33/153, f 409: 23 January 1628) indicates that the Wortleys' plea and demurrer were referred not to a Master, the normal procedure, but to two common law judges because of the importance of the issues involved. But the judges themselves proved unwilling to offer a definite answer (C 38/60: judges' report, 4 July 1628, located using the alphabets for C 38).

In turn, the second C 33 reference (C 33/155, f 694: 20 April 1629) indicates that the matter was then referred to Lord Keeper Coventry. He appears neither to have reported nor decided speedily because the next C 33 reference (C 33/161, f 324: 9 Febuary 1632) is a notation that the Lord Keeper is to be reminded of the matter - presumably, a reminder moved by the Eyres. And on 19 April 1632, after having heard counsel for both sides on the matter, the Lord Keeper ruled that the defendants must formally answer the complaint - in effect, overruling their plea and demurrer and so prompting the long-delayed answer put in by the Wortleys on 13 June 1632.

After nearly five years, then, the litigation could proceed, and the rest of the entries in C 33 for 1632 concern the taking of depositions from witnesses. Here, again, there were disputes about procedure and also some slightly unusual arrangements. Not only did both parties individually receive the Court's permission to use depositions taken in the earlier case (as indicated above), but in addition the defendant petitioned and was allowed to put in evidence the (sworn) answer of Elizabeth Sanders (now deceased) from that former suit as well.

In addition to the depositions taken in the earlier suit, a commission was now issued for the taking of testimony at Salisbury and witnesses in London were also deposed. Given the incompleteness of the index (IND 1/9115-9121) for town depositions (C 24) for this period, it was decided to go directly to the records (they are organized chronologically by term and can be called for box by box). Search of the likely boxes yielded in C 24/581 a set of interrogatories to be put to witnesses and five witnesses' depositions (the latest dated 9 September 1632) concerning the quarrels between the deceased and the plaintiffs and the circumstances under which the second will had been made. The witnesses included a judge of the Prerogative Court of Canterbury, a member of the Barber-Surgeons Company of London who may have been in attendance at the deathbed, and a barrister of the Inner Temple.

The search for Country depositions for this stage of the proceedings proved less fruitful. As noted above, the finding aids for those classes are organized as alphabets and the entries are undated. But no more 'Eyre v Wortley' depositions could be traced, even though the authorization of a commission in November 1632 to take depositions in the country suggested there might be others. Either the commission was never activated or whatever depositions were taken have not survived.

In any event, once whatever depositions were taken were returned (sealed), and a day for publication set in late January 1633, the cause finally had a hearing on 25 May 1633 (C 33/163, f 609). Much to the disgruntlement of the Wortleys, the plaintiffs won their claim for legacies and also were awarded compensation for the defendants' failure to pay the legacies earlier. A Master was instructed to determine the appropriate amount of compensation; he reported on 6 June and his report (traced to C 38/75) was confirmed on the 17th. However, on 29 June the Wortleys indicated that they were not clear which Eyre children (in terms of date of birth) were the appropriate recipients of the legacies. Certificates of their respective dates of birth were submitted by the plaintiffs on 9 July (also filed at C 38/75) and at length the Court confirmed its decree in detail on 17 July 1633.

But this was not quite the end of the matter (and this is often the case!). Further entries in C33/163 - that is, for the legal year 1632-1633 - and also in C 33/165 and C 33/167 reveal that Sir Francis Wortley was very loath to pay and sought to shield himself behind a privilege he claimed as a royal servant. Contempt process, and related costs, account, therefore, for the final string of references in C 33 running up to 25 March 1635.

In addition to the documentation in C 33 generated by the enforcement of the decree, this decree was also enrolled; its final text in parchment is to be found at C 78/458/5. No entry was usually made in C 33 as to whether a decree would be enrolled, so that searching for an enrolment of a decree is a speculative process, and also a difficult one, since the surviving decrees are not easily accessible when all that the searcher knows is the parties' names and the likely date. Nevertheless, it can be done by working through the finding aids for the decrees in C 78 (and, if necessary, the alphabet for additional decrees in C 79). In this instance, since 'E' is a relatively small letter, the search was not a very protracted one.

However, to make this effort in the Eyre case would yield very little. The enrolled decree in this case can tell the searcher no more than has already been gleaned from the pleadings, the depositions, the Masters' reports, and the text of the decree in C 33. Rather, the point of locating a decree is either to fill in gaps in the history of the case for which the relevant documentation cannot be traced or, alternatively, to start from a known decree and trace the suit backwards into the other classes of records.

2. Cope v Hooker - mid-1680s: the plaintiff Sarah Cope, widow of Thomas Cope, of London, dyer, was suing Robert Hooker, merchant tailor, and others, seeking to obtain from them assets of her husband as her entitlement as widow

In searching for a suit in the pleadings of the later seventeenth century (C 5 through C 10), it may be necessary to plough through as many as six separate lists, organized as alphabets for the most part. (The need to do so, however, should be obviated in the near future by recourse to the PRO's Equity Pleadings Database since the initial input into this database will consist of the existing C 5 - C 10 lists; thus, a single search of the database should pull up all similarly-named suits - eg Kendal v Jones. However, it should be noted that this input, with the possible exception of the second half of C 6, will be from the existing finding aids, *not from the documents*, and hence will represent no improvement for subject searches.)

For the present, and for the sake of expedition, it makes sense to start with the list for C 9 since it is a modern (ie, fully alphabetical) index. If nothing is found there, the searcher must painstakingly work through the other lists *unless* the suit in question concerns the personal estate of a deceased. On the face of it, this suit does concern a personal estate, but search of the indexes to personal estates for C 6 (part only), C 7, C 8 and C 10 yielded nothing.

So after the C 9 list and the indexes to personal estates, the searcher should proceed to the C 5 alphabet, and to the remainder of the alphabets for this group of classes but leaving to last the C 6 alphabets (as the most difficult). In fact, Cope v Hooker, despite its omission from the index of personal estates in C 7, is listed in the C 7 alphabet at C 7/64/26.

The file C 7/64/26 contains a bill dated 26 November 1685, two answers, and an affidavit. The answers are respectively from Hooker (who describes himself as a trustee of the deceased Thomas Cope) and the third defendant John Stephens, a dyer of London (who describes himself as 'administrator' of Thomas Cope). (The term 'administrator' indicates that Cope died intestate, one of the facts set out in the plaintiff's bill.)

The next step is to try to trace the course of the suit via C 33 and its alphabets. C 33/265, the book of orders for the legal year 1685-1686 for the first half of the alphabet, contains in fact no fewer than ten references. The first two, in order of date, are an order of 23 April (then confirmed on 30 April) for publication of depositions and for a hearing on the suit in the coming term (Trinity).

So alerted to the likelihood of depositions, but without any indication that a commission was taken out for depositions in the country, the searcher has two choices. One is to use the alphabets to C 24 for this period (IND 1/9115-9121) but bearing in mind their incompleteness. The second is to call for the six boxes of C 24 for Hilary, Easter and Trinity terms, though this will entail considerable time. In fact, it is only a box for Trinity term (C 24/1101) that yields any reward - two sets of interrogatories and the depositions of three witnesses for the plaintiff and six for the defendant, with the former being asked chiefly about the plaintiff's marriage settlement, the latter about the deceased's finances.[12]

Returning to the references accumulated from the C 33 alphabets, the third reference, C 33/265, f 644 (dated 4 June), is an entry stating that a related cause - Hooker v Cope & Stephens - was to be heard along with this suit. From this entry, it might be well be inferred that the second bill was a cross bill filed by, in this instance, one of the defendants against both the plaintiff and another of the original defendants. (The normal practice was to file a cross bill in the same Six Clerk's division as the original had been filed - ie, in C 7 in this dispute.)

Search of the C 7 list for Hooker v Cope is, however, only partly successful. No bill could be located but C 7/580/44 is an answer, dated 1686, of a *Mary* Cope to a bill of Robert Hooker. Mary, it appears from the document, was the widow of William Cope (Thomas's brother), and judging from her answer Robert Hooker's suit concerned the same transactions as those involved in Cope v Hooker, with Robert seeking compensation from William's estate. (Attached to Mary's answer is a schedule of her husband's debts and credits [she is the executrix] which makes it clear that though styled a 'mariner' Robert had been involved, probably as a shipmaster, in trade to Antigua, Barbados, etc.) So since the Cope in Hooker v Cope is Mary, not Sarah, this is not after all a cross bill, and the Court did separate proceedings on the two after its initial order (see for Hooker v Cope thereafter - C 33/265, ff 644, 867, and C 33/267, ff 23, 322, 518).

Thus, unencumbered by Hooker v Cope, Cope v Hooker proceeded to its conclusion in the following months. Both parties deposed witnesses (the documents from C 24/1101). The C 33 entries in the case indicate that in early July, the Court heard the cause, decided in favour of the plaintiff, and instructed a Master to take account of the estate of Thomas Cope and to compute the amount Hooker owed the widow (C 33/265, ff 655, 757, 834). In the early autumn, the Master made his report (located via the alphabet, IND 1/1955 for the year 1686, at C 38/223). The report was ratified and confirmed by the Court in late October 1686 (with this decree subsequently enrolled at C 78/1558/7).

However, further search of the C 33 alphabets, always a useful follow-up precaution in case of rehearing or other post-decree action, indicates that this was not quite the end of the matter. In June 1687, the widow sought release from the security of two hundred pounds she had earlier been required to submit for due administration of the estate (C 33/267, f 533). The Court was so inclined, subject to a Master's inquiry, and this second Master's report in the case, located in C 38/226 (28 June 1687), was favourable, thus bringing to a close the proceedings in Cope v Hooker.

3. 'DaCosta v Dubois' - 1718 *et seq*

Unlike the two previous searches, chosen from among the in the sample sets for 1627 and 1685, this case first attracted attention in the course of searching C 33/333 (1719-1720) for entries in another case. In the process, a long entry (ff 224-225, 16 February 1720), relating to a dispute growing out of the winding-up of the Old East India Company, caught the searcher's attention. The entry concerned a hearing that ended with an order in favour of the defendants

---

12 Note that the C24 class list mistakenly identifies box 1101 as from Easter 1686.

(Charles Dubois *et al*, trustees for the old Company) as against John Mendoza da Costa and other shareholders of the old Company (which had been merged with the New East India Company in 1708-1709). The order was subject to a reference to Master Holford to review the accounts of the trustees and to oversee the dispersal of any remaining funds to the plaintiffs and other shareholders of the old Company.

This, then, is a search started *in medias res*, knowing at a minimum that there had been pleadings filed prior to the 1720 hearing and anticipating, if the parties had persisted, that it should be possible to locate a detailed Master's report subsequent to the hearing. But the process of tracing both earlier and later stages turned out to be unexpectedly complicated.

The first step was to try to locate earlier and later C 33 entries. A number of post-hearing entries were found (up to the mid-1720s), but only one prior one. In that entry, the Court gave permission to the plaintiffs to amend their original bill by substituting for an original defendant (and trustee) Jonathan Andrews, now deceased, his daughter Judith and her husband John Davenport.

The second step was to try to find the pleadings in C 11 by searching under the title of 'Da Costa v Dubois'. A good many Da Costa entries for plaintiffs turned up in the C 11 lists (some dated, and some not, underlining the difficulties of using the C 11 lists), but no 'Da Costa v Dubois'. This was frustrating since it seemed clear from the hearing entry in C 33 that the suit should be so titled. However, because pleadings might be misfiled or lost, it seemed logical at this juncture - that is, in a time period where there is a continuous run of bill books and a nearly complete sequence of cause books - to search these records of filed pleadings for clues about the seemingly missing bill.

Initially, this third step of consulting the bill books and cause books proved equally frustrating. No bill or other pleading titled 'Da Costa v Dubois' turned up in these sources for the period 1714-1720, a most puzzling outcome in the light of the hearing entry from which this search had started and given that the cause books supposedly record *all* pleadings filed, whatever their subsequent fate. The other possibilities seemed to be either (1) that the bill was filed before 1714, and hence would have to be searched in the C 5 - C 10 lists, or (2) that there was a problem with the plaintiff's name. Once the problem was formulated in these terms, it seemed plausible to search the cause books under 'Mendoza' rather than 'Da Costa', and the search quickly yielded results. Indeed, in the cause book for the division in which the plaintiff's bill was filed (IND 1/4109) the pleadings were noted and summarized as: bill filed April 1717, bill then amended by substituting the Davenports as plaintiffs, bill answered jointly by most of the defendants in May 1718 (with three schedules attached to their answer), and with the plaintiffs' replication being filed shortly thereafter.

This information from the plaintiff's Six Clerk's cause book suggested that it would be appropriate to go back to C 11 and now search for '*Mendoza* Da Costa v Dubois'. But before doing so, a quick check of the bill book for 1717 to see how the bill was titled there seemed sensible. Frustration at not finding it there either under Da Costa or Mendoza as the first plaintiff and Dubois as the first defendant was considerable. So it was back to the remaining five cause books for 1717 to locate the entry for the defendants' joint answer, and in IND 1/4146 the answer was noted *but* under the title of 'Mendez da Costa v *Davenport*'. In turn, a search of the billbook for 1718 (when the Davenports had been added as defendants) did yield for Michaelmas 1718 a bill styled 'Mendoza v Davenport'.

Here, then, is one and the same case with different names for the first defendant (Dubois or Davenport) and the same name, but differently construed, for the first plaintiff. Or to put it slightly differently, the deputy registers who made up the indexes to the order book logically chose 'Da Costa v Dubois'; with slightly less logic, the clerk who made up the plaintiff's Six Clerk's cause book chose 'Mendez v Dubois'; and with more dubious logic, the clerk who made up the defendant's Six Clerk's cause book chose 'Mendez v Davenport' (as did the clerk who made up the bill books). Further, it is apparent that the confusion over the first defendant's name arose out of the addition to the suit of the Davenports via the route of the amended bill which, as amended, was entered in the bill books under 1718 rather than the original filing year of 1717.

With this additional information, it was back to the C 11 list where the suit as 'Mendez v Davenport' was finally located at C 11/1988/18. As the plaintiff's Six Clerk's cause book indicated, the file contained not only the (amended) bill and answers but some very informative schedules put in by the trustees. The replication, although noted in the cause book, was missing. (In fact, many eighteenth-century replications have gone astray; the replication seems to have been regarded as a *pro forma* matter and so filing the document ceased to be a matter of moment; by then, virtually the only significance of the replication was to signal the end of the pleadings and an advance to the proofs and hearing stages.)

Nor was there any indication either in C 11 or in C 33 that either party at this stage sought to depose witnesses. In this case, the proofs in the hearing would depend on the evidence supplied by the trustees in their answer and attached schedules; apparently, and not surprisingly, the shareholder plaintiffs had no independent source(s) of evidence to bring forward.

However, there seemed no reason to end the search with the order in favour of the plaintiffs; there was, after all, still the report to be made by Master Holford on the reference of February 1720. The likelihood is that it would yield further data about the old Company's affairs and the trustees' conduct of their onerous tasks. In following up the C 33 references, first for 1722, and then for 1725-1728, it becomes apparent that the process of investigation in Master Holford's office was prolonged and contentious. More specifically, the C 33 references (337, f 311; 345, ff 335, 359; 347, ff 13, 31, 334; and 349, f 132) indicate that the plaintiffs initiated a series of examinations (under the Master's aegis) of some of the trustees and others, and kept pressing for the submission of more accounts and records, in the hope of finding something to modify or to overturn the order of 1720. Nonetheless, in July 1728 a rehearing sought by the defendants produced a clear-cut negative from the Chancellor; he saw no reason to alter the decree of 1720 and declared that the defendants should forfeit the deposit that Chancery rules required be made by a party seeking a rehearing.

What, then, of further proceedings? The entry for the rehearing is the last that can be located in the C 33 alphabets under the title 'Da Costa v Dubois'. And a check of the alphabets to C 38 found no later entries under that title either. Nonetheless, it seemed worthwhile and relatively quick to scan a few of the post-1728 indexes to C 38 with particular attention to all notations of reports made by Master Holford to see if there were any among them in which a 'Dubois' was the defendant. This process yielded an entry for a report by Holford under the title of 'Morse v Dubois' made in Michaelmas term 1729.

Who was Morse? In the original bill of 1717 one John Morse had figured as the third-named plaintiff. Apparently, Da Costa had died shortly after the 1728 rehearing, the second-named plaintiff in the original bill was already dead, so now Morse became first-named plaintiff ten or eleven years after the suit was launched.

There was, then, a report after all. But where was it? The alphabet volume for C 38 for 1729 has a 'Morse-Dubois' entry with a marginal note that it had been put 'in the box unbundled' (IND 1/1998). What had happened was that the report was a large document, set aside for special handling, and so is now to be found in C 39 - the supplementary class to C 38 for oversize Masters' reports. Organized chronologically, C 39 begins in 1703, and the 1729 report was located without difficulty in C 39/1.

Can the case be traced any further? To this question, three different answers may be returned. First, further search of the C 33 alphabets through the next three years under 'Morse v Dubois' yielded nothing. Second, it might be concluded that having found the original pleadings, with their schedules, and also the report of 1729, it is hardly likely that the purpose of this search - a fuller understanding of the finances of the old East India Company - would be greatly furthered by any other documents generated in the course of the suit. That is to say, given what had been found and the low level of probability of finding anything else of substance, it would hardly be worth the time to search further. Third, the original cause book entry for the suit contained a clue that the case had not been terminated, at least in this stage - that is, it notes that a bill of revivor in the matter was filed in 1754!

Would the bill of *revivor* yield anything more? Searching for the pleadings under the name of the plaintiff Vincent (named in the original cause book entry) v Dubois (a hope, not a well-founded expectation), pleadings in 'Vincent v Dubois' were found at C 11/2150/49. And this is, indeed, the bill of revivor file. Vincent was claiming as an assignee of one of the original plaintiffs, James Clarke, and suing Charles Dubois's executors - Charlotte Dubois and Stephen Harvey (whose joint answer is filed with the Vincent bill) - and also Clarke's executors. Vincent's bill sets out the origin of his claim as assignee and the prior history of the litigation including the hitherto-undiscovered information that Holford's 1729 report was eventually ratified and confirmed by the Court in mid-1735 (C 33/364, ff 345, 549). Since then, the suit had been dormant. In addition, the joint answer of Dubois's executors supplies a little further information about the handling of the trust since Dubois's death in 1740. However, it does not appear that Vincent persevered with his claim. A search of the indexes to C 33 for 1755-1759 drew a complete blank.

No attempt to trace the revived suit beyond 1759 has been attempted. Even so, something more survives for this case, though perhaps not adding a great deal to the materials already located. The additional materials consist of the interrogatories and answers of the witnesses examined in Master Holford's proceedings. As explained in Chapter Three, there are - scattered among the Masters' Exhibits - several runs of boxes containing Masters' examinations. Some of these runs are carefully listed, others only very briefly noted. C 105/40-50 constitutes an unlisted run of Holford's papers (though not identified as such in the list to C 105). In turn, a search of these unlisted boxes yields examinations and depositions of Sir Nathaniel Gould and Sir Gilbert Heathcote taken in 1722 (C 105/40) and depositions of the trustees along with additional schedules of payments to them by factors in India from 1725-1726 (C 105/49).

On the one hand, this further set of finds in C 105 suggests the richness and complexity of the Chancery records. And if a given Master's report or, more likely, C 33 entries (as here) suggest that there may have been extensive examinations taken in the course of a reference, it is probably worth scanning the list of case names in those runs of Masters' 'Interrogatories' that have been listed in any detail (eg, C 112/212-247 and C 128 - C 129). On the other hand, given the state of the C 105 list, it was in fact only an investigation of the contents of these boxes as part of a different inquiry that yielded these further materials in 'Da Costa v Dubois'. To be accessible, C 105/40-50 (and the nineteenth-century boxes of Masters' 'Interrogatories' that follow in C 105/41-58) need to be listed.

4. Alpress v Alpress, mid-1780s

This is a suit with a very brief life, and seemingly with very little action. There proved to be no problem in identifying the suit in the C 12 lists, and the file (C 12/1261/2), when called up, tells the following story. The plaintiff was Jane Eleanor Alpress, daughter of Samuel, a wealthy Jamaican planter. As yet under age (hence, her 'next friend' in the bill Major General Samuel Townsend, of Upper Wimpole Street), she was seeking an account of her inheritance from three defendants - her widowed mother and the other two executors of Samuel's will. Jane's bill, dated 14 January 1785 (though recorded in the cause book IND 1/4138 as 14 November 1784), also sought the provision of a proper allowance until she came of age. But this is the sum and substance of the pleadings; the file itself includes only the bill, and recourse to the cause book confirms that no answer was submitted in the case.

Nor do the three C 33 entries, dated between 29 January and 12 February, seem to throw much light on the matter. The widow Alpress did respond to the bill by filing a petition asking that her daughter and one Richard Bulkeley esq be summoned to attend the Court, and the entry of 12 February indicates that the matter of the petition was to be put off till the following term when it was ordered that Bulkeley should bring the plaintiff before the Lord Chancellor. But this is the last that can be found of the suit in C 33.

Nonetheless, some sense of what was going on in this case can be derived from other Court records - the affidavits. By the later eighteenth century, the register of affidavits, if kept, no longer survives, so the searcher is dependent on the extant originals in C 31. Because they are boxed by the term in which they were made (not the term in which the associated suit was begun), searching them, even with the alphabets for this class, can often be tedious and frustrating. But in the Alpress case, the time-frame is a brief one and the search rewarding. Use of the alphabet to C 31 (in this case IND 1/14570) yields no less than six references to Alpress v Alpress, all in C 31/236 (nos 14, 37, 81-82, 150, 611), the earliest of 26 January 1785 and the latest of 9 April 1785. In turn, the story that can be reconstructed, somewhat tentatively, from the affidavits is familiar enough. In form, the deponents are mainly recounting their unsuccessful efforts to serve notice of Mrs Alpress's petition on Bulkeley and the plaintiff. But at the same time, they tell of Bulkeley first being received and then barred from Mrs Alpress's house, and later of Bulkeley hiring a post chaise and horses for a trip northward with the young lady. It would appear, then, that this minor heiress had fallen out with her mother over Bulkeley, that very possibly her lawsuit was initiated at Bulkeley's instigation, and that the reason it never went beyond the initial stage was that the plaintiff and Bulkeley journeyed to Scotland to escape the limitations on clandestine marriages imposed by Lord Hardwicke's marriage act of 1753.

Whether or not this reconstruction is altogether accurate, two related points are worth reiterating in the context of Alpress v Alpress. The first is that the majority of Chancery suits never got beyond the pleadings, and a substantial minority exist only in the shape of bills of complaint. The second is that the affidavits, though generally concerned with matters of process (eg, service of subpoenas, etc), can on occasion be informative, especially when usually richer veins (pleadings, proofs, and reports) fail to yield much of import.

II For particular subjects

Subject searching is very difficult for most classes of Chancery equity proceedings. Yet there are two ways into the records that have been under-exploited. One involves starting from within the manuscript records; the other involves starting from without.

In the first place, the searcher may make considerable progress with a subject matter search by investigating the more than 2,200 decree rolls for the seventeenth and eighteenth centuries in C 78. As indicated, the alphabets for C 78 occasionally yield subject information for rolls of the later 1600s and the 1700s, especially IND 1/16955 (the first one-third roughly of this run of rolls from 1300 to 1644), 1/16956 (rolls 1645-1890), and 1/16959 (rolls 1941-1990). In addition, the nearly 800 rolls listed by Professor Maurice Beresford's team in the 1970s provide subject matter information for something in the neighbourhood of 10,000-12,000 decided cases, almost wholly of the seventeenth century. To be sure, the enrolled decrees in C 78 may not altogether mirror the distribution of subjects of the large body of Chancery suits but they do cover a diverse range of subjects. Professor Beresford's interest was in enclosure controversies and agreements, and his team found a sizeable number of relevant decrees. Equally, one might expect a substantial harvest of business and commercial cases, along with even more numerous land and estate cases, judging from the listings in Beresford as well as from the sample sets.

Normally, an enrolled decree will provide the searcher not only with the text of the decree or order but also a summary of the original pleadings and some account of other matters of fact derived from depositions and/or Masters' inquiries. Furthermore, by furnishing the names of the original parties (though not always their status/occupation or place of residence), the enrolment can help the searcher to identify the original pleadings and to locate other materials associated with the case.

The second route for subject-matter searches depends upon the printed reports of Chancery decisions. Approximately 12,000 Chancery cases from the mid-sixteenth century to 1800 have been printed in easily accessible form in the early twentieth-century reprint series known as the *The English Reports*. Though not indexed save by title, all the Chancery decisions are grouped together in one run of volumes (nos 21-31 for the cases of the seventeenth and eighteenth centuries) within the larger series.

Not all is easy going with the printed cases. For one thing, since they were selected and printed because of their legal interest, they are not a representative sample of Chancery decided cases, much less of all Chancery suits.[13] Even so, a rough sense of the distribution by subject areas of these cases can be derived from the data from the bill samples summarized in Chapter Two. For a second, many of the early reports focus narrowly on matters of legal interest so

---

13   See comparison of the distribution of subject matter in the printed reports, in the decrees, and in our samples of bills at note 14, chapter II.

that the searcher often does not get a clue as to the subject in dispute. However, this habit of the early reporters is modified substantially over the course of the seventeenth century. For a third, in the absence of an index by subject to the reprint series, the searcher must page through these large volumes in quest of whatever topic is being pursued.[14]

One other feature of the later (ie, post-1660) printed reports is worth underlining. In many, though not in all instances, the reporters supply a specific reference to the books of orders - eg, Book A, 1735, and folio number - thus enabling the searcher to work back easily into the Chancery records.

In addition to the Chancery decisions printed in *The English Reports*, a much smaller number of appeals (numbering in the hundreds) from Chancery to the House of Lords are printed in the same series (vols 1-3), intermingled with appeals from other central courts of England, Scotland, and Ireland. The Lords began to consider appeals from Chancery in the 1620s, and by the last quarter of the seventeenth century, the process was becoming routinized. Among the rules for appeals was that the parties submit printed 'cases' stating their arguments and evidence. Hence, in addition to the printed appeal cases themselves (and the law reporters did not print all Chancery appeals), there are also from 1698 onwards printed copies of each side's case for all appeals from Chancery.[15] A complete series is preserved in the House of Lords Record Office (and there is also a somewhat less than complete series in the British Library), and these items sometimes add significant details to the printed cases in *The English Reports*.[16]

However, it is not always easy to follow these House of Lords appeals from Chancery back into the Court's record. A case in point is that of 'Ashton v Smith' where, in fact, the report of the appeal itself is very brief, the appeal being decided on a point of law. This case, which involved a dispute among a syndicate of London wharfingers, went to the House of Lords in March 1726 and the defendants' case (first encountered in a longhand copy in the family records of a descendent of a member of the syndicate) alluded to 2,000 pages of depositions taken in Chancery - quite a prize if they could be located![17] The difficulty was that while an outline of the course of the litigation was provided by the parties in their cases presented to the Lords, including the submission of the original bill in 1707, the filing of a cross bill by the defendants, a hearing of 1713, and a Master's report of 1719, documents from the earlier phases of the suit could not be traced via the usual finding aids for Chancery records.

---

14 There is *A Digested Index to the Modern Reports in Chancery* [1690-1705] (2nd edn, 1807); the page references are to the contemporary printed reports but those page references can be followed up in *The English Reports* since the volumes are double-paginated, with one set of page numbers being that of the original printing.

15 Some more detailed sense of the materials available can be gleaned from the volumes of *The House of Lords Manuscripts*, new series, vols 1-12, spanning the years 1693-1718. See also Maurice Bond, *Guide to the Records of Parliament* (1971), pp 114-120. For 1712-1718, roughly three-fifths of decided appeals from Chancery are reported in *The English Reports*. In addition to the decided cases that went unreported, appeals that were initiated and not pursued would, nevertheless, often generate printed 'cases'.

16 A substantial number of these 'cases' are also available in the microfilm series 'The Eighteenth Century Short Title Catalogue' produced by Resource Publications.

17 For a discussion of the controversy, see Henry Roseveare, '"Wiggins Key" Revisited: Trade and Shipping in the Later Seventeenth Century Port of London', *Journal of Transport History* 16 (1995), 1-20.

At this stage, recourse was had to the four cause books surviving for the year 1707-1708, and the searcher was fortunate enough to locate the entry for the original bill. The problem, in some ways comparable to those encountered in tracing Da Costa-Dubois, was that the original defendant was not Smith but Sir John Fleet (who died early in George I's reign). With the title of Ashton v Fleet, it proved relatively simple to find the original pleadings in C 9, and also a cross bill (Fleet v Ashton) and two other related bills in C 9, and then to locate the depositions (via IND 1/9115 & 9117) - admittedly, not 2,000 pages but still close to 200 pages of information about the London wharves and the syndicate's chequered history. And in addition, more information was located in two different segments of the Masters' Exhibits in C 110.

C. Conclusion

As should be evident from these examples, the rewards of a successful search in Chancery equity proceedings can be substantial. But the task is rarely simple. It is hoped this handbook will be of assistance to searchers, partly by indicating the range and character of the Chancery materials and partly by way of introduction for the relatively inexperienced searcher. However, to make this vast cache of material fully accessible will require detailed and comprehensive indexing by name, place and subject of the major classes of records.

APPENDIX ONE:
Memorandum on the Filing of the Pleadings

This memorandum by the long-serving Six Clerk Samuel Reynardson is undated; Reynardson served as a Six Clerk between the mid-1730s and the 1780s, and had previously served briefly as a Sworn Clerk. It is printed to illustrate what was regarded in his day, and in many respects in the seventeenth century as well, as the normal procedure for filing pleadings. A text of this memorandum was previously printed by E A Fry in his introduction to *Index of Chancery Proceedings, Reynardson's Division, 1649-1714* (British Record Society, Index Library, 1903-1904).

> C 173/4, unlabelled bundle [modernized spelling]
> Endorsed: 'The method of filing and keeping bills, answers and depositions'
> [then next line in different hand] 'by Mr Reynardson in his own hand writing'
> *Full transcription* Words in square brackets are additions in later hand. Words in parentheses are conjectural readings. Words in italic are underlined in the original.

When a bill is brought into the office the plaintiff [solicitor] carries it to any one of the Sworn Clerks or waiting Clerks he thinks proper; who is then called the plaintiff's Clerk in Court; and such sworn or waiting clerk ought immediately to put the day of the month and year upon the bill; and carry it into his Six Clerk's Study; who enters the names of the plaintiffs and defendants in a book (called the cause book) kept by him in an alphabetical manner, and then the Six Clerk writes his surname upon the top of the bill and puts it in a file in his study; and from this time such Six Clerk is and continues the Six Clerk for the plaintiff in such cause notwithstanding any change of the Sworn Clerk or solicitor: and if any abatement of suit happens by death of plaintiff or defendant or otherwise and a bill of revivor of the former suit is brought, it ought to be filed with the first Six Clerk in manner before mentioned: that the records in the same cause may be together; and that one Six Clerk may be enabled from time to time to certify to the Court the state of the proceedings in each cause.

When the defendants [solicitor] come to enter an appearance they retain one or more of the Sworn Clerks as each defendant thinks proper: The Sworn Clerk writes a note of the name of the cause, his own Six Clerk's name (or any other of the six Clerks' Names he thinks proper if his own Six Clerk happens to be for the plaintiff) and his own name. This note he delivers to the Six Clerk for the plaintiff; and takes the bill from the file and gives a receipt for it in a book kept for this purpose; and the Six Clerk from the note enters the name of the defendant's Six Clerk and Sworn Clerk in his cause book over against the entry by him before made of the Plaintiff's and Defendant's names and this discharges the plaintiff's Six Clerk of such bill.

The bill then remains in the possession of the defendant's Clerk in Court until an answer is put in thereto. When the bill and answer are affixed together [they] ought immediately to be carried into that Six Clerk's study in whose name the defendant appeared and such Six Clerk enters the name of the plaintiffs' and such as of the defendants' as are mentioned in the answer together with the day of the month and year in his cause book; signs his name to each skin of the answer, and then delivers bill and answer together to the plaintiff's Six Clerk [if this answer is properly taken and signed]; who immediately enters the name of defendant who answers and the day of the month and the year in the same part of his cause book, where had before entered the parties' names from the bill.

The answer being thus entered tis said to be filed; and during the term it came in the bill and answer together lie open upon a table in the plaintiff's Six Clerk's study from where the plaintiff's Clerk in Court takes the same to copy the answer but first gives the Six Clerk a receipt for the same and when the answer is copied it ought to be returned into the study of the Six Clerk for the plaintiff; and amongst the records of the term in which the answer was filed.

At the end of every term the records of the term are bundled up by each Six Clerk [and recordkeeper] and a label of the term affixed thereto; The single bills to which no appearance is entered by themselves and bills and answers in another bundle, and were the records returned to the Six Clerks [according to the order of the Court] when copied by the Sworn Clerks and put into the bundle of records of the term when filed the Six Clerks' books would be an exact index or calendar to the records; and any record would be found with ease.

When the defendants have answered if the plaintiff would reply thereto his Clerk in Court carries a replication (to all or either of the defendants' answers) to the Six Clerk for the plaintiff; who enters the names of defendants replied to in his cause book where the first made; and puts the day of the month and year on the replication and in his book; then signs the replication and carries it to the defendant's Six Clerk; who makes the like entry and puts the replication upon a file in his study where the same remains. From these entries the Six Clerks are enabled (when required) to certify to the Court the state of proceedings in every cause so far as relates to the time of filing bill, answer or replication.

When witnesses are examined by commission in the country such commissions when returned into Court *ought by the orders of the Court* to be delivered to the Six Clerk of the party who sued out such commission (or his deputy) to be safely and secretly kept and unopened till publication is passed; when the same ought to be opened in the presence of such Six Clerk or his deputy; and delivered to the Clerk in Court to be copied; and all records when copied *ought immediately* to be (?returned) to the Six Clerk from whom the same was received. And *all copies* of records when made should be brought to the Six Clerk *to be signed before the same are delivered out to any clients.*

This is the method prescribed by the Orders of Court for the due filing and keeping and copying of records; and which the Six Clerks observe to the utmost of their power, but are not so well observed on the part of the Sworn and Waiting clerks by which tis apprehended many inconveniences arise not only to the Suitors but to the Officers of the Court.

First as to single bills. These are taken out by the Clerk in Court who first appears for any or either of the defendants who make a copy of it but never returns it to the Six Clerk; but instead thereof delivers it over to any other Sworn or Waiting Clerk who appears for any other defendant by which means such other Clerk copies it; and *if no answer happens to be filed by such last Sworn* or Waiting Clerk, his Six Clerk *never comes to the knowledge of the copy* made by him; by which means the Six Clerk *is deprived of his fees*; and the bill remains in the custody of a Clerk whose name does not appear in the Six Clerk's books so as to charge him with the record of the bill; but the same when wanted is to be traced from one Sworn or Waiting Clerk to another.

Whereas if the record of the bill was to be returned by the Sworn Clerk who first took the same to copy; to the Six Clerk from whom the same was received and the like method observed by every Clerk who appears for any defendant as is by the Sworn or Waiting Clerk who first takes the bill to copy; the bill in case of no answer filed would remain in the term's bundle in which it was filed. And the Six Clerks would be enabled to know how many copies of such bills were made.

Secondly, as to answers.

They are frequently copied before they are filed; and by that means often not filed at all; for by copying the answers before filed the Six Clerk who (in case the answer was filed) would have been entitled to a copy has not an opportunity of charging the plaintiff's Clerk in Court with such copy. And in case the cause is not like to be proceeded in such answers often remain unfiled.

Such answers as are regularly filed, the plaintiff's Clerk in Court takes from the plaintiff's Six Clerk to copy; and ought to be returned when copied to the same Six Clerk, and put into the same term's bundle from whence taken; *but this method not being observed it occasions great confusion* amongst the records; for it frequently happens that answers when copied by the plaintiff's Clerk in Court are not returned to the Six Clerk in many years; and by this means such answers are never put into the proper term's bundle; But in case of the death of such Clerk in Court his records are delivered to his Six Clerk; but not in the order or method observed by the Six Clerks in keeping their records; so that the Six Clerks can only take an alphabetical list of such records; and this occasions the records in the Six Clerks' record rooms to be under two different heads. One entituled Study Matters and the other Pleadings.

The first class are such records as are by the Six Clerks respectively sent out of their offices or studies into the record rooms; and which is for the most part so contrived as to have always the records of five terms in their studies. So that were the records that are copied but returned before the end of five terms the inconveniences which arise from their not being returned to the Six Clerks would be avoided; and should any one have occasion to search for a record in any cause at any distance of time; if the plaintiff's name and the term when the cause began was but known; the plaintiff's Six Clerk's book would immediately shew in what term's bundle any particular bill answer or other record was remaining.

But as great numbers of records are never or at least not in many years returned to the Six Clerks; if any occasion to resort to any such records the first step to be taken is to search the cause book of the Six Clerk was concerned for the plaintiff where is to be found what answers have been filed; and in particular when filed; then search is to be made into that term's bundle for the particular record wanted (and which if regularly returned would be there to be found) but not being to be found there; search must again be made in the Six Clerk's books of delivery of records to see what Clerk in Court took such answer to copy; if the same person who take such answer be then in the Office the answer may be found without any great difficulty; but if it happens to be a record of long standing that is wanted it may happen that the plaintiff has several times changed his Clerk in Court or the seat of such Clerk may have several times changed its owner; and in such case a record is to be found with great difficulty if at all: This is the case when a record is taken out by a Clerk in the division of the plaintiff's Six Clerk; but as plaintiffs often change their Clerk in Court it frequently happens that a record is taken from this

Clerk by a Clerk who comes into the Cause for the plaintiff; who is neither in the division of the plaintiff's or defendant's Six Clerk. This occasions a greater inconvenience still; for in case of the death of such last mentioned Clerk in Court his records are or ought to be possessed by his Six Clerk; and never come back to the Six Clerk who was concerned in the cause; in which case they are scarce ever to be found.

Thirdly

Commissions to examine with the interrogatories and depositions to be taken therein never come to the hands of the Six Clerk either before or after publication notwithstanding the several orders for that purpose, unless in the case of a death of a Clerk in Court: And what is most extraordinary *although depositions* seem to be of the greatest consequence; They do not so much as appear in any of the Six Clerks' books; nor are the records thereof ever signed with the Six Clerks' names as other records are: and unless the cause wherein such depositions are taken is set down to be heard; the Six Clerks have no knowledge of the copies thereof; and are deprived of their fees for the same; and there are great numbers of depositions in causes which never come to be tried (and) depositions in causes after hearing; which not being brought to the Six Clerks according to the orders of the Court, the Six Clerks are deprived of their fees for the copies thereof.

APPENDIX TWO:
The Samples

As the term suggests, the samples - though they involve the making of lists - do not themselves cover fully any sizeable segment of any single class of Chancery equity records. The procedures for drawing them and their contents are briefly explained below. The sample data are published in *Samples of Chancery Pleading and Suits: 1627, 1685, 1735 and 1785* (List and Index Society, vol 257, 1995), ed Henry Horwitz and Charles Moreton.

The three principal objectives in taking the samples were to generate indicators of (a) the subject matter of litigation, (2) the identity of the litigants, and (3) the subsequent course of suits after the filing of pleadings. An additional aim was to provide guidance to searchers as to how often they might anticipate locating documents in addition to the pleadings in the relevant Chancery classes.

The samples were drawn from years which were judged to be ordinary ones, undisturbed by national upheavals, local disasters in the capital (plague, in particular), or upsets in the Court itself. (Only when the work of sampling was well-advanced did it become evident that 1785 might have been an unusual year because of the revival of sharp strife between the Six Clerks and the Sworn Clerks; even so, as the figures on loss discussed in Chapter Three indicate, that upset does not appear to have markedly affected the filing of bills.)

Samples of pleadings were drawn, then, from four individual years which spanned the seventeenth and eighteenth centuries - 1627, 1685, 1735 and 1785. Sample size was intended to take into account the volume of business in those years: the 285 sets of pleadings in the 1627 sample and the 250 sets of pleadings in the 1685 sample constitute roughly five per cent of the total of new bills for those years; the 294 and 140 sets of pleadings in the 1735 and 1785 samples constitute about ten per cent of the new bills for those years.

The process of drawing the sample pleadings was not a simple one, given the complexities of the existing organization of the records and the limitations of available finding aids. Most difficult were the 1627 and 1685 samples: the former had to be drawn from two differently-organized classes (C 2 and C 3, neither of them with finding aids giving the years of the files); the latter involved drawing from six separate classes (C 5 through C 10). There was also a concern to sample in rough proportion to the character of the existing pleading files - in particular, to match, or nearly match, in the samples the proportion of bill-only files for the year in question. The appropriate proportions could be gauged from the cause books for the 1735 and 1785 samples; in the absence of such evidence for 1627 and 1685 much cruder approximations, based on the exploration of the dozens of boxes of pleadings, had to be employed. Answer-only files were, on the other hand, excluded. Thus, specific items in the respective samples were selected by identifying, either from lists or by direct inspection, those boxes in the relevant classes with substantial numbers of files for the years in question.

Once the 969 sets of pleadings were drawn, read and listed, all the 1627 and 1785 suits were followed through the other relevant PRO classes till the cases either disappeared from the records (especially the books of orders) or were formally concluded. Had there been sufficient time, the same procedure would have been adopted for the 1685 and 1735 sample pleadings; in the event, it was possible to trace only about one-half of the 1685 sample pleadings (that is, those in which the first plaintiffs' surnames begin with the letters A-K). All told, then, 571 suits (285 from 1627, 146 from 1685, and 140 from 1785) have been traced in this fashion. The resulting listings for the traced suits include, in addition to the summary of the contents of the bill (and any responses filed with it), documents from the deposition classes, the Masters' reports and other Masters' papers, the affidavit classes (selectively), as well as all entries concerning the suits to be found in the books of orders.

The frequency with which other documents were generated in the sample suits can be briefly summarized as follows. Depositions were located in 30 of the 285 suits from 1627 (with entries in the books of orders of process for the taking or publishing of depositions in 15 more), in 21 of the 146 suits from 1685 (with process entries in 6 more), and in 16 of the 140 suits from 1785 (with process entries in 9 more). Masters' reports were located in 41 of the 1627 suits (with orders for references in 17 more), in 23 of the 1685 suits (with orders for references in 4 more), and in 42 of the 1785 suits (with orders for references in 2 more). Further breakdowns of the types of references are provided in Chapter One. And some of the broader implications of these findings are also considered in the analysis of wastage and loss of records in Chapter Three.

Whatever the limitations of such relatively small samples taken from so large a body of material, the dual process of the sampling of pleadings and the tracing of suits more than fulfilled the original objectives. In addition to making possible the analysis of the composition of litigation, the characteristics of litigants, and the workings of the Court, the results should provide guidance to searchers as to the likely benefit of pursuing their inquiries beyond the pleading classes *once they have been able to determine* whether the suit proceeded to proofs and references. Furthermore, the research uncovered quite significant changes in the mix of suits, the identity of the litigants, and the speed at which suits were processed over the course of the two centuries - changes discussed principally in Chapter Two. In turn, the analysis in Chapter Two was extended and refined in a number of important respects by drawing upon the results of a similar inquiry carried out independently by Dr Patrick Polden: taking suits from the legal year 1818-1819 with first-named plaintiffs whose surnames began with the letter 'M' as his sample, he traced 149 suits (roughly 7 per cent of all the new bills for that year), forward and, when they involved bills of revivor, backwards as well.

BIBLIOGRAPHY

I   Printed Sources: Chancery and Equity Records
II Other Printed Works, pre-1850
III Secondary Works on the Court of Chancery and on Equity (Books, Articles and Dissertations)
IV Printed Guides/Calendars to Chancery Equity Records, in addition to those listed in Appendix One
V   Manuscript Materials relating to the Court of Chancery outside the PRO

I   Printed Sources: Chancery and Equity Records

The Ancient State Authoritie and Proceedings of the Court of Requests by Sir Julius Caesar (1975), ed Lamar Hill

[Carew, George], 'A Treatise of the Maisters of the Chauncerie', *A Collection of Tracts relative to the Law of England* (1787), ed Francis Hargrave. And see W J Jones, 'The Treatise of the Masters in Chancery', *National Library of Wales Journal* 10 (1957-1958), 403-408

The English Reports (1900 ff): vols 1-3 contain House of Lords cases for the 17th-18th centuries; vols 21-31 contain printed Chancery cases for the period. See also *A Digested Index to the Modern Reports in Chancery* [1689-1805] (2nd edn, 1807)

The Manuscripts of the House of Lords [printed by the Historical Manuscripts Commission and continued by the House of Lords from 1694 to 1718; thereafter, reference must be had to the printed *Lords' Journals* and to the manuscript materials in the House of Lords Record Office]

Monro, C, *Acta Cancellariae; or, Selections from the Records of the Court of Chancery Remaining in the Office of Reports and Entries* (1847)

Lord Nottingham's Chancery Cases (2 vols, Selden Society 73 & 79: 1957 & 1962), ed D E C Yale

Lord Nottingham's "Manual of Chancery Practice" and "Prolegomena of Chancery and Equity" (1965), ed D E C Yale

Reports of Cases Decided by Francis Bacon, ... in the High Court of Chancery (1617-1621) (1932), ed John Ritchie

St. German's Doctor and Student (Selden Society 91: 1974), ed J L Barton

St. German on Chancery and Statute (Selden Society, supplementary series 6: 1986), ed John A Guy

Sanders, G W, *The Orders of the High Court of Chancery* (1845): the best edition for the period up to the date of its publication

Select Cases in the Court of Chancery 1364-1471 (Selden Society 10: 1896), ed W P Baildon

Squibb, Lawrence, "A Book of All the several Officers of the Court of Exchequer...", ed William H Bryson, *Camden Miscellany xxvi* (Royal Historical Society, Camden Society Publications, 4th series, 14, 1975)

II   Other Printed Works, pre-1850

(A) Works relating to reform of the law and of Chancery;
(B) Printed materials relating to the quarrels of the Six Clerks and the Sworn Clerks, and to the situations of other Court officers;
(C) Manuals written for practitioners and treatises on doctrine.

Call numbers are for the British Library, unless otherwise indicated; Wing references are to the printed Short Title Catalogue for 1640-1700; Eighteenth Century Short Title Catalogue references are from the CD-ROM version (some of these items not given locations in England are available on microfilm from Resource Publication's 'Eighteenth-Century Short Title' series). Wing and ESTC references are usually provided when no British Library copy exists or, if in the catalogue, could not be produced by the Library. The Law Society Library also has broad holdings, and, for mid-seventeenth century items, the London Library has proved useful as well.

(A) Works relating to reform of the law and of Chancery

Animadversions upon the present laws of England (1750) 518 h.14(4)

Antiquity of the High Court of Chancery (1654, 1658) Wing P2005A (cf Fabian Phillips, philazer of Common Pleas, *The Antiquity, Legality, Right, Use ... of fines, paid in Chancery upon the suing out ... of original writs* (1663) London Library, Pamph 626 #10

Atkyns, Sir Richard, *Inquiry into the jurisdiction of the Chancery in causes of Equity* (1695) 515 k.9

Burt, Nathaniel, *An Appeal from Chancery* (1653) E697(21)

Certain Quaeres for the Publike Good, Concerning the Avoiding of Multitudes of Unnecessary Orders, Delays, Charges and Troubles in Courts called English Courts or Courts of Equity (1647) Wing C1747 (BL: Thomason tracts)

Collins, Richard, *The cause of England's mercy* (1698) no location

Considerations touching the dissolving or taking away the Court of Chancery (1653) 518 b.3(3) [London Library, Pamph 626: endorsed - 'by Fabian Phillips who was afterwards publicly thanked for it by Lenthall']

Continuance of the High Court of Chancery Vindicated (1654) E809(2)

Cooper, Charles P, *A Brief Account of some of the most important Proceedings in Parliament relative to the ... Court of Chancery* (1828), and see below *Parliamentary Papers*

D., L. *Exact Relation of the Proceedings of the late Parliament Dissolved, 12th Dec 1653* (1654) E729(6)

An Essay on the Amendment and Reduction of the Laws of England (1724) - see below *Law Quibbles*

Fitzsimmondes, Joshua, barrister, *Free and Candid Disquisitions, on the nature and execution of the Laws of England, Both in Civil and Criminal Affairs* (1751) 115, f 34

Leach, William, *An Abatement of most of the motions and orders in Chancery* (1652) 518 i.3(10)

Leigh, Edward, 'gent', *Second Considerations Concerning the high court of Chancery*, 1658 London Library, Pamph 626 #9 - this is a virtual reprint of 13 pp of his earlier *Some Considerations* (below)

Locusts or the Chancery painted to the Life, 1705 Bodleian Library (quoted extensively in Parkes) ESTC gives two entries: (1) a BL loc [not mentioned on Resource Publication reel 2140#20]; (2) Guildhall Library, G 13505(3)

Norbury, George, 'Abuses and Remedies of Chancery' (c 1626, addressed to Lord Keeper Williams) in *A Collection of Tracts Relative to the Laws of England* (1787), ed Francis Hargrave, pp 425-448

Observations concerning the Chancery with some Proposals for the Redress of the Inconveniences in the Practices thereof (1653-sic, but after the Chancery Ordinance) E821(12) [dated Jan 1 1654[-5] by Thomason]

Observations upon the dilatory ... proceedings in the Court of Chancery in relation to the bill now depending ... for lessening the number of attorneys and solicitors (1701) Cambridge University Library

Parliamentary Papers
1810-11 (244) iii Causes of delay in Chancery
1812 (273) ii Causes of delay in Chancery, 2nd report
1812-13 (28 & 29 & 32) xiii Accounts of decrees ... causes ... bills in Chancery
1826 (143) xv, xvi Royal Commission on practice in Chancery
1836 (370) xliii State of business in Chancery and Exchequer 1750-1835

The Present State of the Practice and Practisers of the Law (1750)

Proposals concerning the Chancery (1650/51) E593(19) and 518 i.3(7) (reprinted as *Proposals presented to the hon. committee for regulating courts of justice on 18 Oct 1650* E615(21))

Proposals humbly offered to the Honourable the House of Commons, for remedying the great charge and delay of suits at law and in equity (1706) 3rd edn (1724) 515 h.14(5)

Report of the Lords Commissioners on the Court of Chancery (1740, reprinted in *Parliamentary Papers*)

The Representative of diveres well-affected ... touching the present laws, and government ... with xxxix new proposals (1649) 518 i.3(6)

(Philostratus Philodemius), *Seasonable Observations on a late book intituled System of the Law, so far as it relates to the High Court of Chancery and the Fees and proceedings thereof* (1653)

Some Considerations concerning the High-Court of Chancery (?1654) 1490 d22 (and see above under Leigh, Edward)

Tancred, Christopher, *Essay for a general regulation of law* (1727)

View of the Regulations of the Chancery (1640 and 1654) 518 b.33(2)

[Walter Williams, MT barrister] *Reasons Humbly offered ... the Commons of England, ... for their speedy endeavour to Regulate the Proceedings of the Court of Chancery with a Proposal how it may be legally done without an act of Parliament* (endorsed 'in case the bill now before them should not pass') (1693-1699?) 816 m.15(62)

(B) Printed materials relating to the quarrels of the Six Clerks and the Sworn Clerks, and to the situations of other Court officers

1. Six Clerks etc

a. the 1650s

Printed paper of some of the under clerks in Chancery, intitl'd, Reasons to be offered touching the fees mentioned in the table annexed to the Ordinance related to the intended attornies in Chancery (1654)

Reply to a Paper written by one of the Six Clerks, Intituled, An Answer to a Printed Paper of the under-clerks in Chancery dated 'Feb 1654'[-55] E826(17)

b. 1667-68: under-clerks' bill

Reasons for the Bill for Regulating the Six Clerks Office in Chancery, with an Answer to the Six Clerks case (nd) 816 m.15(63)

c. re the act of 1706 and the attempt the following year to repeal the clause re copy bills

The Case of the Six Clerks of the High-Court of Chancery. In relation to a clause in a Late Act of Parliament, Intituled, an act for the amendment of the Law &c (nd) 816 m.15(64)

The Answer of the Sworn Clerks ... to the Six Clerk's Case (nd) 816 m.15 (65)

The Six Clerks' Reply to the under-clerks (nd) 816 m.15(66)

A modest computation of the loss which the Under-Clerks in Chancery may sustain by taking away of the Dedimus Bill (nd) 1879 c4, (and also as *The True State of the Case of the Six Clerks in Chancery, with Reference to the Under-clerks, and a Bill now depending in Parliament* in PRO, C 173/2 and C 173/4)

d. re the act of 1748/49 for renewing and amending the 1729 act for the registration of attorneys and solicitors

The Case of the Sworn Clerks and Waiting Clerks of the Six-Clerks Office (nd) 213 i.1(88)

Reasons against a Clause in the expiring Law-Bill, Tending to increase the numbers of Attorneys and Solicitors (nd) 213 i.1(89)

Answers of the Sworn and Waiting Clerks ... To the Solicitors' Reasons (nd) 213 i.1(90)

e. re the disputes of the 1780s

In Chancery: The Six Clerks, one of two versions is endorsed 'Notice set up in the office 28 Feb. 1786'; both versions at PRO, C 173/36

Whereas the Six Clerks have entered an agreement, two versions, dated 19 July 1785 and 16 August 1785 respectively, at PRO, C 173/11 and C 173/36

2. The Masters

The Accompts of the Several Masters of the High Court of Chancery, ... (1725) 509 i.15 [this reprinted in various places, and see below *Report of the State*]

Bennett, W H, *A Short Dissertation on ... The Masters' Office ... with Directions for Carrying the Most Usual References to a Master into Effect* (1831)

Burroughs, Samuel, *The History of the Chancery ... and the Rights of the Masters* (1726) 883 g.20

Burroughs, Samuel, *The Legal Judicature in Chancery Stated. With Remarks on A Discourse of the Judicial Authority* (1727) 510 d.20

Coldham, P W, 'Genealogical Resources in Chancery Records - 2: Documents of Masters in Chancery', *Genealogical Magazine* 19 (1977-1979), 514-520

Hardwicke, Philip Yorke (1st earl), *A Discourse of the Judicial Authority belonging to the office of Master of the Rolls* (1727 - alternatively attributed to Joseph Jekyll) 2nd edn, 1728 = 884 i.15, with reply to Burroughs

Reasons, humbly offered, for an alteration of the present method of practice of the Masters in Chancery [?1760], BL Add MS 35879(300)

Report of the State of the Offices of the Deficient Masters (1725) and see above *Accompts*

The Reports of the Commissioners appointed to Inspect the Accounts of the Masters in Chancery ... (1725) Harvard Law Library (ms copies at British Library, Additional MS 6726, ff 124-144 and at PRO, SP 35/54, no 24)

3. Miscellaneous

The Case of the Proprietors of the Sub-poena Office in the High Court of Chancery (nd but early in Anne's reign) 1890 b.4(4)

(C) Manuals written for practitioners and treatises on doctrine

Acherley, Roger, *Jurisdiction of the Chancery*, (?1731) 883 e.19(2)

Bagot, Daniel, *Precedents of Decrees in Chancery* (17??) King's Inn Library, Dublin

Ballow, Henry, *A treatise of equity* (1737) 6192 aa.1 [for 1793 and later editions, see Fonblanque, John, *A Treatise of Equity*]

Barton, Charles, *Historical treatise of a suit in Equity* (1796) 518 k.6(3)

Beames, John, *Elements of Pleas* (1818) 511 c.15

Beames, John, *Doctrine of the Courts of Equity re Costs* (1822) Law Society Library

Bohun, William, *Cursus Cancellaria* (2nd edn, 1723) 883 h.17

Bohun, William, *Practising attorney: or, lawyer's office* (2nd edn, 1726) Law Society Library [see also Richardson, Robert, *Practicing Attorney: or, Lawyer's office* (4th edn, 1737); and see *Practicing Attorney and Solicitor: Containing the Lawyer's Office in Equity* (4th edn, 1737), both at Law Society Library]

[Boote, Richard], *The Solicitor's Compleat Guide in the Practice of the High Court of Chancery* (1776) 883, ff 22-23

Boote, Richard, *Solicitor's Practice in the High Court of Chancery* (1775) 513 c.30(2)

[Booth, William], *Compleat Solicitor* (5th edn, 1683 [first edn probably 1660]) 1608/979. A variant edition is *The Compleat Solicitor Performing his Duty* (1672)

Brown, William, *The Clerk's Tutor in Chancery* (first edn, 1688) 3rd edn, 1705, at 513 b.1

Brown, William, *Practice of the High Court of Chancery as now regulated by act of parliament* (1702 and 1706) Lincoln's Inn Library

Brown, William, *Praxis Almae Curia Cancellariae* (first edn, 1694) 1714 edn, at 513 b.2

Clerk's Associate: containing an account of the High Court of Chancery (1738) 883 e.20

[Young] Clerk's Magazine ... appendix relating to business in Chancery (first edn, 1739) 4th edn, at 1489 p 66

Collection of Interrogatories for the Examination of Witnesses in Courts of Equity (1776) Resource Publications reel 2867 #6

Complete Attorney (1654) Cambridge University Library

Costs in the High Court of Chancery 1779 edn at 513 c.11(2)

Coventry, Thomas Lord, *Perfect and exact directions to all those that desire to know the true and just fees of Common Pleas and Chancery* (1641) Wing C6625

Equity Pleader's Assistant (Dublin, 1796) [mainly Irish]

Fowler, David Burton, *The Practice of the Court of Exchequer, upon proceeding in equity* (1795) 228, ff 26-27

Francis, Richard: *Maxims of Equity* (1727) 509 h.6 [modern reprint edn of 1978]. And see Roscoe Pound, 'On certain maxims in equity', *Cambridge Legal Essays in Honor of Bond, Buckland, and Kenney* (1926), p 267

Gilbert, Geoffrey, *Two Treatises on the proceedings in equity, and the jurisdiction of that court* (Dublin 1756-1758). And see M Macnair, 'Sir Geoffrey Gilbert and his Treatises', *Journal of Legal History* 15 (1994), 252-268

Gilbert, Geoffrey, *History and Practice of the High Court of Chancery* (1758) [Dublin edn at 1608/2387; London edn at 510 e.7 (with ms annotations)]

Gilbert, Geoffrey, *The Law of Uses and Trusts ... from the reports of adjudged cases ... with a treatise of dower* (1734) 514 d.9

Grounds and Rudiment of Law and Equity (1749) Law Society Library

Hake, Edward, *Epieikeia A Dialogue on Equity in Three Parts*, ed D E C Yale (1958), and see Raymond B Marcin, 'Epiekeia: Equitable Lawmaking in the Construction of Statutes', *Connecticut Law Review* 10 (1978), 377

Hands, William, *Solicitor's Assistant in the Court of Chancery* (1809) Law Society Library

Harrison, Joseph, *The Accomplished Practicer in the High Court of Chancery* (5th edn, 1779) 516 c.55 (Law Society Library has edn of 1741)

Hinde, Robert, *The Modern Practice of ... Chancery* (1785) 510 d.4

Historical Essay on the Jurisdiction of the Court of Chancery (1735) 1241 G.19(1)

[Jacob, Giles], *The Compleat Chancery Practicer* (1730) 510 d1-2

Jacob, Giles, *A New Law Dictionary* (1732 and ff)

Maddock, Henry, *A Treatise on the Principles and Practice of the High Court of Chancery* (2 vols, 1820)

Mitford, John, *A Treatise on the Pleadings in Chancery* (1780) 518 h.15(1)

Parker, Wilmot, *Analysis of the Practice of the Court of Chancery* (1794) 510 e.8

Parkes, Joseph, *A History of the Court of Chancery* (1828)

Points in Law and Equity...[for] all persons concerned in trade and commerce (Dublin, 1793)

Powell, Thomas, *The Attourneys Academy* (1623) C113 b.3

The Practical Register in Chancery (1714) 228 g.31 [reprinted with additions in 1800 by John Wyatt as *The Practical Register in Chancery with the addition of the Modern Cases*]

The Practice of the High Court of Chancery Unfolded (1652) E 1292[2]) dated 'Nov. 6. 1651'

Present Practice of the High Court of Chancery 1741 (by a gent of the Six Clerks' Office) 510 a.33-34

Sanders, Francis Williams, *An Essay on the nature and laws of uses and trusts* (1791) 574 d.10

Sheppard, William, *Faithful Councellor* (1651, 2nd part 1653)

Sheppard, William, *England's Balme* (1656) E1675(2)

Solicitor's Practice in the High Court of Chancery Epitomized (6th edn, 1791) Law Society Library

Spence, George, *The Equitable Jurisdiction of the Court of Chancery* (2 vols, 1846)

Story, Joseph, *Commentaries on Equity Jurisprudence, as administered in England and America* (1839)

T G, *Practick Part of the Law: shewing the office of an attorney, and a guide for Solicitors in the Courts of Chancery...* (1652) 519 a.33

[Turner, Samuel], *Costs in the Court of Chancery; with practical directions and remarks* (1791) 1241 g.5

Turner, Samuel, *Epitome of the Practice of the High Court of Chancery* (2nd edn, 1809) Law Society Library

View of the Regulations of the Chancery (1640, 1654) 518 b.33(2)

Viner, Charles, *A General Abridgement of Law and Equity* (1746)

[Walker, Maynard Chamberlain], *Equity Pleader's Assistant* (1796) King's Inn Library, Dublin

West, William, *Three Treatises, of the second part of Symbolograephia... whereto is annexted another Treatise of Equitie...* (1594) 1586/9026

Williams, William, *Jus Appellandi ad Regum ipsum a Cancellaria* (1683)

Wyatt, John, see *The Practical Register*

III Secondary Works on the Court of Chancery and on Equity (Books, Articles and Dissertations)

In general, the best short guide is

Baker, John H, *An Introduction to English Legal History* (3rd edn, 1990), chapter 6. In turn, Baker's bibliography gives the relevant volumes and pages of Sir William Holdsworth's *History of English Law* (16 vols, 1922-1966)

More specialized works include

Avery, M E, 'An Evaluation of the Effectiveness of the Court of Chancery under the Lancastrian Kings', *Law Quarterly Review* 86 (1970), 84-97

Avery, M E, 'The History of the Equitable Jurisdiction of Chancery before 1460', *Bulletin of the Institute of Historical Research* 42 (1969), 129-144

Ball, R M, 'Tobias Eden, Change and Conflict in the Exchequer Office, 1672-1698', *Journal of Legal History* 11 (1990), 70-89

Baker, John H, 'The Common Lawyers and the Chancery: 1616', reprinted in his *The Legal Profession and the Common Law Historical Essays* (1986), 205-229

Barbour, W T, *The History of Contract in Early English Equity* (Oxford Studies in Social and Legal History 4: 1914)

Birks, Michael, 'The Perfecting of Orders in Chancery', *Cambridge Law Journal* 14 (1955), 1-12 [TO BE USED WITH CAUTION]

Brooks, Christopher W, 'Interpersonal conflict and social tension: civil litigation in England, 1640-1830', *The First Modern Society* (1989), ed A L Beier *et al*, pp 357-399

Brooks, Christopher W, *Pettyfoggers and Vipers of the Commonwealth* (1986)

Bryson, W H, *The Equity Side of the Exchequer Its Jurisdiction, Administration, Procedures and Records* (1975)

Busch jr, Allan J, 'Bulstrode Whitelocke and Early Interregnum Chancery Reform', *Albion* 10 (1979), 317-330

Busch jr, Allan J, 'The John Lisle Chancery Manuscripts: The "Abridgements" [&] "The Pleas and Demurrer"', *Journal of Legal History* 10 (1989), 317-342

Carlton, Charles, 'Changing Jurisdictions in 16th and 17th Century England: The Relationship Between the Courts of Orphans and Chancery', *American Journal of Legal History* 18 (1974), 124-136

Champion, W A, 'Recourse to law and the meaning of the great litigation decline, 1650-1750: some clues from the Shrewsbury local courts', *Communities and Courts in Britain 1150-1900* (1997), ed C W Brooks and Michael Lobban, pp 179-198

Churches, Christine, '"Equity against a purchaser shall not be": a seventeenth-century case study in landholding and indebtedness', *Parergon* new series 11 (1993), 69-87

Churches, Christine, '"The most unconvincing testimony": the genesis and historical usefulness of the country deposition in Chancery', *Seventeenth Century*, XI (1996), 209-227

Croft, Clyde E, 'Lord Hardwicke's Use of Precedent in Equity', *Legal Record and Historical Reality* (1989), ed Thomas G Watkin, pp 121-155

Croft, Clyde E, 'Philip Yorke, First Earl of Hardwicke - An Assessment of his Legal Career', PhD Cambridge, 1982

Guy, John A, 'Law, Equity and Conscience in Henrician Juristic Thought', *Reassessing the Henrician Age* (1986), ed Alistair Fox and J Guy, pp 179-198

Guy, John A, *The Public Career of Sir Thomas More* (1980)

Haskett, Timothy, 'The Presentation of Cases in medieval Chancery Bills', *Legal History in the Making* (1991), ed W M Gordon and T D Fergus, pp 11-28

Haskett, Timothy, 'The medieval English court of Chancery', *Law & History Review*, 14 (1996), 245-313

Henderson, Edith G, 'Legal Rights to Land in the early Chancery', *American Journal of Legal History* 26 (1982), 97-122

Henderson, Edith G, 'Relief from Bonds in the English Chancery: Mid-Sixteenth Century', *American Journal of Legal History* 18 (1974), 298-306

Heward, Edmund, 'The Early History of the Court Funds Office', *Journal of Legal History* 4 (1983), 46-53

Hill, Lamar, *Bench and Bureaucracy: The Public Career of Sir Julius Caesar 1580-1626* (1987)

Holdsworth, Sir William, *Charles Dickens as a Legal Historian* (1928)

Hoffer, Peter Charles, *The Law's Conscience Equitable Constitutionalism in America* (1990)

Horwitz, Henry, and Polden, Patrick, 'Continuity or Change in the Court of Chancery in the Seventeenth and Eighteenth Centuries?', *Journal of British Studies* 35 (1996), 24-57

Horwitz, Henry, 'Recordkeepers in the Court of Chancery and their "record" of accomplishment', *Historical Research* 70 (1997), 34-51

Jones, Neil G, '*Tyrrell's Case* (1557) and the Use upon a Use', *Journal of Legal History* 14 (1993), 75-93

Jones, Neil G, 'The influence of revenue considerations upon the remedial practice of Chancery in Trust Cases 1536-1660', *Communities and Courts in Britain 1150-1900* (1997), ed C W Brooks and Michael Lobban, pp 99-114

Jones, William J, 'Conflict or Collaboration? Chancery Attitudes in the reign of Elizabeth I', *American Journal of Legal History* 5 (1961), 12-54

Jones, William J, 'Due Process and Slow Process in the Elizabethan Chancery', *American Journal of Legal History* 6 (1962), 123-150

Jones, William J, *The Elizabethan Court of Chancery* (1967)

Jones, William J, 'A Note on the Demise of Manorial Jurisdiction: The Impact of Chancery', *American Journal of Legal History* 10 (1966), 297-318

Jones, William J, 'Palatine performance in the seventeenth century', *The English Commonwealth 1547-1640* (1979), ed Peter Clark *et al*, pp 189-204

Kerly, D M, *Historical Sketch of the Equitable Jurisdiction of the Court of Chancery* (1890)

Knafla, Louis A, *Law and Politics in Jacobean England The Tracts of Lord Chancellor Ellesmere* (1977)

Knight, Marcus, 'Litigants and Litigation in the Seventeenth Century Palatinate of Durham', PhD, Cambridge, 1990

Langbein, John, 'Fact Finding in the English Court of Chancery: A Rebuttal', *Yale Law Journal* 83 (1974), 1620-1630

Lemmings, David, *Gentlemen and Barristers: The Inns of Court and the English Bar, 1689-1730* (1990)

Levack, Brian, *The Civil Lawyers in England 1603-1641* (1973)

McDermott, Peter, 'Jurisdiction of the Court of Chancery to Award Damages', *Law Quarterly Review* 108 (1992), 652-673

Macnair, Michael, 'The Law of Proof in Early Modern Equity', DPhil, Oxford, 1991

Macnair, Michael, 'Common law and statutory imitations of equitable relief under the later Stuarts', *Communities and Courts in Britain 1150-1900* (1997), ed C W Brooks and Michael Lobban, pp 115-131

Matthews, Nancy L, *William Sheppard: Cromwell's Law Reformer* (1985)

Metzger, Franz, 'The Last Phase of the Medieval Chancery', *Law-Making and Law-Makers in British History* (1980), ed Alan Harding, pp 78-89

Milhous, J, and Hume, R, 'Eighteenth-century Equity Lawsuits in the Court of Exchequer as a Source for Historical Research', *Historical Research* 70 (1997), 231-246

Powell, Damian X, 'Why was Sir Francis Bacon Impeached? The Common Lawyers and the Chancery Revisited: 1621', *History* 81 (1996), 511-526

Pound, Roscoe, 'The Progress of the Law, 1918-1919—Equity', *Harvard Law Review* 33 (1920), part iii at 941-942

Prest, Wilfrid, 'Law Reform in Eighteenth-Century England', *The Life of the Law* (1993), ed Peter Birks, pp 113-123

Prest, Wilfrid, *The Rise of the Barristers A Social History of the English Bar 1590-1640* (1986)

Pronay, Nicholas, 'The Chancellor, the Chancery, and the Council at the end of the Fifteenth Century', *British Government and Administration*, ed H Hearder and H R Loyn (1974), pp 87-103

Shapiro, Barbara, 'Law Reform in Seventeenth Century England', *American Journal of Legal History* 19 (1975), 280-312

Stretton, Tim, 'Women and Litigation in the Elizabethan Court of Requests', PhD, Cambridge, 1993

Thomas, G W, 'James I, Equity and Lord Keeper John Williams', *English Historical Review* 91 (1976), 506-528

Thornton, Tim, 'Local Equity Jurisdictions in the Territories of the English Crown: The Palatinate of Chester, 1450-1540', *Courts, Counties and the Capital in the Later Middle Ages* (1996), ed Diana E S Dunn, pp 27-52

Tittler, Robert, 'Sir Nicholas Bacon and the Reform of the Tudor Chancery', *University of Toronto Law Review* 23 (1973), 383-395

Turner, R W, *The Equity of Redemption* (1931)

Veall, Donald, *The Popular Movement for Law Reform* (1970)

Whitaker, S, 'An historical perspective to the "special equitable action" in *in re Diplock*', *Journal of Legal History* 4 (1983), 3-45

Yale, David, 'The Revival of Equitable Estates in the Seventeenth Century: an Explanation by Lord Nottingham', *Cambridge Law Journal* 16 (1957), 72-86

Yale, David, 'A Trichotemy of Equity', *Journal of Legal History* 6 (1985), 194-200

Yeazell, Stephen C, 'Default and Modern Process', *Legal History in the Making* (1991), ed W M Gordon and T D Fergus, pp 125-144

Yeazell, Stephen C, *From Medieval Group Litigation to Modern Class Action* (1987)

IV Printed Guides/Calendars to Chancery Equity Records, in addition to those listed in Appendix One

Beresford, Maurice, 'The Decree Rolls of Chancery as a Source for Economic History, 1547-c.1700', *Economic History Review* 2nd ser 32 (1979), 1-10

'A Calendar of Chancery Depositions before 1714', ed F S Snell, *The British Archivist* 1 (1913-1920), supplement 2 (covers 495 consecutive suits of the letter 'A' from C 22) (copy at Guildhall Library is indexed)

'A Genealogist's Kalendar of Chancery Suits at the time of Charles I', *The Ancestor* 1-12 (1902-1905) (covers 441 suits from early bundles of C 2)

Gerhold, Dorian, *Courts of Equity A Guide to Chancery and other Legal Records* (1994: Pinhorn Handbooks: Ten)

Goulden, R J, *Some Chancery Lawsuits: An Analytical List* (of eighteenth-century printers' cases in C 11) (1982/1983) BL 205/1260

Lawton, Guy, 'Using Bernau's Index', 3 parts in *Family Tree Magazine*, VIII (2-4: 12/1991-2/1992), pp 42-43 in each

Lawton, Guy, 'Using Bernau's Notebooks', 3 parts in *Family Tree Magazine*, X, 2-4 (12/1993-2/1994), pp 44, 21, and 15

Mann, J H, *Chancery Depositions taken by Commission A Complete List of All Such Depositions for the County of Devonshire as are Filed among 'Chancery Proceedings 1714-1758' at the Public Record Office, London* (1950) BL 6003 i.6

A Register of English Theatrical Documents 1660-1737, compiled and edited by Judith Milhous and Robert D Hume (2 vols, 1991)

Samples of Chancery Pleadings and Suits: 1628, 1685, 1735, and 1785 (List and Index Society, vol 257, 1995), compiled by Henry Horwitz and Charles Moreton

V Manuscript Materials relating to the Court of Chancery outside the PRO

There are extensive holdings of manuscript reports of seventeenth and eighteenth century Chancery cases widely dispersed in the United Kingdom and in the United States. Some, undoubtedly, contain additional and/or variant material to the printed legal reports. Much of this material has been listed by Professor J H Baker of St Catharine's College, Cambridge, and some of it is available on microfiche. See his *English Legal Manuscripts in the United States of America A Descriptive List Part II 1558-1902* (Selden Society, 1990) with cross-references to items available on microfiche. For similar materials in England, see J H Baker, *English Legal Manuscripts* [microfiche series], part ii - manuscripts in Lincoln's Inn, the Bodleian Library, and Gray's Inn.

In addition, the following specific collections contain much relating to Chancery or to Chancery cases:

British Library: papers of Lord Chancellor Hardwicke, esp Additional MSS 36045-36069, 36105, 36118, 36148, 36175-36178, 36180-36182, 36276-36281

Harvard University Law Library: primarily early seventeenth-century materials, including 6 mss volumes listed under 'Munro'. See also MS 5026 (collection of Six Clerks' documents overlapping with Six Clerks' materials in PRO, C 173/2 and C 173/10)

Henry E Huntington Library, Bridgewater MSS (papers of Lord Chancellor Ellesmere)

House of Lords Record Office: material relating to appeals from Chancery after 1718

Finally, it should be noted that the records of the Accountant-General from 1725 onwards, never deposited in the Public Record Office, are held by the Court Funds Office.

A Guide to Chancery Equity Records and Proceedings 1600-1800

INDEX

Entries relating to the Court of Chancery are grouped under 'Chancery, Court of'. Entries relating to other courts are grouped under 'Courts, other'. Entries relating to the Court of Chancery's records presently in the Public Record Office are grouped under 'Public Record Office', usually by their class number.

Alpress, Jane Eleanor 101
Alpress, Margaret Eleanor, widow 101
Alpress, Samuel 101
Andrews, Jonathan 98
Andrews, Judith 98
Attorney General 35, 40 n 21

Bacon, Sir Francis 9 & n 5, 10
Bacon, Sir Nicholas 10
Barber-Surgeons, Company of 95
Barbon, Sir Nicholas 8
Bateman, Harry Charles 53
Bell, John 21 & n 37
Beresford, Maurice 86-87, 102
Beresford Calendar (C 78) 86-87 & n 37, 102
Bernau, Charles A 61
Bernau Index (*and see* Dwelly Index) 61-62 & n 25, 68, 71, 72-73, 76-77
Bernau Notebooks (C 11) 72-73, 77
Bladen, Martin 51 n 1
Bohun, William 12
Boote, Richard 12
Bowyear, Francis 88
Bridgeman, Sir Orlando 14, 15
British Library 103
Brown, William 12
Bulkeley, Richard 101

Chancery, Court of
  Cases Cited
    Alpress v Alpress 101
    Ashton v Smith 103-104
    Boehm v De Tastet 10 n 8
    Coates v Myers 78
    Cope v Hooker 96-97
    DaCosta v Dubois 97-101
    Eyre v Wortley 4 n 17, 93-95
    Hooker v Cope 97
    Smythe v Lomax 85 n 35
    Turpin v Bernard 52 n 4
    Vincent v Dubois 100
  Cases in print 36 n 14, 102-104
  Indexes to records, see Public Record Office

Litigants (in general 30 n 1, 41-50)
  Commercial/artisanal 41-45, 49
  Farmers 41-45
  Gentlemen, and above 41-45
  Minors 42-43, 93-94, 101-102
  Professionals 41-45
  Representative parties 41 n 26 (*and see* 'next friend')
  Residence of 41 & n 26, 45-50
  Women 22, 41, 42, 43, 93-94
Miscellaneous
  Bankruptcy 43, 49 & n 38
  Business, of court 5-6, 9, 25, 32-35, 48-50
  Civil lawyers 2
  Confederacy 14 & n 16
  Counsel in 2, 4, 11, 13, 34 & n 10, 60, 95
  Critiques, of court 1, 2 & n 6, 5, 16, 21, 30-31 & n 2, 34 & n 10, 53-54
  Enclosure, decrees 102
  Estates 35-38, 44 n 29, 48 & n 36, 93-97
  Executors 38 n 16, 41 n 26, 48, 97, 100, 101
  Fees and the purchase of offices 9, 16, 17, 18, 24, 30, 34 & n 10, 55-56, 74, 80, 108
  Judges, shortage of 9
  Jurisdiction, and nature of cases 4-5 & n 14, 30-40, *and see* Subject Matter
  Location of offices 11, 13, 15, 20
  'Next friend' 101
  Origins 1-2
  Practice Manuals 12-24 & n 15, 40 n 24
  Progress of Cases 11, 28, 29, 31, 33-35, 48-50
  Recordkeeping and its deficiencies 6-7, 18, 23, 25 & n 47, 50-56, 105-108
  Relations with the common law (courts and judges) (*see also* Injunctions) 1-2, 3 & n 9, 4 nn 12-13, 15, 23, 32, 38 7 n 15, 48, 94
  Samples, nature 24-25 & n 46, 109-110
  Samples, results 25-29, 35-48, 47, 55-56 & n 21, 78 n 28
  Solicitors 10-11 & n 11, 14, 20 n 33, 52, 56 n 20, 74, 89, 105
  Stages, of a suit 11-29, 30-31
Offices, Officers (the office of Lord Chancellor is not indexed)

Index

Accountant-General 9 n 5, 80 n 30, 81
Affidavit Office 11, 78
Clerks in Court (*see also* Sworn Clerks, Waiting clerks) 9 n 4, 11 n 11, 12, 14, 74, 105-108
Commissioners (for taking answers or depositions in the country) 3-4 & n 10, 20-21 & n 33, 52 n 4, 60, 75, 76, 77, 88, 94, 95
Examiners and Examiners' Office 4, 11, 20, 30 n 2, 60, 76, 77
Judges (common law) 2, 9, 11, 94
Masters, Extraordinary 4, 80 n 29
Masters, Ordinary 2 & n 5, 3, 4, 9, 16, 18, 22 & n 39, 24, 27, 52-53, 80-81, 83, 84
Masters' clerks 22, 84
Masters' offices ('the Public Record Office') 11, 51
Master of the Rolls 2, 4, 9, 11, 19, 21, 34, 53, 54, 71, 89
Petty Bag 1 n 2
Register (and deputy registers and their clerks) 11 & n 13, 15, 18, 21, 59, 60, 80, 93-94, 99
Register's (Report) Office 11, 18, 49, 56, 71
Rolls Chapel (*see also* Tower of London) 11, 15, 18, 20, 51, 53, 54, 86, 88
Six Clerks 9, 10 & n 9, 14-15, 16, 18 & n 29, 18, 23, 30, 34 n 11, 52-56, 60 n 23, 85, 86, 88, 89, 105-109
Six Clerks' offices and record rooms 11, 14, 18, 51 & n 1, 53, 55, 107
Subpoena Office 11, 15
Sworn Clerks (and their employees) 9 & n 4, 14-15, 16, 18 & n 29, 23, 34 & n 11, 52, 53, 48, 59-60, 71, 74, 86, 89, 105-109
Tower of London (as record repository) 18, 51, 53, 54, 62
Under-clerks *see* Sworn Clerks, Waiting Clerks
Usher 20-21, 71
Vice Chancellor 49
Waiting clerks 9 & n 4, 14, 74, 105

Process and Remedies
Appearance 14
Arbitration 88-89
Calendar 12 & n 12
Collusive (or consent) proceedings 8 & n 2, 15, 16 & n 25, 26 n 49
Contempt 5, 16, 26 n 48, 95 (*and see* Attachment, Sequestration)
Costs 10, 11 n 11, 16, 24, 39
Damages 5 n 17
Decretal order (unenrolled decree) 22-23, 85, *and see* Decrees and Orders, Decrees Enrolled
Default, judgement by 16 & n 23
Demurrer 11 n 12, 14-15, 27 & n 50, 93, 94
Disclaimer 14-15
Discovery 8
Dismission 8
Enforcement 5, 13, 95 (*and see* Contempt)
'English bill procedure' 3, 5
Equitable title to land 5
Equity of redemption (of mortgages) 5 n 15, 35
Examinations *viva voce* 20, 22
Exceptions (to reports) 22, 82
Feigned issue 4 n 13, 21 & nn 35-38
Further directions 11
Hearings 13, 21-22, 26, 28, 59-60, 94, 95, 97-98, *and see* Rehearings
Imprisonment 5
in forma pauperis 5 n 19
Injunctions 3 & n 10, 5, 13, 19 & n 30, 27, 40 & n 23, 60, 81
Interlocutory matters *see* Injunctions, Motions, Petitions
Interlocutory relief 19, 27, *and see* Injunctions
Judgments 10, 95, 97, 102-103, *and see* Decrees, Decrees Enrolled
Motions 13, 19, 20, 21, 28, 34 n 10, 59
'Necessary Party' 14 n 16, 17
Orders, enforcement of 59
Penal bonds, and relief thereof 36 & n 16, 88
Petitions 13, 19, 28, 59, 60, 79-80, 101
Plea 11 n 12, 15, 27 & n 50, 93, 94
Pleadings, scandalous 17 & n 27, 27
Pleadings, sufficiency 14, 17, 27, 81, 94
Proofs 3-4, 13, 20-21, 75-78
References (to Masters) 3, 4, 11, 22, 30, 60, 81-82, 94
Rehearings 13, 23 & n 42, 24, 52, 60, 63, 79, 99
Rules 10, 11-12
Sequestration 5
Settlements out of court 25
Specific performance 5
'Study matters' 52, 107
Subpoenas 2, 10 n 10, 13-16, 25, 41, 59, 60, 78
Testimony *see* Depositions, Proofs
Trustees 96, 98-100
Witnesses *see* Depositions, Proofs

Records (*see also* Public Record Office)
Affidavits 41, 78-79, 91, 96, 101-102, 110
Agreements 8, 25, 88-89
Answers (and further answers, demurrers, disclaimers, and pleas) *see* Pleadings
Attachments (schedules) 16 & n 26, 20, 27 & nn 51-52, 99
Awards 88-89
Bills (original, amended, supplementary, cross) *see* Pleadings

121

Bill Books 18, 29 & n 6, 31, 32 & n 6, 46, 48, 52-53, 74, 75, 80, 98, 99
Bills, copy *see* Pleadings
Bills, cross 15, 97, 103, 104, *and see* Pleadings
Bills of Review 23 & n 42, 26-27, 79
Bills of Revivor 22, 24, 26-27, 52, 60, 74, 75, 100, 110
Book of [Decrees and] Orders (*and see* Decrees and Orders) 3, 4, 15, (12), 19, 23, 33, 51, 59-60, 85, 91, 93-97, 99, 100, 103
Cause Books 18, 25, 53, 74, 75, 98-99, 100, 101, 105, 109
Clerk in Court Books 74
Decrees, and orders (*and see* Book of [Decrees and] Orders) 2-3, 10, 13, 21-23, 26, 27, 36 n 14, 93
Decrees, Enrolled 2, 10, 21 & n 38, 22-23 & n 43, 27-28 & nn 53-54, 85-88, 95-96, 97, 102
Depositions 3-4 & n 11, 5, 7, 20-21 & n 34, 22, 26 & nn 48-49, 55 & n 18, 58, 60, 75-78, 91, 94-95, 96-97, 103-104, 108, 110
Docquets 58, 85-86, 88
Interrogatories 20, 72, 75-78, 91, 95, 96, 100, 108, *and see* Masters' Interrogatories
Masters' Accounts 58, 82
Masters' Documents 84-85
Masters' Exhibits 80, 82, 83, 91, 92, 100, 104
Masters' Interrogatories 22, 76, 82, 84, 100-101
Master' Reports 3, 4, 7, 17, 19, 21-23, 27 n 52, 51, 55-56, 80-82, 94, 97, 98, 99-100, 103, 110
Pleadings (*and see* bills of review and bills of revivor, above) 2, 3, 7, 10 n 10, 12-18, 24-27 & n 50, 51-55, 60-62, 68-75, 81, 97-99, 105-108
Rebutters *see* Pleadings
Rejoinders *see* Pleadings
Replications 93 n 11, 94, 99 *and see* Pleadings
Rule Books 75
Schedules *see* Attachments
Surrebutters *see* Pleadings
Surrejoinders *see* Pleadings
Subject matter of suits
Business 35-37 & nn 13-14, 43
Debts and Bonds 35-37 & nn 13-14, 38 & n 15
Estates 24, 29, 35-37 & nn 13-14, 38 & n 16, 40 n 25, 44 n 25, 44 n 29, 48 & n 36, 49, 93-97, *and see* Estates, index to cases
Land 4-5 & nn 15-16, 35-37 & nn 13-14, 43
Tithes 21 & n 37, 35, 40
Chancery Lane 11, 13, 18
Clandestine marriage 83
Clarke, James 100

Coke, Sir Edward 2
Coldham, Peter Wilson 62, 69-70, 84 & n 33, *and see* Estate cases, index to
Collison, Benjamin 53
Cope, Mary 97
Cope, Sarah 96, 97
Cope, Thomas 96, 97
Cope, William 97
Courts, other 1-2, 4, 15, 39, 40, 47
   Admiralty, Court of 2 n 5
   Canterbury, Prerogative Court of, and other church courts 38, 47, 93, 95
   Chester, court of equity 39
   Common Pleas, Court of 1-2, 47
   Dover, Court of Chancery 5, 39
   Duchy of Lancaster, Court of 39, 47 n 33
   Durham, court of equity 39 & n 18, 47 n 33
   Exchequer, Court of (equity side) 6, 19 n 30, 21 nn 35 & 37, 39-40 & nn 20-25, 47 n 35, 83, 85
   King's Bench, Court of 1-2, 3 n 9, 47 & n 34
   Lords, House of, appellate jurisdiction: 23 & nn 41-43, 85, 103 & nn 15-16
   North, Council of 5, 39
   Requests, Court of 2 & n 5, 5 & n 19, 6, 30, 39
   Star Chamber, Court of 5, 6, 30
   Wales, Council of 5, 39
Coventry, Thomas, first baron 94
Cremer, Six Clerks' employee 88
Cromwell, Oliver 6, 31

DaCosta, John Mendoza 98, 99
Davenport, John and Judith 98
Devonshire, deponents from 77
Dickens, Charles 1, 49
Dubois, Charles 97-100
Dubois, Charlotte 100
Dulken, S van 70 (*and see* Pembrokeshire)
Dwelly Index 71(*and see* Genealogists, Society of)
Dwight, John 90-91

Earls Colne (Essex) 90
East India Company (old) 97-100
Eldon, first Earl, John Scott 10, 49
Ellesmere, Sir Thomas 2, 10, 68
England, population of 31
English Reports 102-103
Erickson, Amy 92
Estate cases, index to 62, 69-70, 96, *and see* Coldham, Peter Wilson
Eyre, Christopher 93
Eyre, Robert 93, 94
Eyre, Thomas 93, 94
Eyre, William 93, 94

Index

Fleet, Sir John 104
Fry, E A 62, 69, 71, 105

Genealogical Society of Utah 61, 72
Genealogists, Society of (London) 61, 71, 72, 77
Gerhold, Dorian 91-92
Gilbert, Jeffrey 12
Gould, Sir Nathaniel 100
Goulden, R J 73

Hale, Sir Matthew 38 n 15
Harrison, Joseph 12
Harvey, Stephen 100
Hatton, Sir Christopher 2 n 4
Heathcote, Sir Gilbert 100
Heward, Edmund 55-56 & n 19
Holford, Richard 98, 99
Hooker, Robert 96-97
Hotson, Leslie 92 & n 8
House of Lords Record Office 103
Hume, Robert 92

Jackson, Clerk of Court 12
Jekyll, Sir Joseph 60 n 23
Jones, Clyve 91
Jones, W J 7, 39
Justices of the Peace 20 n 33

Kingston, Alfred 87-88

Lawton, Guy 61, 62 & n 25, 73
Lincoln's Inn Hall 11 n 12
London, Survey of 91
The London Gazette 16
Lowther, Sir John 14 n 16

Macclesfield, first earl of, Thomas Parker 9 n 5
Macfarlane, Alan 90
Maddock, Henry 19
Mann, J H 77
Marescoe, Charles 91
Marriages, clandestine 101
Milhous, Judith 92
Mitford, John, first Baron Redesdale 12, 38 n 16
More, Sir Thomas 2
Moreton, Charles 7, 109
Morse, John 99-100

Norbury, George 30 n 2
Norfolk, deponents from 77
Nottingham, first earl, Heneage Finch 20 n 33, 38

Ordinance, of 1654 6, 31

Ossulston, second baron (and first Earl of Tankerville), Charles Bennett 91

Parliament, acts (*and see* Ordinance)
   1696-1697 (8-9 Will III, c 11) 38
   1705-1706 (4/5 Anne c 3) 16, 31, 38
   1730 (3 George II, c 30) 9
   1732 (5 George II, c 25) 16 & n 23
   1765 (5/6 George III, c 28) 22 n 39
Parliamentary Papers 1 & n 1, 21 nn 36-37
Parliaments (*and see* Chancery, miscellaneous, critiques of)
   'Long Parliament' 39
   'Nominated' Parliament 30
Pembrokeshire, cases 70
Polden, Patrick 7, 28, 110
Powell, Thomas 12 n 15, 16
Proby, Edward 8
Public Record Office
   Classes of Equity Records and associated Finding Aids
      See Beresford Calendar; Bernau Index; Bernau Notebooks; Estate cases, index of
   Classes, in general 6-7
   Finding aids, in general 56-58
   IND 1 (contemporary lists and alphabets, etc) 32, 56, 57, 58, 59, 74-75, 77 & n 28, 81, 84, 85, 87 & n 38, 88, 94, 95, 96, 98, 101, 102, 103, 104
   Lists & Indexes 58, 60, 62, 68, 70
   Losses, of records 51-56
   'Moris' 57
   Standard List (SL) 56-62, 69-89
   Search Procedures (in general) 56-58. For specific classes, see below, and for specific searches, see Chapter Four
   Individual PRO Chancery classes (and groups of classes)
      C 2 - C 12 (Pleadings): 51, 56, 60-62
      C 2 - C 10: 60 n 23
      C 2: 52, 57, 60, 61, 62, 68, 93, 94, 109
      C 3: 52, 57, 60, 61, 68-69, 93, 94, 109
      C 4: 57, 60, 68, 69
      C 5 - C 10: 60, 69-71, 72, 91, 92, 96, 98, 109
      C 5 - C 12: 92
      C 5: 57, 69, 71, 91
      C 6: 10 n 9, 52 nn 4&7, 57, 69, 70-71, 91, 96
      C 7: 57, 69, 70, 91, 96, 97
      C 8: 57, 69, 70, 96
      C 9: 57, 69, 70, 78, 85, 104
      C 10: 57, 69, 70, 96
      C 11 - C 12: 54 & n 15, 55, 57, 60 & n 23, 71 & n 26, 73, 75-76, 77
      C 11: 54 & n 15, 55, 57, 60 n 23, 61, 71-73, 77, 98, 99, 100

C 12: 25, 54 & n 15, 57, 73
C 18: 56 n 22
C 21 - C 25 (Depositions and Interrogatories): 56, 75
C 21: 57, 61, 76, 78, 94
C 22: 57, 76-77, 78
C 23: 58, 78
C 24: 55, 57, 77 & n 28, 78, 91, 94, 95, 96-97
C 25: 57, 78
C 27: 57, 89
C 28: 57, 79
C 28 and C 36 (Petitions): 79
C 31: 57, 79-80, 101
C 31 and C 41 (Affidavits): 56, 78-79, 91, 101
C 33: 3, 23, 33 & n 8, 57, 58, 59-60, 80, 91, 93, 94, 96, 97, 99, 100
C 33 and C 37 (Books of Orders, Clerk in Court's Books): 59
C 36: 57, 79-80
C 37: 57, 60
C 38: 55-56, 57, 80, 81, 94, 95, 97, 100
C 38 and C 39: 3 & n 8, 80, 94
C 38 - C 40 (Reports and Exceptions): 56, 80
C 39: 57, 81, 100
C 40: 57, 82
C 41: 57, 78, 79
C 42: 57, 88-89
C 48: 57, 89
C 78: 57, 85-88, 94, 97, 102
C 78 - C 79 (Enrolments): 2, 27 n 53, 57, 85
C 78 - C 79 and C 96 (Enrolments and docquets): 85-86
C 79: 57, 86
C 96: 58, 88
C 98: 56 n 22
C 101 - C 129 and C 171 (Masters' materials): 56, 80
C 101: 58, 80, 82
C 102: 57, 82, 84, 89
C 103: 57, 80, 83
C 103 - C 116 and C 171 (Exhibits): 80, 82, 83, 91
C 104: 57, 83
C 105: 57, 83, 84, 100-101
C 106: 57, 83
C 107: 57, 83, 84
C 108: 57, 80, 83
C 109: 57, 83
C 110: 57, 83
C 111: 57, 83
C 112: 57, 83, 84, 101
C 113: 57, 83
C 114: 57, 83
C 115: 57, 83

C 116: 57. 83
C 117: 57, 85
C 118: 57, 85
C 119: 57, 86
C 120: 57, 85
C 121: 57, 84, 85
C 122: 57, 85
C 123: 57, 80, 85
C 123: 57, 80, 85
C 124: 57, 80, 85
C 125: 57, 85
C 126: 57, 85
C 127: 57, 84
C 128: 57, 84, 101
C 129: 57, 84, 101
C 171: 57, 83
C 173: 57, 89
C 240 (Orders to Usher): 57, 89
J 90 (Exhibits): 83 n 32

Redesdale, first baron *see* Mitford, John
Reynardson, Samuel 52 n 5, 105-108
Roseveare, Henry 91
Roupell, George Boone 21 n 37

Salisbury, City of 93, 95
Saunders, Elizabeth 94, 95
Shadwell, Sir Lancelot 54
Snell, F S 77 & n 27
Stephens, John 96
Survey of London 90, 91
Symonds' Inn 20

Temple, Inner 95
Theatre, history of 92 and n 8
Tower of London *see under* Chancery
Townsend, Major General Samuel 101
Trevor, Sir John 53
Turner, Samuel 12
Turton, William 54

Vesey, Francis 54, 55
Victoria County History of England 90

Wedgwood, family of Burslem, Staffs 91
Wilkinson, —— 53
Wolsey, Thomas, Cardinal 1
Wortley, Sir Christopher 93-95
Wortley, Lady Hester 93-95